Training & Development
Group Human Resources
Lloyds Register
71 Fenchurch Street
London EC3M 4BS

Published by DDI Press, c/o Development Dimensions International, World Headquarters—Pittsburgh, 1225 Washington Pike, Bridgeville, PA 15017-2838.

Manufactured in the United States of America.

Library of Congress Cataloging in Publications Data
Byham, W.C.

Grow your own leaders
Acceleration pools: a new method of succession management/William C. Byham, Audrey B. Smith, Matthew J. Paese

1. Business   2. Succession Management

ISBN 0-9623483-9-2

10 9 8 7 6 5 4 3 2

D0493484

DEDICATION

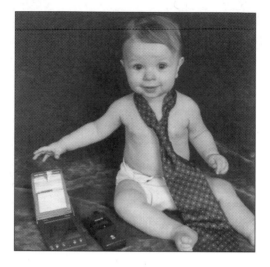

To a future leader—

Spencer Charles Lehman—

my first grandchild
and the apple of my eye,
born on February 29, 2000.

WCB

CONTENTS

GROW YOUR OWN LEADERS WEB SITE

www.ddiworld.com/growyourownleaders

Development Dimensions International maintains this web site for people who are interested in succession management. We invite you to visit the site, which includes:

- Information and implementation advice that supplement this book.

- A link to which you can e-mail suggestions about the book. We plan to revise *Grow Your Own Leaders* periodically, and we welcome your input.

- A discussion forum on succession management where you can ask questions, make comments, share your ideas and best practices, and explore issues.

- Information about what's new in succession management best practices, legislation from around the world, events, and more.

We hope you find the web site useful.

Introduction

Today, more and more organizations face a shortage of leaders at both the executive and general management levels. This shortage is driven by a variety of factors, including rapid growth, a dramatic rise in retirements, poaching of key people by competitors, and the difficulty of retaining talented people. And it's happening at a time when leadership is increasingly important to an organization's success.

To contend with this reality, organizations essentially have three options: 1) intensify their efforts to hire hard-to-find, increasingly expensive people from outside their organization; 2) do nothing and likely experience a competitive decline, which could lead to being acquired or going out of business; or 3) tap into the quality people already in their organization, thus growing and keeping their own leaders.

The third option is, of course, the most desirable. By finding effective ways to grow their own leaders, companies can make sure they have the executive talent they need in an increasingly competitive world. They can reduce the time and resources that they devote to attracting outside talent. And, they can improve their ability to retain their best and brightest employees. In today's opportunity-rich economy, talented leaders enjoy a myriad of alternatives. Research has shown that a primary reason people leave companies is lack of personal growth and job challenge opportunities (Axel, 1998; SHRM, 1997 [as cited in AMA, 1997]). By growing your own leaders, you give high-potential people the chance to pick up new skills and knowledge and take on new responsibilities. You

denotes that information on this topic is available at the *Grow Your Own Leaders* web site (www.ddiworld.com/growyourownleaders).

give them clear opportunities to reach for bigger and better things, and in so doing you give them a solid reason to stay with your organization.

The benefits of being able to grow your own leaders are clear. Nevertheless, many organizations try to do so by using traditional "climb the corporate ladder" approaches and replacement-planning programs— systems that are increasingly out of place in a fast-paced, ever-changing leadership environment.

In this book we provide a more systematic and targeted method for identifying and developing high-potential individuals. We call this approach the Acceleration Pool^{SM}. Compared to traditional approaches, it is:

- **Faster and simpler,** requiring less paperwork and management time (e.g., eliminating the yearly replacement-planning forms that have long plagued managers).

- **More accurate** in terms of getting the right person in the right job at the right time to meet organizational needs.

- **More developmental,** with improved diagnoses of development needs, a sharper focus on building skills and knowledge, and better support for change and growth.

- **Fairer** by providing greater integrity and transparency, minimizing "old boy network" influences, and creating more diversity by encompassing high-potential people wherever they are in the organization.

- **More closely linked to business plans and strategy.** The focus is on the development of leaders who can run the organization as it will be, not necessarily as it is now.

- **More involving.** Participants decide whether they want to join the Acceleration Pool, share in the responsibility for creating and executing their development plans, and are consulted relative to their assignments.

- **More flexible** because it can accommodate late bloomers, work-life conflict considerations, and people from outside the organization who are coming into middle- and senior-management positions.

- **More contemporary in its approach to retaining top talent.** It provides the job challenges that top talent crave as well as the appropriate support. Top talent feel they are growing in terms of skills and responsibilities.

- **More tailored to specific organizational situations and needs.** It is not a "one size fits all" approach.

Traditional Replacement Planning

To understand the value of Acceleration Pools, it helps to take a look back at the more traditional approach. For decades replacement planning has concentrated on preselecting backup people for key positions and then charting a series of job assignments to prepare them to fill the positions. One company called this approach "bus planning," as in "What would we do if Joe were hit by a bus?" It was not a bad system for the times. Back then:

- Organizations were stable, large, and hierarchical; there were few changes in job titles, job responsibilities, or organizational direction.

- Organizations employed many middle managers, most of whom had time for assignments outside their regular job duties.

- Technical and competitive changes occurred much more slowly.

- Human resource staffs were large, and control of personnel systems was more centralized.

- Succession planning was largely an HR-managed means of knowing who would replace departing leaders.

- Typical career path options within an organization were generally understood and rarely deviated from. People changed jobs and moved to new towns when asked to do so.

In such an environment managers could tolerate—not necessarily enjoy— a forms-driven system that consumed days or even weeks of their time each year. One study in the 1980s found that line managers at Exxon spent as much as *one-third* of their time on succession-planning and human resource development activities (McManis & Leibman, 1988).

Today it is impossible to conceive of devoting even a fraction of that much management time to replenishing managerial talent or other related HR activities. For business in the 21st century, the landscape is far different from the relatively stable times of two or three decades ago. In today's business world:

- Organizations are flatter, with horizontal career paths taking an increasing importance in addition to vertical paths.

- There are fewer middle managers—and those who remain have multiple demands that compete for the time required to develop themselves or coach and mentor their direct reports.

- Rapid change is occurring in all sectors—technology, competition, distribution, globalization, etc.

- There is greater decentralization of business units, resulting in fragmentation of HR initiatives.

- Top executives face myriad pressures that severely restrict the time they can spend on leadership development and succession management; yet, shareholders and board members show an increasing interest in the quality of the organization's executive talent.

- Quarterly pressure to meet Wall Street's expectations is enormous for some companies, often leading to short-term thinking relative to the development of leadership talent.

- Talented individuals expect unique attention that addresses their personal goals and aspirations, not just the promise of promotion if solid performance persists.

What We Believe About Growing Leaders

Grow Your Own Leaders describes a new system for managing leadership development and succession that we believe is essential in this rapidly changing and highly demanding world. We have used these beliefs to shape the Acceleration Pool approach.

Reasons for Succession Management

- Business strategy can be implemented only if appropriately skilled and experienced leadership is in place.

- Decisions about filling positions are more accurate when candidates are from inside the organization.

- Effective succession management systems operate as both talent-*growth* and talent-*retention* mechanisms; both are central to the system's success.

- Organizations don't have the time or resources to develop the leadership skills and organizational savvy of *all* their people. They must concentrate on those who will benefit most.

Identification of Talent

- Organizations need to actively identify high-potential individuals. We do not subscribe to the "bubble-up" theory, which maintains that the best leaders inevitably move upward and gain the skills and experiences needed to meet the increasingly complex challenges of today's organizations.

- Organizations should cast a wide net in choosing people to be developed. Companies can't afford to miss good people, wherever they are. Although relatively young individuals will be the primary source for Acceleration Pools, leaders in later stages of their careers should also be eligible.

- Accurately selecting the talent to bring into the organization is critical. Everything depends on the developability of the organization's talent.

Diagnosis of Development Needs

- Diagnosis of individual development needs is critical. A "one size fits all" development plan is a waste of money and fails to produce results.

- Diagnosis should cover experience and knowledge required at the executive level, executive competencies derived from organizational strategy, and executive derailers (personality attributes that can cause executives to fail).

Meeting Development Needs

- Executives can change behavior and develop new skills if they are motivated and provided with the required resources and support.

- High-potential individuals (high potentials) should be responsible for their own development.

- High potentials should be consulted regarding their job assignments and development plans.

- Leadership development is a continuous process—not a one-time event.

- Developmental assignments that stretch people, such as challenging job responsibilities and task force membership, have more impact than training experiences.

- High potentials should have development goals for each assignment or training activity and a plan for immediately implementing their new skills or knowledge in the workplace.

- Development initiatives should have a measurable impact on job objectives, not be an extra responsibility added to people's job objectives.

Managing the Succession Management System

- Senior management should own the succession management system and be fully accountable for its success. As part of their involvement, senior managers should teach special programs for high potentials and show their support in other ways. Top managers should be given incentives to be active participants in the succession management process and to develop the leaders below them.

- The best way to grow your own leaders is *not* to earmark specific backup people for specific jobs. It is much more effective to identify and develop a pool of people who have the potential to fill multiple senior management positions, except of course for the very top leadership positions in the organization, for which specific backups *should* be identified.

- Good performance is required in every job—there is no room for "crown princes" or "princesses" who move through their jobs with no real responsibilities. Individuals operating below their potential or the organization's standards need management attention and corrective action.

- The role of the Human Resource department is to facilitate the succession management system. It should support the executives who are identifying and working with high potentials and help those individuals manage and monitor their own development.

- Forms and meetings should be minimized. Executive time should be focused on high-impact activities that directly support high-potential identification and development.

General

- Every organization has unique succession management needs based on its size, growth rate, number of expected openings, organizational structure, management commitment, and most of all, strategic direction.

Why Should You Listen to Us?

The ideas expressed in this book are based on more than three decades of experience that Development Dimensions International (DDI) has had in helping organizations find and nurture leaders and managers. In those 30-plus years, DDI has worked with 19,000 organizations throughout the world, including 470 of the *Fortune* 500 companies. Distinguishing hallmarks of DDI's practice include our ability to help clients both *identify* and *develop* high-potential individuals and our extensive research evidence that confirms the effectiveness of our systems.

Although most of our experience has been with large, publicly owned companies, we believe the ideas presented in this book can be put to work in all types of organizations—large and small, new and old. Indeed, DDI has applied them in health care systems, schools, religious groups, and government agencies—in dozens of countries.

How This Book Will Help You

Grow Your Own Leaders is designed to help you understand and implement systems that will identify talent and develop the high-potential people your organization needs to grow and prosper—and to do it at "Web speed." As most senior executives realize, organizations need more good leaders, and they need them now.

Grow Your Own Leaders describes a complete succession management system (Acceleration Pools), but an organization need not adopt the entire approach to benefit from this book. In fact, organizations just starting an Acceleration Pool have the freedom to begin their efforts through many different doors. For example, they can pilot a streamlined version of the Acceleration Pool and build toward a more comprehensive strategy as buy-in grows. Many organizations will benefit by using the ideas discussed here to tune up their already-effective succession management systems. Other organizations fighting for survival (e.g., young dot-com companies) might

---

Targets for Acceleration Pools

Much of this book concerns filling positions at the level of general manager or above—positions in which executives must be strategic, transcend functional or technical silos, make broad organizational decisions, and lead autonomous business units. We use the terms *executive* and *general manager* interchangeably to denote individuals in general management positions. When we refer to *senior executives,* we mean the CEO and the level that reports to the CEO (typically the executive committee, the operating committee, etc.).

Acceleration Pools also can be aimed at filling positions below the general manager level. Various uses of Acceleration Pools are discussed in Chapter 2.

view the concepts we describe as a premature focus for them. While such organizations might gain the most from focusing on near-term market windows, they should not neglect the future. Remember that Cisco Systems was a dot-com start-up just a few years ago, but now that it's a dominant computer-technology player, it has recognized that it must play catch-up to build a competitive, long-term leadership bench.

Who Is This Book Written For?

In his recent book, *On Writing,* author Stephen King (2000) describes an "ideal reader" as one whose anticipated interests and reactions help to shape his novels. While the authors of this book do not claim to be as mesmerizing writers as Stephen King, we too wanted to shape our book around the needs of our "ideal readers." We considered two constituencies: 1) **CEOs and other executive stakeholders** (i.e., decision-making groups), such as members of the Executive Resource Board, and 2) **HR practitioners,** who are often the unsung strategic partners in organizations and serve as a cultural insurance policy for identifying and implementing sound people or leadership practices.

Writing about Acceleration Pools for two very different target audiences proved to be a more daunting challenge than we anticipated. Any comprehensive treatment of succession management reveals a kaleidoscope of questions, issues, and opportunities that, in practice, reflect unique vantage points, interests, and agendas that the different stakeholders have for outcomes.

As our book evolved, the many layers of the Acceleration Pool "onion" made it difficult to focus our discussion on the tactical execution challenges that HR professionals might face in implementing Acceleration Pools while we also tried to make the book interesting for the executive reader.

The "onion layers" analogy for succession management emerged over the last several years as customers came to us with seemingly different needs (on the surface), varying levels of organizational readiness or commitment, and a range of desired points of entry. Some organizations requested support on focused interventions, such as building executive competency models, facilitating selection processes following reengineering, providing 360° assessment and executive coaching, and planning executive learning events. Others came to us with broader (and sometimes amorphous) requests for help, such as establishing succession management systems, identifying (nominating) next-generation talent, or creating a culture that drives learning and accountability.

In some cases clients were surprised at the extent to which we viewed sound executive assessment, development, and succession management as culture change initiatives. At the same time, we were continually intrigued at just how different both the questions and initial focus were, depending upon whether our "client" was the chief executive or senior HR player.

Listening to a broad array of "presenting needs" during the last five years led us to conclude that communicating one simple path for solving unique organizational talent challenges would oversimplify a complex imperative. Our challenge was constantly to balance comprehensiveness against the risk that any given reader might not identify with our book or care about the content.

Ultimately, we decided to maintain our comprehensive approach to describing Acceleration Pools because there are so few up-to-date "road maps" available for the two constituencies. Therefore, we apologize in advance for our (perhaps overly conservative) bias toward inclusion, and we recommend that you focus on the sections of our book that will add the most value to your own objectives.

How This Book Is Organized

We have incorporated several navigational tools to help you locate information of interest and have formatted the book into these five broad sections:

I. Leadership Talent: Crisis and Proposed Solution

Chapter 1 offers an orientation to the business and societal dynamics that have led to a worldwide leadership crisis. In Chapter 2 we propose a unique approach for organizations wishing to expand their leadership bench strength (the Acceleration Pool) and describe how it works. Chapters 3 and 4 elaborate on issues relative to an Acceleration Pool's operation and explain why various features of a pool overcome traditional problems with succession management systems.

Chapter 1 The Growing Leadership Shortage: Building the Case for Acceleration Pools

Chapter 2 Acceleration Pools: The Basics

Chapter 3 Seventeen Reasons Acceleration Pools Work

Chapter 4 Acceleration Pools: Fundamental Questions and Rationale

II. Identifying High Potentials

Our chapter in this section focuses on best practices associated with initial identification of high-potential Acceleration Pool members.

Chapter 5 Identifying High Potentials

III. Understanding Organizational Talent

This section defines the basic activities and best practices associated with diagnosing the development needs of high-potential pool members. First we describe the *executive descriptors* (i.e., organizational knowledge, job challenges, competencies, and derailers) that define successful executive performance and highlight an array of assessment tools/practices for supporting an in-depth diagnosis of development priorities. We then deal with the very important—and often neglected—issue of translating an individual's diagnosis into a commitment to action.

Chapter 6 Defining the Executive of the Future

Chapter 7 Diagnosing Strengths and Development Needs

Chapter 8 Understanding and Prioritizing Development Needs

IV. Strategies for Accelerating Development

The first chapter in this section overviews development strategies available to fill pool members' development gaps, with emphasis on developing competencies. These four strategies for facilitating pool member growth and development (assignments, short-term experiences, training/executive education experiences, and professional growth through short-/long-term coaching) are discussed at greater length in Chapters 10 through 13.

Chapter 9 Development Options

Chapter 10 Growth Through Assignments

Chapter 11 Growth Through Short-Term Experiences

Chapter 12 Growth Through Training/Executive Education

Chapter 13 Growth Through Professional Coaching

V. Ensuring Acceleration Pool Success: Key Processes, Roles/Accountabilities, Meetings, and Other Mechanics

Our last section focuses on the processes and logistics associated with successful and enduring implementation of Acceleration Pools. The important development-facilitator roles of supervisors and mentors are described in Chapter 14. Chapter 15 discusses tactics to maximize the effectiveness of talent review discussions (where placement and development decisions are made), and Chapter 16 explores in detail the important role of the CEO. Finally, succession management, HR, and consulting practitioners will appreciate Chapter 17's discussion, Getting Started.

Chapter 14 Key Partners: Supporting Growth

Chapter 15 Optimizing Your Talent Review Discussion

Chapter 16 The Role of the CEO and Measures of Acceleration Pool Success

Chapter 17 Getting Started

Throughout this book we describe what we believe are best practices in areas related to successful succession management. For virtually every practice we could have reported that "some do it this way, and some do it the other way" and let the reader choose. Instead, with a few exceptions, we have hammered a stake in the ground and detailed what our experience has shown to be, out of the spectrum of possibilities, the best practices.

Additional Information Available on the Web

After we finished *Grow Your Own Leaders*, it was much longer than we thought it should be. To get the book to a manageable length while still assuaging our need to be as complete as possible, and to provide forms and lists of steps as appropriate, we have included additional information on various subjects on the Web. Throughout the book we have placed the symbol ☞ to denote that you can find additional information about that particular subject at a special *Grow Your Own Leaders* web site (www.ddiworld.com/growyourownleaders). This web site also provides people who are involved in succession management a place where they can follow new developments and exchange views and best practices. More information about the web site is provided at the end of the book.

A Few Final Remarks

We all know that today's business environment, with its warp-speed change, has a way of forcing reactive behavior and a focus on near-term performance. Yet we have witnessed the competitive advantage enjoyed by organizations that have successfully matched their stated values regarding talent advocacy with Acceleration Pool practices, and have been willing to step up to the long-term investment challenges associated with building their leadership bench. We fervently believe that the long-term winners are the organizations that recognize and act as if their business strategy and future viability depend on their current and future talent.

Finding Your Topic

If you are a senior executive concerned about the future leadership of your organization . . .	Read Chapters 1–3, 10, 15–16.*
If you want to know what's new in succession management . . .	Read the entire book.
If you are an HR executive who has decided to implement all or part of an Acceleration Pool system . . .	Read the entire book and review the supplemental information on the DDI web site (www.ddiworld.com/growyourownleaders).
If you are a manager or mentor responsible for the development of an Acceleration Pool member . . .	Read Chapters 1–3, 6–14.
If you want more information about a specific area only (e.g., diagnosing development needs or prescribing appropriate development options) . . .	Read Chapter 2 and the appropriate chapters pertaining to your interest.
If you are an Acceleration Pool member . . .	Read Chapters 2–3, 9–14.

---

* These chapters have been printed on gray paper for easy identification by CEOs and other senior executives.

SECTION I

LEADERSHIP TALENT: CRISIS AND PROPOSED SOLUTION

Chapter 1 offers an orientation to the business and societal dynamics that have led to a worldwide leadership crisis. In Chapter 2 we propose a unique approach for organizations wishing to expand their leadership bench strength (the Acceleration Pool) and describe how it works. Chapters 3 and 4 elaborate on issues relative to an Acceleration Pool's operation and explain why various features of a pool overcome traditional problems with succession management systems.

Note: Pages printed on gray paper contain information that will be of particular interest to CEOs and other senior executives.

Chapter 1

The Growing Leadership Shortage: Building the Case for Acceleration Pools

"The thing that wakes me up in the middle of the night is not what might happen to the economy or what our competitors might do next; it is worrying about whether we have the leadership capacity and talent to implement the new and more complex global strategies."

—David Whitwam, Chairman, President,
and CEO Whirlpool Corporation

This book was written to help executives like David Whitwam sleep better. We do so by helping them find ways to prepare leaders with the right skills, motivations, and experiences to assume management positions when needed.

Having moved into the new millennium, virtually every executive faces the same daunting dilemma: The demand for leadership talent far outstrips the supply. In fact, the dearth of people qualified for important leadership positions has become one of the foremost challenges facing managers today. For instance:

• When The Conference Board asked CEOs in the United States, Europe, and Japan for their top concerns, competition for talent was ranked among the top five (Csoka, 1998).

☞ denotes that information on this topic is available at the *Grow Your Own Leaders* web site (www.ddiworld.com/growyourownleaders).

- In a study by McKinsey & Company (Chambers, Foulon, Handfield-Jones, Hankin, & Michaels, 1998), three-quarters of the executives in the 77 companies studied said their company either didn't have enough leadership talent at times or was "chronically short of talent."

- A majority (76%) of the 252 organizations surveyed by the Corporate Leadership Council (2000) were less than fully confident in their ability to staff leadership positions across the next five years. While 64 percent report that their CEOs strongly agreed that leadership was a top priority, only 18 percent felt it was a low priority.

Not surprisingly, revenues for search and recruitment agencies have grown twice as fast as the gross domestic product during the past five years (Chambers et al., 1998).

Does Your Organization Need to Worry About Leadership Talent?

☐ Does your organization have the leadership bench strength to staff its growth plans?

☐ Has your company experienced a long-term vacancy in a key leadership position (general manager or above) in the last year? Did you have to go outside to fill the position? What was the cost to the organization?

☐ Has the organization had to compromise on leadership quality to fill certain positions?

☐ What percentage of your leaders would be selected if they were applying today for their current positions?

☐ Have the business challenges faced by your top leaders changed significantly during the past 5–10 years?

☐ Would your current executives say that they felt adequately prepared for their top management role when they first took it on?

☐ How many people who are ready or are being groomed for promotion typically leave the organization before they get that promotion?

If your answers to these questions leave you feeling a bit uneasy or, worse yet, if you simply don't have the answers, it might be time to make the search for leadership talent a priority in your organization. While most growing organizations typically will need more leaders, during the next 10 years, an increasing number of companies will face an unusually large shortfall in leadership talent caused by an inordinately large number of people leaving senior management through retirement and resignation. The authors know of hundreds of large private and public organizations that will lose 30 to 50 percent of their key leaders in the next five years—many in the next three years.

To gauge the impact of this dilemma on your organization, ask your Human Resource department to give you a report on your company's projected retirements—and then assume that reality will be worse than the projections. Although workers today can choose to remain in their jobs longer (in the United States forced retirement constitutes age discrimination), managers and executives are retiring earlier. What's more, the trend is accelerating in the executive ranks because a strong economy has put a financially secure retirement within reach of many high achievers. Others are taking advantage of the widespread availability of part-time and full-time jobs and consulting opportunities to supplement retirement income. And many managers in their 50s are simply looking forward to applying their skills in other fields—perhaps ones that offer the opportunity of a big payoff.

Even if your organization is not growing and is not projecting a higher percentage of retirements, you still have cause to worry. Because other organizations will be feeling the impact of the leadership shortfall, they will be intensifying their recruiting efforts—meaning that you are likely to lose key personnel to companies looking to fill their leadership void. Some organizations devoting increased attention to building their leadership bench are likely to be your direct competitors.

The 1998 McKinsey study concluded that the most important corporate resource during the next 20 years would be talent—smart, sophisticated business people who are technologically literate, globally astute, and operationally agile. The study noted that even as the demand for talent escalates, the supply is spiraling downward, culminating in a corporate "war for talent." To win the war, organizations will have to be very skilled at hiring and promoting people and—even more important—at keeping them.

Most Organizations Are Not Ready

A number of situations are making it difficult for organizations to fill key leadership positions:

• As organizations become more complex and global, the number of competencies (behavior, knowledge, and motivations) required for success at senior levels is growing beyond the traditional business and leadership skills. Companies are looking for visionary individuals who excel at collaboration and partnering, grasp the big picture, are able to handle vast ambiguities, can deal with international issues, and can produce rapid results. Above all, organizations want good leaders and people developers—not just good managers.

- The standard for all senior management competencies has risen because the positions have become more challenging. Senior managers always needed to be good communicators. Now they must be *exceptional* communicators; they need to be able to sell the organization's vision so they can help employees understand *WIIFM* (what's in it for me). Senior managers have long been required to be effective at managing organizational change. Now they must be adept at driving near-constant change and effectively managing resistance to it.

- The ideal executive candidate in the coming years will need a broader range of job experiences. For example, many organizations will insist on candidates' having experience with a start-up, merger, or acquisition; a fast-growth organization; a unionized environment; implementing a change or a new technology; or leading and living outside of their home country. Why? Because people can't be adaptable, agile, and comfortable with the unfamiliar if they have been confined to a functional silo or have only a one-country or regional perspective.

- Downsizing has dramatically reduced the field of possible internal replacements. According to a 1996 American Management Association (AMA) survey entitled *Corporate Downsizing, Job Elimination, and Job Creation,* middle managers made up just 5–8 percent of the workforce in 1995 through 1996, but they represented 15–20 percent of the positions eliminated in downsizing. Furthermore, outplacement specialists Challenger, Gray & Christmas (1997) report that in 1986 just 27 percent of their clients were middle managers; by 1996, that number had risen to 60 percent. In short, during the last several years, many people who by now would have been logical candidates to fill higher leadership positions were given incentives to leave. Consequently, an age gap is often present between top management and the new cadre of middle managers—a group that top management perceives to be young and unprepared.

- As organizations have become flatter, top management has faced increasing difficulty determining whom to promote. Many traditional development positions that led to top management roles—such as

"Assistant to" and "Deputy"—have been eliminated. Traditional hierarchical companies kept the rungs of their organizational ladders closer together, making it easier to assume that excellent performance at one level would predict excellent performance at the next. In flattened organizations the rungs are farther apart, requiring very different competencies at each level (e.g., operational competencies at middle management and strategic competencies at senior management). Thus, because requirements for success are so different at each managerial rung, it is no longer clear that a successful middle manager will be a successful senior manager.

- In the late 1980s and early 1990s, many organizations scrapped their formal succession management or replacement-planning programs. Their thinking was, "Why should we worry about succession when we are downsizing the organization and laying off people?" A 1999 DDI survey of 260 organizations revealed that 39 percent had no succession management system in place (Rioux & Bernthal, 1999). When there is no succession management system in place, the net effect is that many middle managers lack the breadth of experience required for higher-level positions. For example, a manager might have had all of his or her experience in one area, such as sales, but no working knowledge of the marketing, finance, or international operations.

- Some potentially excellent candidates for senior management simply don't have the motivation to step up to the next level. Increasingly, middle managers are happy to avoid the long hours, outside commitments, extensive travel, and other hassles that have become part of life for those in senior management. Many feel that as middle managers, they can still make significant contributions to the organization, earn good pay, and enjoy the potential of long-term benefits, stock options, and other perks without incurring the headaches of top leadership—and they can!

- Many younger members of the workforce are bringing a different work ethic to the job—one that has also become a factor in the leadership shortfall. Many "Generation Xers" have less organizational commitment than their older counterparts, are more concerned with work-life balance, and value experiencing life even if there are economic consequences, such as limited advancement or less-lucrative positions. For many members of this age group, the responsibilities of management hold no appeal.

A Senior HR Executive Describes the Situation

"Things are going from bad to worse in terms of filling middle and senior positions. The people who would naturally replace managers who are retiring or leaving either don't have the breadth of experience they need or the management skills required, or both. We often compromise and end up with important positions filled with people who are very parochial (they can't get out of their 'silo'), [who] don't think or act strategically, and who make a lot of poor decisions. I feel we are batting about .500 in our appointments, and that's not good enough."

Why Grow Your Own Leaders?

All in all, finding and attracting leadership talent is getting harder all the time. That fundamental reality has led us to the core concept behind this book—that is, growing your own leaders.

Given all the elements that work against organizations as they try to replace leaders from dwindling pools of external and internal candidates, the grow-your-own-leaders approach seems like an obvious strategy for a number of reasons. For one, having pre-identified leadership "bench strength" in place helps your organization meet both long-term and emergency leadership needs at all levels. It also ensures continuity of management, which helps your company to implement a consistent strategy and set of values and to follow through with planned changes consistent with them. Looking for outside candidates takes time as well, leaving your organization with open positions. That, in turn, leads to lost opportunities and/or the inability to carry out planned business initiatives. And growing your own leaders makes it easier to achieve your organization's diversity goals by ensuring that it has an appropriate gender and ethnic mix of candidates in the selection pipeline.

Reasons for Succession Management Systems

- Provide a source of in-house replacements for key leadership positions.
- Retain key talent.
- Prepare individuals for future challenges (e.g., growth or implementing new strategies).
- Align executive resources to new organizational directions.
- Increase the organization's human capital.
- Accelerate the development of key individuals.
- Provide challenging, growth-oriented, and rewarding career opportunities.
- Ensure a continuity of management culture, which is difficult to maintain when many executives are brought in from the outside.
- Avoid lost productivity while a new person is learning a job.
- Control costs: Developing internal talent is less expensive than hiring from the outside (e.g., costs of recruitment and relocation, higher starting salary).
- Make the organization more attractive to job candidates.
- Monitor and help attain diversity goals.
- Increase stock value: Investment analysts are becoming concerned with organizations' processes for filling top positions.
- Increase chances of survival: The alternative might be decline or collapse.

A key benefit to growing your own leaders is the positive message it sends throughout your workforce. Promoting people from within is good for morale—and essential to a positive company culture. People want to join and stay with an organization that develops its own people. A primary reason high potentials leave is that their rate of advancement is too slow. Promoting from within is consistent with an empowerment philosophy that encourages people to take on responsibility, assume risk, measure outcomes, and grow through their achievements. Conversely, by failing to promote from within, companies risk losing good people and their intellectual capital—often an organization's most valuable resource.

A grow-your-own strategy is also much less expensive than a policy of searching for the best external candidates. The starting compensation of people promoted from within is almost always lower than the compensation paid to outsiders. And don't forget to factor in the cost of executive searches and the time it takes for an outside recruit to learn the new job and the organization.

In general, your organization will usually have a clearer sense of an internal candidate's strengths and weaknesses as well as access to more and better data on that person's performance than you would with outside candidates. Therefore, you'll be able to make more informed and accurate selection decisions. This is especially important when looking for a senior leader. Hiring mistakes at the senior level are not only costly, they can also be devastating to the organization, in terms of everything from poor morale to plummeting stock value.

Finally, identifying and accelerating your leadership bench strength might provide a significant Wall Street advantage. Leadership development is no longer a simple HR imperative. The viability of future leadership has become a significant, ongoing concern to boards and investors and is an important factor in driving stock value.

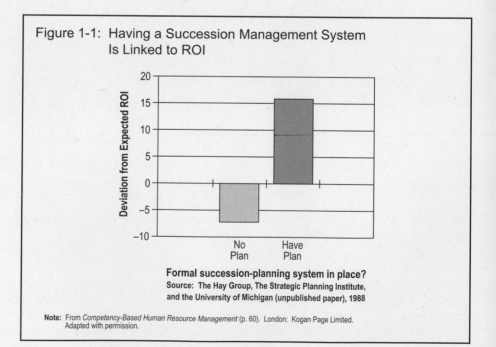

Figure 1-1: Having a Succession Management System Is Linked to ROI

Formal succession-planning system in place?
Source: The Hay Group, The Strategic Planning Institute, and the University of Michigan (unpublished paper), 1988

Note: From *Competency-Based Human Resource Management* (p. 60). London: Kogan Page Limited. Adapted with permission.

Higher-Performing Organizations Have Succession Management Systems

Studies in 1988, by the Hay Group along with the University of Michigan and the Strategic Planning Institute (as cited in Mitrani, A., Dalziel, M.M., & Fitt, D., 1992/1996), and in 1999, by Sibson & Company and McKinsey & Company, showed that organizations with better operating statistics are more likely to have succession management programs (see Figures 1-1 and 1-2). Of course, correlation does not mean causation.

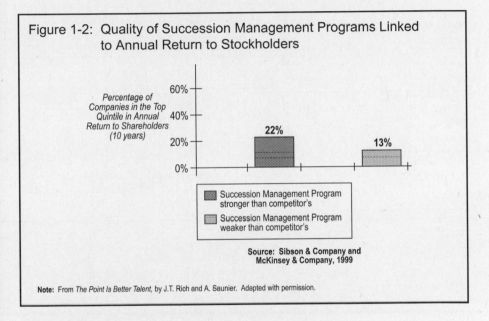

Figure 1-2: Quality of Succession Management Programs Linked to Annual Return to Stockholders

Source: Sibson & Company and McKinsey & Company, 1999

Note: From *The Point Is Better Talent*, by J.T. Rich and A. Saunier. Adapted with permission.

Why Worry About Having Enough Organizational Talent?

Some organizations aren't concerned about a shortage of internal talent, believing that they can always hire from outside or that the situation will work itself out. Table 1-1 lists some of the rationales used by senior managers who hold this opinion as well as our view of the particular situations.

If you are getting the idea that we believe in the value and viability of organizations growing most of their own leaders, you're right. Every organization will need to go outside to get new ideas, special skills, and experience, but a strong bench-strength strategy is required for long-range success. The remainder of this book describes a new system—the *Acceleration Pool*—of doing exactly that.

Table 1-1: Contrasting Rationales Relative to Developing Internal Talent

Rationale for Doing Nothing	The Grow-Your-Own Leaders View
Why limit ourselves to people from our own company? There is a world of talent out there.	There is talent, but bringing them into your organization is more expensive and riskier—failure rates for new executives have been estimated at up to 50 percent (Corporate Leadership Council, 1997 [as cited in Graddick, 1998])—and can lead to internal morale problems.
The best talent will rise to the top on their own.	Top leaders need a wide variety of experiences that they will unlikely get by chance. Without a systematic approach to developing leaders: • Many talented people will never experience having an effective leader who can act as coach, model new and changing behavior, and clear the way for job achievement. This type of leadership is a prime factor in an individual's success. Unfortunately, such leaders are few and far between. • People's skill development can be haphazard and fail to prepare them for the challenges they will face at the next level. For example, an individual with no development plan in place might receive five assignments in which he or she learned and reused the same skills and abilities; in contrast, a person with a solid development plan would get a series of assignments, each designed to build new skills. Also, some experiences provide an opportunity for a great deal of self-insight—encouraging development actions—while others do not.
People treated as high-potential talent will want more money.	High-potential individuals will want compensation commensurate with job success, and they will expect to be paid more than those who are not high performers. They will also want more challenges, experiences, senior management exposure, and appreciation of their successes from their manager. In addition, they will want to know that the organization is interested in their long-term retention and development.
People who are told they are high potential will set their sights on even bigger opportunities in other organizations.	If people know they are high potential and are treated as such, they are actually more likely to stay in the organization. Too often, high potentials leave because they fail to understand the extent of their opportunities or see no new challenges.

Table 1-1: Contrasting Rationales Relative to Developing Internal Talent (cont'd)

Rationale for Doing Nothing	The Grow-Your-Own Leaders View
Determining who has potential and developing them is a waste of money because many employees end up leaving before reaching senior management.	In today's competition for talent, up to 50 percent of those who enter high-potential pools do leave before they actually get into high-level jobs, especially if the pool has many relatively young people in it. Nonetheless, having a pool is still a good investment if it is run correctly. Everyone should earn his or her compensation while in the developmental assignments, and you still have the remaining 50 percent to promote. Also, having a pool increases the organization's ability to attract top talent from outside the company because of developmental and job opportunities.
Leaders are born, not made. There is nothing you can do to develop them.	Being born with certain leadership characteristics and innate skills is a great advantage, but it's not enough. Even the best leaders improve their abilities through training, stretch assignments, and experiences that push them to develop new skills and get further training.
People can't change. You can't teach someone who's "middle-aged" new tricks.	The positive impact of training and developmental assignments on people's organizational performance can be measured. Naturally, people who start with the most talent benefit more than others, but everyone benefits from an appropriate combination of training and experience.
Selection is the key. If we spend our money on selecting the best people, we'll be OK.	Selection, while very important, is only part of the answer. The sticking point is that the people who really could be your great leaders might not have the experiences required to be successful. Thus, you risk having too few candidates to choose from.
You know a good leader when you see one.	It is easy to overlook good people or assume that a person's success at one level will lead to success at the next. Our experience in assessment proves that the best communicators aren't necessarily the best leaders. Also, leadership competencies are changing, which makes recognizing good leaders more difficult. Tomorrow's high-level jobs will be markedly different from those of today.

Table 1-1: Contrasting Rationales Relative to Developing Internal Talent (cont'd)

Rationale for Doing Nothing	The Grow-Your-Own Leaders View
People with similar job backgrounds are pretty much alike (e.g., all salespeople are alike, all engineers are alike, etc.).	Wide skill and knowledge differences exist among people with similar backgrounds or job titles.
We have no confidence in our internal talent; we *must* go outside.	There are more good people than you think in your organization who have the necessary skills and who know the organization, its operations, and its history. The trick is to find them. Shoring up your identification system is the first step, followed by an improved succession management system to develop your talent.
People know their own development needs.	Accurate self-insight is a skill that some people have, but many don't, as evidenced by the often-large differences in "self" and "others" ratings on multiple-perspective (360°) instruments. Our observation is that new executives have markedly less insight about their personal strengths and development needs than about the businesses they run.
People know what they need to do to develop their skills and knowledge once they are recognized.	People usually don't have a high-level view of where the organization is going. They often choose assignments that are not in their best long-term interest and turn down assignments that will prepare them for a stellar career. One of the reasons for the recent proliferation of executive coaches is that most leaders are less creative about how to develop themselves and others than they are about implementing business strategies.
Bosses know what their individuals need to do to develop skills and knowledge.	Often, the boss is not interested or lacks the skills or insight to develop high-potential employees without higher-level guidance and encouragement.
Productivity will drop because the organization is moving people around to different jobs or assignments.	While individuals learn their new jobs, the gains—from the higher motivation sparked by new challenges, the advantage of having fresh eyes to look at problems, and the knowledge they bring of how other parts of the organization work—far outweigh short-term losses in productivity. There are other creative development strategies that don't even necessitate new jobs (e.g., short-term task force assignments, special projects, etc.).

Chapter 2

Acceleration Pools: The Basics

"We cannot be what we want to be by remaining what we are."

—Max DePree, former Chairman and CEO
Herman Miller, Inc., and author of *Leadership Is an Art*

According to a DDI survey of midsize and large organizations throughout the world, an overwhelming majority of firms want to fill 70 to 80 percent of their executive positions (general manager and above) with internal candidates. Yet most are having trouble doing so (Bernthal, Rioux, & Wellins, 1999).

Several years of corporate downsizing have left companies with fewer middle managers to promote into executive positions. Even more troubling is that many of the remaining middle managers lack the competencies and career experience necessary to run a third-millennium corporation. Much of the shortage of ready-to-promote managers stems from the failure of traditional replacement-planning systems.

Replacement-Planning Systems

In traditional systems senior and middle managers identify potential replacements for themselves, and sometimes for their direct reports, and estimate when those individuals will be ready to move up the organizational ladder. From these inputs the HR department develops a book or a series of charts showing the backups for each position and their readiness.

 denotes that information on this topic is available at the *Grow Your Own Leaders* web site (www.ddiworld.com/growyourownleaders).

Positions with no backups are identified, and meetings are held to do something to fill in the open slots on the charts. That process can consume an inordinate amount of time, with relatively little gain. One major U.S. company discovered that it was devoting 250,000 executive hours a year to completing and discussing replacement-planning forms.

As a rule, companies aren't getting much of a return on that time investment. Replacement-planning systems are often out of touch with organizational strategies because executives are essentially searching for replacements for themselves. That is, they are looking for people to do the same things they are doing in their current jobs. However, this could be at a time when the company might be executing a new strategy that requires an executive with much-different knowledge and competencies, or the organization might even be eliminating the executive's job completely. In addition, there's usually very little focus on skill development; most of the attention is concentrated on job placement. But worst of all, the majority of actual replacement decisions are made outside the replacement-planning system. Most organizations that have done formal research on their

PepsiCo Gives Up Replacement Planning

A research study conducted a few years ago at PepsiCo revealed that its traditional replacement-planning system had burned hundreds of thousands of executives' hours each year as they filled out forms and participated in meetings. Determining that this was an investment far beyond its value to the company, the organization scrapped its traditional replacement-planning system, which for many years had been a benchmark for companies interested in succession management. In its place PepsiCo instituted a system in which high-potential people are groomed for an organizational level rather than a specific job. Decisions about moving high potentials up the organizational ladder are now made by senior executives who balance the organization's needs to fill certain positions and the needs of the individuals being developed.

PepsiCo reports considerable success with the high-potential program, which is in its third year of operation and is fully implemented in a number of divisions throughout the world. In those areas it's been very successful in "fast tracking" high potentials and offering them broader opportunities for advancement. The time-saving is also very much appreciated by PepsiCo executives, who find that they have much more time to devote to "business work" rather than "HR work."

succession-planning process have determined that their designated backups actually fill fewer than 30 percent of the open positions for which they were slotted. Thus, companies are spending a large amount of executive time on a system that is not used when needed.

Acceleration Pools

We propose a different approach to grooming executive talent: the *Acceleration Pool,* which represents a drastic departure from traditional replacement planning. Rather than targeting one or two hand-picked people for each executive position, an Acceleration Pool develops a group of high-potential candidates for executive jobs in general. As the name implies, the development of these pool members is accelerated through stretch job and task force assignments that offer the best learning and highest visibility opportunities. Pool members have an assigned mentor, receive more training, and attend special developmental experiences, such as university executive programs and in-company action learning sessions. They also get more feedback and coaching. The Human Resource group and senior management actively track pool members' development and readiness.

In an Acceleration Pool system, senior executives no longer need to worry about deciding who's going to back up whom in their organization, except for the top positions. The annual chore of completing replacement-planning forms is eliminated, which gives them more time to focus on skill and knowledge development—that is, on cultivating tomorrow's leaders.

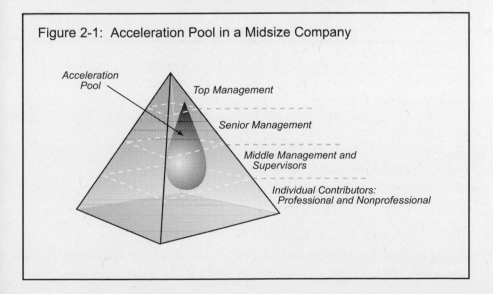

Figure 2-1: Acceleration Pool in a Midsize Company

Acceleration Pool

Top Management

Senior Management

Middle Management and Supervisors

Individual Contributors: Professional and Nonprofessional

The size of an Acceleration Pool depends on the number of positions above it, the number of candidates the organization would like to choose from in filling target positions, and the speed at which the organization is growing. Figure 2-1 on the previous page shows a hypothetical example of a pool that might be found in a midsize company (1,000 to 5,000 employees) preparing candidates for general management positions.

There can be many variations on the basic Acceleration Pool shown in Figure 2-1. A larger organization might have two pools—one starting at the supervisory and professional individual contributor level and one starting at the middle management level (see Figure 2-2).

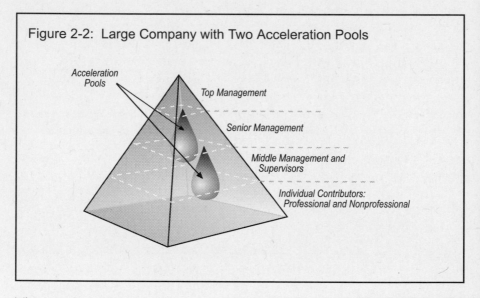

Figure 2-2: Large Company with Two Acceleration Pools

The number of pools often reflects how a company is organized. For example, an Acceleration Pool in a manufacturing organization might exist to fill top plant-management positions, while a pool of middle managers might be designated to fill a range of corporate positions. Often, large strategic business units (SBUs) will have their own Acceleration Pools to fill senior SBU positions in addition to the wider company pool that is aimed at filling senior corporate management positions (see Figure 2-3).

Figure 2-3: Organization with a Pool in Each Business Unit and a Pool for Corporate Positions

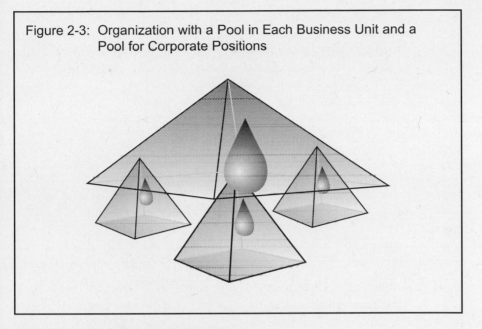

How Acceleration Pools Work

In this chapter we provide an overview of the operation of an Acceleration Pool. In Chapter 3 we'll explain the purpose and importance of various features of an Acceleration Pool system and how Acceleration Pools can uniquely meet the leadership needs of 21st century organizations. We'll then answer common questions about Acceleration Pools in Chapter 4. The remainder of this book will expand on the general description provided in these three chapters. Figure 2-4 shows a flowchart of the Acceleration Pool process described in this chapter along with a listing of other chapters containing additional information, tools, and forms. Table 2-1 lists the people and groups involved in an Acceleration Pool.

Figure 2-4: The Acceleration Pool Process

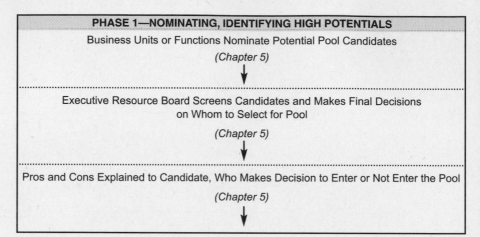

PHASE 1—NOMINATING, IDENTIFYING HIGH POTENTIALS

Business Units or Functions Nominate Potential Pool Candidates

(Chapter 5)

↓

Executive Resource Board Screens Candidates and Makes Final Decisions
on Whom to Select for Pool

(Chapter 5)

↓

Pros and Cons Explained to Candidate, Who Makes Decision to Enter or Not Enter the Pool

(Chapter 5)

↓

PHASE 2—DIAGNOSING DEVELOPMENT OPPORTUNITIES

Assessment of Development Needs, Using an Acceleration Center

(Chapter 7)

↓

Feedback of Assessment Results and Determination of Development Priorities

(Chapters 8, 14)

↓

PHASE 3—PRESCRIBING SOLUTIONS TO DEVELOPMENT OPPORTUNITIES

Executive Resource Board Decides on Pool Member Assignments, Special Training,
or Executive Coaching and Monitors Progress and Completion

(Chapters 8, 15, 16)

↓

Development Goals on Current or New Job Assignment Are Framed Relative to Diagnosis

(Chapters 8, 14)

↓

Pool Member Targets Areas and Strategies for Development with
the Help of Manager and Mentor

(May involve changes in job responsibilities or projects.
Additional development goals may be chosen.)

(Chapters 8, 14)

↓

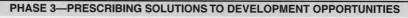

From Phase 5

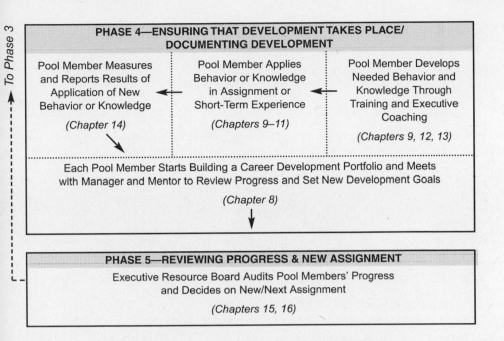

To Phase 3

PHASE 4—ENSURING THAT DEVELOPMENT TAKES PLACE/ DOCUMENTING DEVELOPMENT

Pool Member Measures and Reports Results of Application of New Behavior or Knowledge

(Chapter 14)

Pool Member Applies Behavior or Knowledge in Assignment or Short-Term Experience

(Chapters 9–11)

Pool Member Develops Needed Behavior and Knowledge Through Training and Executive Coaching

(Chapters 9, 12, 13)

Each Pool Member Starts Building a Career Development Portfolio and Meets with Manager and Mentor to Review Progress and Set New Development Goals

(Chapter 8)

PHASE 5—REVIEWING PROGRESS & NEW ASSIGNMENT

Executive Resource Board Audits Pool Members' Progress and Decides on New/Next Assignment

(Chapters 15, 16)

Phase 1: Nominating, Identifying High Potentials

To fill the pool, each major part of the organization (e.g., divisions, business units, etc.) is asked to nominate people, basing the choice on job performance and an agreed-upon criteria of potential. People can be nominated from any organizational level and career stage: supervisor, middle manager, or senior manager. Individuals might be in the Acceleration Pool for anywhere from 1 to 15 years, depending on when they enter and what their development needs are. This approach is quite different from some "high-potential" development programs that admit people only at the start of their career. Recognizing that individuals' and organizations' needs change over time, the Acceleration Pool system is flexible enough to develop leaders at virtually any point in their career or at any time that makes sense for the organization. A senior management committee—which we call the Executive Resource Board and which should include the CEO and/or COO—reviews the nominations against defined criteria and decides who is admitted into the pool.

Invitation into the Pool

After prospective pool members are selected, the pros and cons of participating in the accelerated development program are explained to each person who has been invited. Each person then decides on whether to join

Table 2-1: People Involved in an Acceleration Pool

Pool Member	The person whose development is being accelerated for a target level (e.g., general management).
Pool Member's Manager	The person to whom the pool member reports. This manager can be at any level in the organization. The manager's role is to establish an environment for development and provide guidance, coaching, feedback, and reinforcement.
Pool Member's Mentor	A manager at a level equal to or higher than the pool member's manager. The mentor's role is to provide guidance, support, and organizational and business insights.
Professional Coach (a.k.a. Executive Coach)	An outside professional who is brought in to work one-on-one with a pool member. Coaches help their clients expand self-awareness and understand their development needs. Coaches help pool members develop new behaviors or interpersonal strategies to overcome executive derailers/ competency needs and work with them to measure and monitor growth against desired goals.
Executive Resource Board (a.k.a. Talent Review Board, Talent Committee, Executive Succession Board, Executive Development Board, Leadership Team, etc.)	In organizations with one pool aimed at producing general management-level candidates, the Executive Resource Board comprises the CEO and/or COO and the division, unit, or SBU heads— the group responsible for filling the target-level positions and operating the Acceleration Pool. When more than one pool exists, organizations usually have a different board for each pool (and a different name), although there is some overlap in membership.
HR Representative to the Executive Resource Board	The member of the organization who makes the Acceleration Pool system work. The HR representative acts as a catalyst and quality control expert as well as the expert source of information on all parts of the system.

the pool. It's important to ensure that there is no stigma or penalty attached to opting out of accelerated development. A wide range of family concerns and other considerations (e.g., the perceived risks involved) might make a candidate feel that it's not the right time for a high-intensity, accelerated program. Such situations can change, of course, so the individual who opts out may have a chance to join the pool at another time.

Phase 2: Diagnosing Development Opportunities

Assessment of Development Needs, Using an Acceleration Center

Once they have accepted the invitation to join the Acceleration Pool, the new pool members complete an in-depth assessment of development needs. The members are assessed in terms of four sets of *executive descriptors* that define the leadership needed to make the organization successful in the future:

- **Organizational knowledge**—*What I know*—The functions, processes, systems, and products, services, or technologies of an organization that a general manager must understand. For example, a candidate might be assessed in terms of span of knowledge of company products, how the R&D process operates, or the function provided by the HR department.

- **Job challenges**—*What I have done*—The kinds of situations that an individual entering top management should have experienced or at least have been exposed to. Some examples include carrying a key functional assignment through from beginning to end; being heavily involved with a merger, acquisition, strategic alliance, or partnership opportunity; implementing a companywide change; developing and implementing a plan to cut costs or control inventories; negotiating agreements with external organizations; and operating in high-pressure or high-visibility situations.

- **Competencies**—*What I am capable of*—The clusters of behavior, knowledge, technical skills, and motivations that are important to success in senior management. Some examples include *Change Leadership, Establishing Strategic Direction, Marketing and Entrepreneurial Insight,* and *Global Acumen.*

- **Executive derailers**—*Who I am*—The personality traits that might cause an otherwise effective senior leader to fail on the job. Examples include being aloof, arrogant, overly cautious, approval dependent, distrustful, eccentric, melodramatic, mischievous, passive aggressive, perfectionistic, and volatile (Hogan, 2000; Hogan & Hogan, 1997).

The senior leadership of the organization, based on the organization's strategic direction and values, selects the specific descriptors. A variety of methods, including the Acceleration Center[SM] (a modern-day assessment center), multiple-perspective (360°) instruments, and interviews, are used to diagnose pool members' development needs.

Feedback of Assessment Results and Determination of Development Priorities

A professional explains the results of the diagnosis to each pool member and checks on any personal or retention needs that would shape development. Together, they decide how the pool member can maximize the impact of the identified strengths and prioritize the development needs in each of the four executive descriptor areas, creating a Development Priority List.

Phase 3: Prescribing Solutions to Development Opportunities

The Executive Resource Board or its representative reviews the completed Development Priority Lists and diagnostic summary reports to ensure that areas of development need are covered and that the chosen priorities fit with the organization's strategic direction. This review is important because the priorities determined by an individual pool member might be based on the assumption that the organization is going in a certain direction, when in fact top executives might see it going in a different direction. The new direction might change the relative importance of competencies, organizational knowledge, or job challenges.

After being approved by the Executive Resource Board, the Development Priority Lists become "official"—but that does not mean that they are unchangeable. New insights into development needs usually arise over time, and these should be reflected on the lists. More important, development gaps will be closed as members gain experience in the pool, and this will, of course, change their development needs.

Executive Resource Board Decides on Pool Member Assignments, Special Training, or Executive Coaching and Monitors Progress and Completion

The Executive Resource Board is responsible for placing pool members into situations where they can experience the required job challenges, obtain needed organizational knowledge, develop competencies, and overcome executive derailers. This is accomplished through a combination of short, high-impact, targeted training programs; short-term learning experiences (e.g., attending conventions or hosting a delegation of foreign customers); and, most of all, meaningful, measurable job or task force assignments where the pool member can be held accountable for results and learn from the experience. Jobs, task force membership, and other longer-term assignments are the most important factors in developing Acceleration Pool members because they offer opportunities to satisfy several development objectives at once. For example, in a given assignment, an individual might encounter two job challenges and three areas of organization knowledge, have a chance to develop one competency, and be able to address one derailer. It is very important to note that all development is within the context of high-quality job performance—not something done in addition to an individual's job. There is a clear link from successful development to job success. Both are accomplished at the same time.

The Executive Resource Board also determines who should attend major training events, such as university programs or programs developed exclusively for Acceleration Pool members (e.g., action learning). An action learning program enables pool members to work in teams as they confront major organizational issues and make recommendations to senior management. Strategy-orientation programs represent another training alternative often tailored for Acceleration Pool members. The Executive Resource Board also decides whether it is appropriate to make an executive coach available to specific pool members. The board uses the Development Priority List and its understanding of individual pool members' personal and retention needs to make these decisions.

The Executive Resource Board typically meets with the heads of organizational or business units at least twice a year to review major personnel movements and discuss talent development. Board members review Acceleration Pool members' progress at that time and consider ways to speed their development.

Because the ultimate goal of the Executive Resource Board is to fill key positions with ready talent, the organization's needs must be in balance with each individual's needs. As specific solutions to individual development needs are considered, business demands and associated job requirements are considered as well. These factors result in a series of trade-off decisions about how to develop a pool member and when to place the person into a key role. The trade-offs often involve people who are not in the Acceleration Pool who are being considered for placement into positions. Organizational movement can be horizontal as well as vertical, and the board relies heavily on task force assignments to minimize moves that would adversely affect a pool member's personal life.

Development Goals on Current or New Job Assignment Are Framed Relative to Diagnosis

After job and training assignments are made, a representative of the Executive Resource Board meets with each pool member (in person or over the phone) to review the decisions and discuss how the assignment or training fits with the person's development priorities and expressed personal interests. This is how pool members learn what specific competencies and challenges they are to work on in their new assignments. Because pool members understand the purpose of the assignment or training and its potential value to their personal development, they are more likely to be enthusiastic about it and be fully committed to its success.

Pool Member Targets Areas and Strategies for Development with the Help of Manager and Mentor

Pool members meet with their current manager (or their manager in their new assignment) and their mentor to pin down the specifics of how to develop the competencies, job challenges, and organizational knowledge suggested by the Executive Resource Board while also accomplishing the objectives of their job assignment. Usually the effective completion of the assignment is itself the principle development goal. Other development goals are always closely tied to assignment success (e.g., the manager, mentor, and pool member might discuss a derailer that could cause problems and ways to avoid it, or they might talk about how the development of a target competency or area of organizational knowledge will contribute to success during the next year). This discussion is where the "rubber meets the road" in making the development come about. The manager and the mentor are prepared for their roles through orientation and training.

In preparation for these meetings, Acceleration Pool members complete the first part of a Development Action Form (see Appendix 2-1) for each of the areas to be developed. This form forces pool members to think about how they will achieve the targeted development (skills, behavior, knowledge), how they can apply the newly learned development targets on the job, and how they will measure the effectiveness of the application (ideally on job performance measures). This encourages pool members to focus on applying skills, behavior, and knowledge rather than on merely learning them in an abstract sense. For example, Acceleration Pool members should not be evaluated on completing a developmental opportunity, such as a training program, but rather on measurements of organizational change brought on by their using the new skills or knowledge back in the workplace. With such *application targets* defined before a training program, pool members are able to focus on applying development goals during the training. They are also in a better position to tap into an instructor's special knowledge or get coaching from other people to help them learn how to apply their new skills or knowledge. Most important, they see the development project as part of their job—to make them more successful—not as an add-on.

As one might expect, a pool member in a new assignment might not know enough about opportunities offered by the job to complete the first part of the Development Action Form for some development targets. The manager and mentor can be a big help in the planning process by talking through issues and possibilities. More important, the meeting helps gain the manager's and the mentor's buy-in and commitment to the pool member's learning and skill application goals. This is important because the manager might have to add or take away job responsibilities or performance goals to facilitate development in an area. For example, a manager might assign managing the budgeting process to someone who needs a better understanding of the process and the organization's long-range planning.

The planning meeting also provides an opportunity for the pool member, the manager, and the mentor to explore additional areas from the Development Priority List that the job assignment might offer. These opportunities typically arise in the form of short-term learning experiences or prescriptive training programs that are open to everyone in the organization. For example, someone in need of presentation skills might attend a course on that topic sponsored by the business unit and then be asked to present a new product at field offices to demonstrate the new skills.

Discussions at the planning meeting and subsequent meetings allow the manager and mentor to remain in touch with the pool member's personal and retention needs so those needs can be considered in the individual's development plans and communicated, where appropriate, to the Executive Resource Board. For example, a pool member might need to return to his or her hometown because an elderly parent is dependent on the person for support and care. Where feasible, the pool member's manager can meet this need by assigning projects near the individual's hometown. However, only the Executive Resource Board would have the authority to move a pool member to a desired location.

Phase 4: Ensuring That Development Takes Place/ Documenting Development

Responsibility for completing and executing the Development Action Form belongs with the pool member alone. The mentor and manager simply provide counsel, open doors, and make resources available.

After completing a development project (e.g., running an R&D team as part of the job assignment) or training program, pool members evaluate success against their defined objectives. They review their accomplishments (or lack thereof) with their manager and mentor, and then record their achievements on the second part of the Development Action Form. As we mentioned, this is typically done at the end of a project. If the project lasts six months or more, intermediate progress should be reviewed to allow the mentor and manager to offer help as needed.

Pool Member Documents Development

Each Acceleration Pool member keeps a Career Development Portfolio, which includes the member's Development Priority List, an up-to-date personal information form, completed performance appraisal forms, and completed and in-progress Development Action Forms. The portfolio serves as a repository for all the individual's development information.

When entering the Acceleration Pool, members agree to make this portfolio's contents available to the Executive Resource Board. In turn, the board agrees to review the portfolios every six months—a relatively easy task if portfolios are posted on the corporate intranet with access limited to respective pool members and the Executive Resource Board.

Phase 5: Reviewing Progress & New Assignment

At least every six months, the Executive Resource Board considers whether pool members will be reassigned, sent to special training events, given an executive coach, or maintain their current assignments for continued development. If some action is decided, the plan is discussed with the pool member. The operation of the Executive Resource Board is discussed at length in Chapter 15, Optimizing Your Talent Review Discussion.

Summary of Process

We believe that Acceleration Pools offer an attractive alternative to traditional replacement-planning systems and are more in touch with the needs of 21st century organizations and managers. An Acceleration Pool approach is not a cure-all, and it's not easy. It's also not as hard as you might think after looking at the flowchart in Figure 2-4. We believe that the Acceleration Pool uses no more top management time than traditional replacement planning yet produces better results. The Executive Resource Board has a more accurate and organized way of making decisions about who gets into the Acceleration Pool and more meaningful information on which to make development decisions about pool members. We have seen the efficiency and quality of discussions of Executive Resource Boards totally change as they've adopted the more behavioral, data-oriented approach provided by Acceleration Pools.

Acceleration Pools take up significantly less time of managers, who no longer have to fill out replacement-planning forms each year. By putting the responsibility of record keeping on the people being developed, and by giving them forms to guide their discussions and planning, we are maximizing the relationship between these individuals and their managers and mentors. And their meetings are much more productive and meaningful.

Most important, you will have the leaders you need. We have seen the ideas endorsed by this book successfully used in organizations of every size and shape. And from a personal standpoint, we know that Acceleration Pools work well because we're using the system within Development Dimensions International.

Appendix 2-1: Sample Development Action Form

Development Action Form

Part 1: Development Plan

Name: _____ Date: _____

Job/Title: _____

Department/SBU:_____

Development goal? Specify job challenge, organizational knowledge, competency, or derailer, and add clarifying information as needed. You can list more than one on this form if they can be developed by the same action. Explain how your development in this executive descriptor will enhance your success in your position:

How will learning be obtained if required (e.g., coaching, observation, training program, membership on a committee)?

Define the support needed to accomplish the learning (if required).

How will the development goal be applied? (Be specific [e.g., project, person, group].)

Define the support needed to apply the development goal.

How will intermediate achievements be tracked (if appropriate)?
(When should next meeting with manager or mentor be?)

Specify the date for completing the application of the development goal, and describe how you will document accomplishment of learning.

Part 2: Development Results

Evaluate the acquisition of learning. If learning goals weren't met, list the reasons why.

Evaluate the application of the behavior, skill, or knowledge. If application goals weren't met, list the reasons why.

What did you learn about developing your skills and knowledge or by changing your behavior?

Probable future application of the behavior, skill, or knowledge:

What additional skills or knowledge was obtained?

What could have been done to make your development process more rewarding?

What general insights into leadership or management did you develop (if any)?

Chapter 3

Seventeen Reasons Acceleration Pools Work

"The best way to predict the future is to create it."

—Peter Drucker, Professor, Author
Claremont Graduate School

Making Corporate Darwinism Fairer

Morgan McCall, a professor specializing in executive development at USC, and others have said that many organizations have relied upon a Darwinian approach to top-management development: identifying the best people and then giving them increasingly difficult challenges until they drop off the organizational ladder or reach the top (McCall, 1997). This is *not* the approach taken in an Acceleration Pool system. Pool members receive appropriate growth and stretch assignments in which they can succeed and are given support along the way to facilitate their success. Some people will still opt out of the pool, but most of the chance factors that so often unfairly affect people's career progress have been eliminated. The organization keeps better track of *how* individuals are doing and *what* they are doing and learning in their job assignments so that both the behavior and the actual results can be evaluated. In contrast, in a Darwinian system, people in job assignments might hit a difficult economic period or run into unusual competition that can make them look bad; the opposite can also be true, with people's poor performance looking seemingly good. We strongly advocate helping individuals learn from their experiences by providing accurate feedback regarding what they did well and what they could improve upon.

☞ denotes that information on this topic is available at the *Grow Your Own Leaders* web site (www.ddiworld.com/growyourownleaders).

The Acceleration Pool system gives pool members training and adequate preparation before they face a challenge so that they will use more of the right behaviors and be successful. Our approach is more analogous to an agricultural model, which is based on nurturing and cultivating the seeds of talent, rather than the "fittest" emerging from a series of tests and challenges. The balance of this chapter focuses on 17 specific reasons that Acceleration Pools offer a superior alternative to corporate Darwinism.

1. Acceleration Pools are 21st century programs.

They are based on assumptions that differ significantly from those that have long underpinned traditional replacement-planning systems. We contrast these two sets of assumptions in Table 3-1.

2. Pool members' buy-in is built in.

In the past large organizations were able to freely move their people around the world without much consideration of their employees' personal needs or desires. IBM was once known by the nickname "I've Been Moved." J.C. Penney would tell a manager on Friday to report to a new assignment in another town on the following Monday—and expect that it would always happen. But today, it's simply not appropriate—or realistic—to assume that people are going to accept assignments without question. More and more people want to match their work situations to their lifestyles, which makes them much more selective about new assignments.

The Acceleration Pool approach acknowledges that reality: Nominees decide whether they want to be in the pool. Once they are in, pool members have a voice in determining what they do. Their career interests and views on their own development needs are collected as part of the diagnosis phase of the Acceleration Pool process. They are told about proposed assignments and why each is a learning opportunity—specifically what development gaps they will be able to fill in a given assignment. Then they can make intelligent decisions about taking on that task. People tend to agree to such assignments because they see how the experience will help them grow.

3. Less paper, time, and bureaucracy.

A major benefit of the Acceleration Pool system is the drastic reduction of the overwhelming paperwork associated with traditional replacement-planning systems. Gone are the annual replacement plans

Table 3-1: Contrasting Assumptions About Traditional Replacement-Planning Systems and Acceleration Pools	
Assumptions About Traditional Replacement-Planning Systems	**Assumptions About the Acceleration Pool System**
• Consistent business strategy.	• Frequent changes or flexibility in business strategy (e.g., new competitors, distribution channels, and alliance partners).
• Stable organizational structure.	• Fluid organizational structure (frequent changes).
• Fixed jobs.	• Fluid jobs (frequent changes in responsibilities and reporting arrangements).
• People move vertically.	• People move vertically and horizontally.
• Upward movement is automatic, as long as people avoid making big mistakes.	• People must pass through an effective selection system for each job they take on.
• Jobs can be planned two or three positions ahead.	• Impossible to plan future jobs with any accuracy. Thus, the focus is on the next assignment— and the balance between organization needs and individual development needs.
• Training is a "rite of passage" (e.g., university executive programs).	• Training is integrated with assignments to provide skills and knowledge that can be used immediately on the job. At higher levels, short one-on-one training experiences are used. University executive programs often are replaced by organizationally specific, action-learning programs.
• People can be moved anywhere, anytime. If they said "no," they were often considered "not active candidates" for future positions outside their current location.	• Family, working spouse, and other circumstances might make physical moves unacceptable.

and the bureaucracy associated with compiling and defending the plans. Gone too are the Individual Development Plans (IDPs) that individuals on their way up in an organization traditionally had to complete after an assessment center or 360° feedback. Acceleration Pools replace the IDPs with two short forms and replace the bureaucracy with a streamlined system.

4. **A better use of time—no additional top-management time required for making job or development assignments.**

Nearly all the midsize and large organizations we deal with have an annual or semiannual human resource review of some kind. Larger organizations conduct the review by SBUs or functions. Midsize companies might review promotions and people development for the whole organization at the same time. The Acceleration Pool system

---

A Former Executive Describes a Now-Discarded Replacement-Planning Process at Xerox

Chris Turner, former Xerox executive and now a consultant, writer, and speaker, described her former company's promotion process in *Fast Company* magazine (1999) as follows:

> Xerox had a horrible process for promotion. Each year, everyone in the organization had to fill out reams of paperwork about what they wanted to be when they grew up. You had to list your one-year, three-year, and five-year goals. And you had to name specific positions that you were shooting for. Well, whose life ever unfolds according to a five-year plan—or even a one-year plan? That practice was absurd—but one that we all completed like mules.

> Finally, I said, "I'm not going to do this anymore. This process perpetuates the type of organization that I don't want to work for." So, for a few years, my boss, a good corporate soldier, filled out the paperwork for me. Other people soon caught on to the absurdity, and eventually everyone on my team quit doing it. Then I got a call from someone in HR who admitted that only 35 percent of all employees complied with the process. When that HR person asked me to start filling out the paperwork again, I told him that everyone knew that being promoted at Xerox had nothing to do with all that paper. To make a long story short, Xerox bagged the process (Muoio, 1999, p. 96).

does not increase the number of talent reviews or hours devoted to them, but it provides additional data, structure, and focus to the assignment decision to ensure that pool members get the best available development opportunities.

5. **Acceleration Centers improve the accuracy of the development needs diagnosis and are perceived as fair.**

Modern-day assessment centers, which we call Acceleration Centers to convey that they are different in several ways from traditional assessment centers, play an important role in Acceleration Pool systems because they help provide an accurate diagnosis of people's development needs. Acceleration Centers force pool members to deal with issues and situations that are typical of general manager and executive positions while professional assessors observe them as they work through the simulations.

A truism of industrial/organizational psychology is that when multiple job-related methodologies are used for evaluation, and when multiple trained people involved in different parts of the evaluation systematically pool their insights to develop a "holistic" picture of an individual, more accurate predictions result. This is how an Acceleration Center operates. Different assessors observe the behavior or the individuals as they go through parts of a set of integrated simulations. The simulations are designed to mirror various challenges or issues appropriate for the target job level. In addition to very realistic, contemporary executive simulations, Acceleration Centers also use paper-and-pencil instruments and behavior-based interviews to round out the diagnosis of individual needs.

In essence, the Acceleration Center lets the pool member "try on" a senior role in a relatively risk-free, simulated environment. For example, in a typical day-and-a-half session, a participant might begin by reviewing a thick folder of information about the simulated company and his or her hypothetical job in it—perhaps a key vice president. As a "vice president," the pool member must prepare a presentation about a new strategic plan to be given the following day. And, in the meantime, numerous memos, e-mails, and voice mails demand attention, forcing the individual to prioritize tasks, organize work time, and make multiple decisions.

Throughout the day the vice president is involved in meetings with individuals, such as:

- Two executives who are not cooperating with each other, thereby putting an important new system in peril.

- The head of the Brazilian operation, whose sales goals are not being met.

- A colleague at a working lunch to begin creating the strategic plan presentation.

- An executive from another firm that could be a profitable strategic partner but that actually wants to buy the company's technology outright.

- An irate major customer who's ready to jump ship.

- A local TV reporter who's heard rumors that the company's product might be linked to pollution problems.

In the evening the participant prepares the strategic plan presentation. After polishing it early the next morning, the person delivers the presentation to a group of other "vice presidents."

All this activity is packed into a demanding few hours. In that time the pool member has developed strategic direction, tested his or her vision, and addressed vendor problems, personnel matters, thorny diversity issues, and professional jealousies.

Acceleration Pool members who participate in this integrated set of simulations receive feedback from the assessors' observations of their behavior and decisions in the simulations as well as from psychological inventories and interviews completed as part of the process. This wealth of feedback gives Acceleration Pool members a clear insight into their strengths and weaknesses at the target level. This insight is enhanced even further when 360° data, based on the same competencies and derailers, are also available to the pool member.

A major advantage of Acceleration Centers is that participants perceive them as being fair and accurate—two considerations that are increasing in importance. Yet, for cost and time considerations, relatively few organizations put all their potential pool members though an Acceleration Center as part of their screening process (see discussion in Chapter 7). However, for some organizations it is clearly the best alternative, as the example on the opposite page illustrates.

Case Study: The Acceleration Center Finds a Diamond

A large global organization decided to put people with certain organizational titles through an Acceleration Center to help identify those with top-management potential. Coming to the center were leaders who managed up to 1,000 employees and a young man who was responsible for only three employees. He got to the center because he was the comptroller of a very small unit of the organization in Nova Scotia. The man had not gone to college, while most of the other managers being evaluated held MBAs from some of the world's leading schools. But the young man performed admirably in the center—indeed, he was one of the very best of the hundreds who went through it.

The organization jumped on the opportunity. It sent the young man to an executive-development program at Harvard, gave him some behavioral training, and promoted him. Every few years, it moved him to different key assignments around the world. In every job he exceeded expectations, and within a few years he was leading one of the largest sectors of the organization.

There are three lessons to draw from this story:

1. All organizations have more good people than they think they do—the trick is to find them.

2. The Acceleration Center method is a very good system for spotting high potentials.

3. An Acceleration Center is an excellent tool for diagnosing specific development needs, which can then be met by targeted training interventions. The young man in the case study was given behavioral training based on needs identified through the center.

6. Development, job, and organizational success are linked.

The most common characteristic of development plans that actually result in measurable changes is that they (creatively) frame pool members' development priorities in the context of the strategic business results for which the person is accountable. While development plans with no tangential relationship to the pool member's business objectives might be appealing in concept, the likely reality is that such plans, well intentioned as they might be, will fall to the bottom of the priority list given the many demands on the pool member's time.

At the start of each job or task force assignment, the manager and mentor ensure that the pool member clearly understands the business results to be achieved and their importance. This is the first topic of discussion in the development planning meeting so that most development activities can be set up to reinforce the performance objectives—not substitute for them. This is a far cry from some traditional high-potential programs, in which people served time in assignments with little pressure for performance.

7. Equal emphasis on selection, diagnosis, and development.

The problem with many succession management systems is that they emphasize identifying talent and diagnosing development needs over development. Many organizations mistakenly believe that selecting people with potential and giving them feedback about their strengths and development needs are all that is necessary. They expect those receiving the feedback to take over from there. Our experience and research do not bear this out. Diagnosis without explicit development actions seldom pays off.

8. Development planning is done at the optimal time.

In traditional replacement-planning programs, high potentials are asked to fill out an Individual Development Plan immediately after completing a diagnostic assessment. At that point, however, they might or might not know what their next job or special assignment will be, much less what development opportunities will be offered. To make matters worse, the high potentials have no idea of what help to expect from their future manager. Most important, people get little help in thinking through possibilities because they have no one to challenge their reasoning or make alternative suggestions. As a result, many completed IDPs tend to be unfocused, vague, and simplistic, such as, "I'll work harder on that" or "I'll take a course that covers that."

In an Acceleration Pool, members formulate their development plans for specific targets suggested by the Executive Resource Board as well as additional targets that they choose for themselves. They do this at the start of each new job or special assignment—when they have a clear understanding of the opportunities and challenges it entails. Because managers and mentors know the assignment, they can offer guidance in making creative, yet realistic plans and are in a position to commit to a certain level of assistance.

9. Acceleration Pools build skills and confidence.

At best, many standard training programs produce minimal skills and confidence. To truly imbed skills into their behavioral repertoire, pool members must apply them immediately and get the appropriate coaching before and after the application. In many organizations the development focus is erroneously placed on completing training programs instead of effectively applying the learning. In an Acceleration Pool, skill application is planned in conjunction with the selection of development activities. That way, skills can be applied immediately.

10. Pool members understand what to learn or accomplish in each event.

In traditional programs we've seen people assigned to a job to learn specific leadership skills from their new manager—but for one reason or another, no one bothered to explain this goal. As a result, these people tend to concentrate on other, relatively unimportant aspects of the assignment. Similarly, people might be assigned to cross-organizational or cross-functional task forces to broaden their knowledge in a specific area. But because they don't know about that goal, they tend to concentrate on the areas in which they are already proficient (the marketer on marketing, the manufacturer on manufacturing, etc.) and let other team members take responsibility for the target learning area. And in training programs people commonly arrive with no idea of why they are there or how they can use the learning on the job.

The use of the Development Action Form eliminates that kind of "assignment ignorance." Acceleration Pool members know precisely what they are to learn from every development event and how they can use the new learning or skill on the job.

11. Support is available.

Pool members often need help understanding the scope and constraints of their new assignments. They also need doors opened, resources and money to apply or practice new skills, and, especially, time to attend training and implement projects. Because pool members meet with their manager to craft their Development Action Forms, they more likely will get the support they need. Either the manager commits to his or her responsibilities relative to the development plan, or the plan is changed. The system prevents pool members from making unrealistic plans. Usually the pool member's mentor also attends this meeting. The mentor provides additional insights and, most of all, applies subtle pressure on the manager to make any sacrifices that are necessary for the pool member's development (e.g., time off for training, special responsibilities, etc.).

Succession Management and Stock Prices

An Asia-Pacific telecommunications company was facing an uncertain future of converging technology, a deregulated marketplace, increased global competition, and increasing customer demands. Although it had a reputation for technical excellence, the company was considered to be highly bureaucratic, unresponsive to customers, and out of touch with the realities of modern telecommunications. In fact, the financial press was often critical of the company's performance and leadership and openly doubted that anyone in the organization had the capacity to take over when the current CEO retired. There was also a real threat that new competitors would very quickly erode market share and take the lead in the most profitable market segments. This would have put the company at the distinct competitive disadvantage of having to maintain a costly telecommunications infrastructure with high-cost/low-profit revenue streams.

Recognizing this very real threat to its future, the organization took a number of steps to improve its position by increasing its focus on regional expansion, improving customer service, and increasing its investment in emerging technologies. The senior team also recognized that the culture needed to change if the company was to cope with a more uncertain and turbulent marketplace. The company would have to improve the public's perception (especially the stock market perception) of its leaders' ability to drive the kind of sweeping change that was needed and the organization's ability to proactively tackle the issues facing it.

As part of their overall improvement strategy, the senior management team adopted a more strategic approach to developing executive bench strength. They contracted DDI to develop and manage an assessment program for middle and senior managers that reflected the corporate capabilities needed to succeed in the future marketplace they envisioned. The aim was to identify managers who could:

• Thrive in this ambiguous and uncertain business environment.

- Help others cope more effectively with change.
- See the opportunities in the issues facing them and drive the business's future success.

DDI assessed 600 individuals and then provided feedback on participants' key strengths and development needs to participants and their managers. Participants then met with their manager and/or coach to construct development plans and review career/placement strategies. In addition, DDI presented group trend data and met with senior management to identify group development needs and implications for business performance.

For the high-potential managers, individual and group development strategies were then initiated to address development gaps, and then they were moved into key positions. Development strategies included traditional training and executive education, plus executive coaching and mentoring, targeted assignments within the company and other organizations (e.g., executives would be exchanged for a period of one to three years), action learning (e.g., a group of high-potential managers would take the role of the top team and be asked to address specific strategic issues), and project work aimed to stretch the individuals' experience and skill development.

Four years after starting the program, the results were visible on many fronts:

- Despite greater global and regional competition, the organization was steadily growing in both revenue and profit.
- The company became an early adapter of emerging telecommunication technology and, as result, was able to establish early market presence in a number of these areas (e.g., the Internet).
- The company greatly improved its image within the marketplace. The financial press was more positive about the organization's performance and prospects, and the stock market remains very bullish about the company's future.
- Perceptions of customer service levels, while still not where the company ideally would have wanted them, improved significantly. Despite heavy advertising campaigns, competitors' penetration into the company's traditional base was limited. Most important, the organization retained its share of the most profitable business segments.
- When the CEO retired, the share price did not falter, which reflected both market and media confidence in the CEO's replacement.

12. **Emphasis is on changing behavior—and proving it.**

Behavior change seldom comes about from a single intervention, such as attending a training program or having a good coach. Multiple input is usually needed. This is exactly what an Acceleration Pool provides. An individual working on a competency might build skills in a training program, be assigned to a job or task force to use the skills, get coaching and support from a concerned manager, and perhaps receive additional practice opportunities from a short-term experience.

Pool members use the Development Action Form to plan how they will apply the target skills, knowledge, and behavior as well as how they will document their application achievements (e.g., a project's results, changes in 360° ratings, etc.). This emphasis on documentation helps to ensure that development focuses on behavior change and is bottom-line oriented. While the emphasis is—and should be—on enhancing skills and behavior, pool members need to feel that they are afforded a safe opportunity for making mistakes. The purpose of documentation is to ensure accountability and credit for achievements—not to make pool members feel as though they are under extreme evaluation scrutiny.

13. **Growth *and* bottom-line achievement are documented.**

To remain motivated, pool members must feel that their efforts are paying off, and they must be able to prove it to others. The second part of the Development Action Form helps them measure and track their progress toward their development goals and document their application of target skills or knowledge for each development activity. This documentation underscores that they are learning and growing—which is increasingly critical to retaining top performers.

14. **Managers' and mentors' roles and responsibilities are clear.**

In traditional replacement-planning systems, the roles of managers and mentors are often vague. Frequently, both the mentor/manager and the individual being developed wait for the other to initiate meetings or wait for a form or memo telling them to do so from those running the succession management program. When they finally do meet, goals for the meeting are often not spelled out, which means that the success of the relationship cannot be measured. As a result of all this uncertainty, few of the people involved are likely to be enthusiastic about taking time out of their busy schedules to participate. Soon the frequency of meetings declines, or they cease entirely.

Managers and mentors in an Acceleration Pool are equipped to support assigned pool members. They are oriented to the expectations and accountabilities associated with their roles and are provided with easy access to support resources, such as online guidance relative to training and development options. Preparing managers and mentors with coaching tools and processes is accomplished through streamlined orientations, one-on-one sessions with HR or more experienced executives, and for some managers short, formal training programs. ☞

15. Retention is a focus of the system.

Many a manager has been shocked to learn that a key employee is leaving the organization for better opportunities elsewhere. In an exit interview the manager then hears how the individual just didn't see a future in the organization—although the manager had seen this person as a high-potential "keeper." The problem was communication—no one ever bothered to tell that employee that he or she was a highly valued contributor facing a bright future with the company.

That scenario does not happen in the Acceleration Pool system because members are aware of the benefits and responsibilities of being in the pool and have been invited to choose whether or not to participate. They know that they are, by definition, seen as high potential. They understand that they are getting special attention from senior management. And they see that they are getting the tools and opportunities to realize that potential, be involved in setting their own goals, and shape their own future.

We strongly believe that the key to retaining people is to make significant learning and training experiences available. Today people want to feel that they are learning and growing—indeed, one of the most common reasons that departing managers give for leaving is "lack of personal growth." People in an Acceleration Pool have tremendous (and obvious) learning and promotional opportunities, which provide a powerful motivation to stay with the company.

16. Top management (finally) has accurate, timely information for key appointments.

A common source of frustration for senior managers is the lack of credible and comprehensive information on candidates for leadership positions. Acceleration Pool members keep an online portfolio of their development needs and accomplishments. The online Career Development Portfolio is accessible only to the individual pool members and members of the Executive Resource Board. DDI believes this portfolio will soon become part of most Acceleration Pool members' personal web pages on their organization's intranet.

This approach solves what historically has been one of the great human resource problems of large organizations: the inability to closely monitor employees' changing skills and knowledge. Most companies simply don't know when their people develop new skills, learn a new language, or experience new challenges. Usually, they ask their employees to complete periodic surveys to update their database, but that's a fairly hopeless task in an increasingly fast-paced world. In the Acceleration Pool system, on the other hand, pool members know they are responsible for the currency and accuracy of such data. And, they know that top management will review these data at least every six months, which gives them a powerful motivation to keep the data current.

17. **The pool is solely line-management driven and not at risk of being seen as another "HR program."**

Senior management is actively involved in ways that maximize the impact of their time. HR supports, advises, facilitates, and does many other important things to make the Acceleration Pool system work, but they don't own the system.

Acceleration Pool System Advantages

Overall, we believe that the Acceleration Pool approach is more effective than traditional replacement-management systems and that it provides a wide range of advantages by comparison. These advantages can be summed up as:

• Faster and simpler.

• Less paper.

• More accurate.

• More focused on development.

• Higher level of involvement and buy-in from pool members and managers/mentors alike.

- Greater integrity and fairness (more open approach, less "old-boy network").

- More flexible—the system takes the individual's needs into account.

- More focused on retaining people, as opposed to simply placing them.

- Linked to business plans and strategies.

This chapter has outlined the Acceleration Pool approach—how and why it works. But there are many variations and nuances that need to be understood to transfer the concept to a specific organization. The rest of this book explores Acceleration Pools in greater detail.

Chapter 4

Acceleration Pools: Fundamental Questions and Rationale

"As you look at our growth projections over time, we're going to need more and more leaders. Leadership is the biggest single constraint to growth at Johnson & Johnson, and it is the most critical business issue we face."

—Ralph S. Larsen, Chairman and CEO
Johnson & Johnson

Remember the "onion layer" analogy used to describe complex situations in which one question or discovery leads to additional questions? For first-time practitioners, implementing an Acceleration Pool system might appear to offer "onion layers" of complexity; however, experienced practitioners will verify that the process seems far more complicated than it actually is.

What is true, and what becomes evident to process stakeholders, are the rich opportunities for alignment and integration of Acceleration Pools with other key systems affecting organizational effectiveness. In fact, in many organizations introduction of Acceleration Pools represents a significant culture change initiative, offering important alignment with the business strategy, their learning culture or environment, accountability, and measurement systems, as well as a system for managing strategic talent and individualized approaches to leadership development.

☞ denotes that information on this topic is available at the *Grow Your Own Leaders* web site (www.ddiworld.com/growyourownleaders).

Not surprising, then, is how early broad questions stimulate new thinking and, in turn, more detailed questions around the implementation. This chapter focuses on some of the broad questions (i.e., the top layer of the onion) that practitioners face in getting started with Acceleration Pools.

When is the best time to identify people for an Acceleration Pool?

Although an Acceleration Pool is open to people at any level or age, there usually is a typical career point or organizational level at which the majority of members enter. Management faces a quandary in defining that typical entry point: It is important to identify people early enough so that they have plenty of time for development; but the longer management waits to identify people, the more accurate the prediction of growth potential will be.

So, while there is no "absolutely right" common entry point, research data indicate that evaluations are more accurate when people have been in work situations for a few years and less accurate when performed on those just entering the organization from a university or some other background.

In a classic research study done by Dr. Douglas Bray and his colleagues at AT&T (Howard & Bray, 1988), a group of college graduates were evaluated twice by an assessment center—once when they entered AT&T and then again eight years later, after most had been promoted twice. The findings from the assessment centers were not shared with the individuals or anyone in management. When the predictions of the two assessments were compared to actual promotions to senior management 10 or more years later, the second assessment proved much more predictive of success than the first. (The results also showed that the first assessment was significantly better than any system AT&T had used up to that time [Howard & Bray, 1988].)

While those results are interesting, there are some important points to bear in mind when applying them today. The study was done when AT&T was a very vertically organized company; people had to "serve their time" in various jobs—no matter how good they were. We believe that it is not so much maturity and time on the job, per se, that lead to more accurate assessments as it is meaningful job experience. Thus, we believe that in today's increasingly flat and empowered organizations, in which people get more responsibility and authority earlier, three or four years of meaningful, diverse experience can be a solid basis for highly accurate assessments of top-level management potential.

Why allow people to enter the pool at any level?

The fact that people at any organizational level can enter an Acceleration Pool reflects an acknowledgement of real issues affecting modern business:

- People mature at different speeds. Some are late bloomers whose potential will be recognized later in their careers.

- Family and other situations might make pool membership impossible for some people at certain times.

- People from outside the organization will likely be brought into middle- or upper-management jobs. Some might benefit from being in a pool.

- To achieve desired diversity at senior levels, some companies might need to dig deeper—perhaps even below the supervisory level—into their organizational ranks to find people to develop.

Given the rapid pace of organizational change, is it realistic to try to prepare leaders for roles they would assume more than five years in the future?

The impact of rapid organizational change on succession management is the reason for developing the Acceleration Pool concept in the first place. Because pool members' progress is not focused on individual jobs but rather on a *job level* defined by a range of job challenges, organizational knowledge, etc., the system is very responsive to organizational changes. The level or type of job challenges, organizational knowledge, competencies, and derailers required of each pool member can be adjusted in response to changing organizational needs and should, in fact, be reconfirmed and adjusted as necessary each year.

If someone is ready for promotion to senior management now, is it necessary to put that person in the Acceleration Pool?

As its name implies, the Acceleration Pool system focuses on people whose development needs to be speeded up. If people are completely ready for promotion to a position at the target level (e.g., general manager), they don't need to be in an Acceleration Pool.

How quickly should an organization grow its Acceleration Pool in the first year?

We strongly advise organizations to start slowly by bringing 12–40 people into the Acceleration Pool the first year, depending on the size of the organization and its leadership needs. This will allow time to gear up systems and get accustomed to the issues that rapid acceleration of key individuals creates for the organization and for pool members.

Why have pools? Why not develop everyone?

There are several good reasons why organizations can't develop everyone for senior management positions:

- Every organization has a limited number of prime developmental positions in which a person can be given an unusual amount of freedom and authority to make decisions.

- Development is expensive. It might mean giving special education opportunities, providing executive coaches, or sending people to conferences.

- Developing people burns a great deal of management energy. In fact, one of the biggest succession management and retention hurdles is getting managers to focus on their development responsibilities. Having too many people to coach and mentor dilutes management's attention; as a result, most people don't get enough help to make a difference in their development.

- If you develop everyone, there won't be enough senior management jobs for individuals to fill. Development money and time will be wasted as frustrated individuals who do not move up leave the organization.

- Not everyone will benefit from development for senior management positions.

- Not everyone wants to be in an Acceleration Pool. The travel, relocation, and heavy workloads are negatives to many prospective pool members.

We believe that organizations with Acceleration Pools should offer plentiful opportunities for *all* associates to learn and grow. The Acceleration Pool system simply acknowledges that there are limited resources available for rapid development and that maintaining a pool that is too large can defeat the purpose by spreading resources too thinly.

Should the existence of an Acceleration Pool be broadly communicated within an organization?

This issue has been hotly debated in many organizations, which seem to be all over the map as to how they handle it. Here are the pros and cons as we see them:

Pros of Broad Communication

- People will volunteer for the program. It will be an opportunity to find people who might have been overlooked.

- Communication about its existence makes people in the pool feel good about themselves. They'll be more likely to stay with the company because they feel part of an elite group.

- Having a pool creates an image of a progressive company. For example, GE, Pepsi, Ford, Conoco, and Delta Airlines talk freely about their programs.

- Managers will be under more pressure to nominate the best candidates.

- Having a pool gives those not in the pool something to work toward. If solid, consistent, job-related selection criteria are used, then it's to the organization's advantage to say that if someone meets the criteria, that person will get into the pool.

- An organization will have an easier time hiring people. The image presented to prospective employees is that of a modern organization—and one that cares about its people.

- People will accept individuals brought into their SBU or department when they understand it is part of a larger plan.

- Stock analysts will be assured that executive continuity is getting high priority.

Cons of Broad Communication

- There will be great pressure to get into the program. Handling this pressure tactfully will take up significant management time and might produce extensive paperwork. Weak managers might let people into the pool because of the pressure exerted on them rather than because candidates are fully qualified.

- Knowing the pool exists might make those who aren't in the pool feel unhappy and unvalued, thus creating high turnover.

We have discovered that if the existence of an Acceleration Pool is communicated, the organization would find it helpful to be more, rather than less, explicit regarding its focus. For example, it would be appropriate for an organization to describe the intent of an Acceleration Pool that is focused primarily on developing individuals seen as likely officer-level candidates in five years. Articulating the role of the pool as well as future opportunities to participate might minimize the frustration of those who realize that they are not yet ready for the pool.

Should members of the Acceleration Pool be told that they're in the pool?

We see no alternative but to tell people that they're in the pool because we want to give them the option not to join and to involve them in planning each stage of their own development. Yet, just more than one-third of the companies surveyed by the Corporate Leadership Council (2000) report that they do so. There is a fear that people who know they are in the pool will tell others who, in turn, will figure out that they are not in it. The Council recommends communication but suggests that the company provide communication guidelines and scripts.

What happens to people who don't get into the pool?

Many executives are concerned about the effect that not making the pool will have on people. Will they bolt from the company? In our experience it all depends on the other available advancement and development opportunities as well as the perceived focus, accuracy, and fairness of the selection system.

Obviously, it's not appropriate to distribute memos detailing who is in an Acceleration Pool and who is not. However, if non-pool members ask about their status, it's certainly appropriate to answer. Smartly run organizations make a point of telling people who are not in the pool that there will be continuing opportunities to get in, depending on their job performance and the organization's needs. And even if people are not designated for the pool, management in these companies makes it clear to them that they have not missed all opportunities for advancement and that they certainly will be considered for future openings. There are always people from outside high-potential lists who get promoted—often because they are in the right place at the right time. So, while those in Acceleration Pools inevitably have a better chance of moving up, being out of the pool does not necessarily exclude someone from advancement— just as being in the pool does not guarantee advancement.

Of course, it is important to note that it isn't wise to publicize lists of Acceleration Pool members. In fact, they should be kept confidential. Over time, though, it becomes obvious that certain people are getting special assignments, attending certain training or developmental activities, and being sent to Acceleration Centers or other formal assessment activities. Remember that such assignments would be made even if an Acceleration Pool were not in place; those who are not chosen would feel the same degree of disappointment or envy whether the assignments were part of a larger plan or not. A basic fact of organizational life is that some people are chosen over others for any particular opportunity.

The method of selecting people for the Acceleration Pool also might play a part in preventing unwanted turnover. The more objective and fair the methodology, the better the acceptance of the results.

It is impossible to weigh the cost of losing high-potential people who perceive that their careers are not being accelerated against the cost of losing average people who resent not getting a particular assignment. But we believe that most organizations would see a greater risk in losing the high potentials.

Can new people from outside the organization be brought directly into an Acceleration Pool?

Yes. When hiring at the middle-manager level and above, it's very appropriate to put people in an Acceleration Pool to help them get a feel for the organization more quickly and to fill in competency gaps discovered during the selection process. One of the advantages of the Acceleration Pool is its flexibility; people can enter or leave at different points in their development.

Are there any issues associated with assimilating new members into an Acceleration Pool?

This is usually not a problem because, in most organizations, pool members rarely interact with one another relative to their career development. Some might attend an orientation together or participate in a team-based action learning event, but generally that would be the extent of their pool-related interactions. In some ways the word *pool* is a misnomer. It *is* a pool from management's perspective but not from the pool members'. Even in organizations that encourage peer coaching and teaching among pool members, few assimilation problems exist.

How do you drop people from the pool?

Fortunately, this is a fairly rare circumstance. The more common situation is that the organization delays someone's acceleration because of the individual's personal needs. However, a person's lack of performance or development sometimes requires that he or she be removed from the Acceleration Pool. This should always be done very carefully and be supported by data and documented discussions. While dropping someone from the pool is a tough decision, the individual usually knows that he or she is not performing to expectations and is rarely surprised. And being dropped from the pool does not mean the organization has given up on its commitment to an individual's development; in an Acceleration Pool system, people can rejoin the pool should their performance or speed of development improve.

What about people who want to opt out of the pool for personal reasons?

This is a more common situation, and it's much easier to handle than you might think. If a pool member has been filling in development gaps and performing well in his or her current job, it's usually possible to just leave the person in that position and reduce the speed of development. Sometimes it's appropriate to move someone to a less developmental position to clear the way for other pool members. It's much better to slow a person's development than to lose the individual.

Why have replacement plans for the top people in the organization?

While we suggest that people in an Acceleration Pool not be groomed for specific positions, it is still appropriate for an organization to preselect backups for the company's very top, "business critical" positions. Decisions to fill these positions might need to be made quickly, so candidates need to be tentatively identified. The people seen as front-runners for positions such as the CEO, COO, CFO, CIO, CTO, and heads of large SBUs will often need some special development to prepare for their specific target positions. Common examples would be exposure to governance issues of a Board of Directors or opportunities to interact with high-level government representatives. Usually these candidates would be members of the organization's Acceleration Pool.

Wouldn't it be prudent to at least identify the likely replacements for all key executives?

In other words, isn't a replacement strategy important for more than just a few people at the top? A few organizations might have large numbers of highly critical, unique jobs for which replacements need to be identified in advance and receive special training. However, we still believe that for most organizations the Acceleration Pool strategy is superior to the replacement-planning strategy for managers below the core senior executive team. It is fine to say that Jane is the best replacement for Jack if he wins the lottery tomorrow, but the danger is that by virtue of that designation, Jane's development is restricted because she is seen as being developed only for Jack's job. We feel that approaching Jane's development from an enterprise perspective rather than from a job perspective will yield both enhanced readiness for Jane in assuming Jack's position as well as enhanced readiness for other positions within the organization.

Should small companies have Acceleration Pools?

Succession management is more critical to the viability of a small company than to a large company because every position counts more. Although small organizations don't always need a formal succession management system, it's still a good idea for them to concentrate development efforts on a few people who will benefit most. Even very small organizations should develop a list of executive descriptors (job challenges, organizational knowledge, competencies, and derailers) and define a method for evaluating high potentials. Acceleration Centers are available throughout the world to evaluate individuals relative to competencies and derailers. Job rotations and development assignments are sometimes more difficult for small organizations, but their lack of size should provide the people being developed with a broader view of how the organization operates, more contacts with top management, and earlier opportunities for meaningful responsibilities and decision making.

Summary

Depending on your specific interests, we are sure you will want to peel more layers off the onion that is the Acceleration Pool concept. The rest of this book allows you to do that, depending on your particular interests.

If you don't want or need to read the entire remainder of this book, we suggest you look at Figure 2-4 to select chapters of interest about the Acceleration Pool process and its management. If you only want to know how to start an Acceleration Pool, read Chapters 6 and 7.

SECTION II

IDENTIFYING
HIGH POTENTIALS

Our chapter in this section focuses on best practices associated with initial identification of high-potential Acceleration Pool members.

Chapter 5

Identifying High Potentials

"You can't make a silk purse out of a sow's ear."

Selecting the right people for the Acceleration Pool—that is, identifying high-potential individuals—is essential to a successful succession management effort. Identifying those individuals who are most likely to strengthen an organization's leadership bench—and thus, its future—can be compared to recruiting the best draft choices for a professional football team, building a solid foundation for a home, or choosing the right ingredients for a cake. If the selection process is not accurate, efficient, and fair, the Acceleration Pool system will fail.

The goal is to find people who will yield the highest return on the company's investment in development resources. A sound identification process will accurately pinpoint people who have the right combination of skills, ability, and motivation to take advantage of, and benefit from, the special growth opportunities afforded to Acceleration Pool members.

A large communications company asked us to examine its "high-potential" program. Individuals were recruited from within the company into an eight-year development program intended to prepare them for senior leadership positions. We found that after running it for 15 years and involving nearly 300 individuals, the company had only 3 members of senior management who were graduates of the program, and none of the designated backups for senior positions actually came from the program.

There were many things wrong with the company's succession management program, but most flawed was the selection process.

☞ denotes that information on this topic is available at the *Grow Your Own Leaders* web site (www.ddiworld.com/growyourownleaders).

Internally nominated individuals lacked the skills and often the motivation to make it to top management. Candidates were selected into the high-potential program because of their technical and sales skills as well as concern for their retention rather than for their proven potential to grow to higher levels. Bottom line: The company had invested considerably more than $100 million with very little to show for it. A small investment in better selection of candidates would have produced a tremendous measurable return.

The selection and development system in that communications company never worked very well and had grown increasingly out of sync with today's business realities. Other companies are also finding that the selection system that once produced plenty of qualified candidates is suddenly failing. The people coming through the system have the necessary skills and motivation, but there are not enough of them. In the past companies could overlook a few high-potential people in their search for future executives because there were usually more than enough talented people to groom for senior management positions. Not so in the lean business environments of today. What's more, when high potentials are overlooked, they often leave in search of other opportunities, thereby aggravating the retention problems of their former organization. Companies today can't afford to waste good people— most need every highly talented individual they have. Obviously, the ability to accurately identify high-potential individuals is crucial.

Our recommendations for nomination systems are more general than detailed. We do not provide specific forms, tools, or procedures for how to structure and administer the perfect nomination process. We have supported implementation of hundreds of systems, and no two are alike. Every organization has different needs and requirements based on size, structure, culture, past practices, etc. Instead, we intend to provide a series of recommendations that will help to focus nomination activities on the most critical variables, so that nomination efforts might be made fairer, more accurate, more efficient, and, at the same time, more organizationally accepted. In keeping with these guidelines, the remainder of this chapter focuses on answering the following questions:

- What characteristics can we expect to measure reliably with a nomination process?

- What should be taken into consideration when designing a fair, efficient, and effective nomination process?

- Who should be involved in a nomination system?

- How can decisions about candidates be made most efficiently?

Nomination Criteria

To make the nomination process work, the organization needs a uniform set of criteria against which candidates can be evaluated. These criteria are usually included on the nomination form that is filled out for each candidate. As the nomination process progresses, these forms work their way up the organization to the Executive Resource Board, which uses them as an aid in making its final Acceleration Pool selections. For starters the form should include the "must have" criteria required for Acceleration Pool membership, such as:

- Minimum education requirements. But be careful—this could eliminate a disproportionate number of older managers from consideration.

- Minimum time with the organization.

- Required supervisory/management experience (within or outside the organization).

- Performance appraisal ratings at a specific level—but only if the performance management system is effective.

- Specific training, experiences, or skills.

- International experience—family circumstances might make this impossible for some individuals.

- Geographic mobility; willingness to relocate.

Beyond such basics, which differ greatly from organization to organization, the form would include predictors of executive success, such as:

- Bottom-line results/Track record (career achievement)—specific measures of revenue growth, sales effectiveness, innovation, and process improvements.

- Developmental orientation (i.e., being coachable, a history of learning from experiences, speed of learning new tasks in new situations).

- Modeling of organizational values.

- Strategic thinking (if the individual has had the opportunity).

- Motivation to be a strategic leader/general manager or otherwise perform at the Acceleration Pool's target level.

- Business acumen/Entrepreneurial ability.

- Identification with management.

- Interpersonal and leadership skills.

Most organizations use six or fewer predictors of organizational success. Obviously, the nomination criteria should be reconsidered as the organization's business strategy evolves and as experience with Acceleration Pools increases. This reconsideration of the predictors will usually occur naturally as nominees are discussed and as the Executive Resource Board looks for additional information.

Communication of the evaluation factors is exceedingly important. Everyone who will use them should have a definition as well as examples of high and low behavior of each factor.

We often are asked whether the organization should list its executive descriptors (see Chapter 6) on the nomination form, particularly the competencies required. It is tempting to get a head start on diagnosing development needs in the four descriptors (i.e., job challenges, organizational knowledge, competencies, and executive derailers). However, doing so is not a good idea for two reasons:

1. Nominators will probably have very different standards for each of the descriptor categories, which would lead to inaccurate ratings.

2. Nominators often won't have enough information to accurately evaluate a candidate on many of the descriptors because the nominee lacked the opportunity to demonstrate proficiency in all areas. For example, a person in a midlevel position probably would not have had an opportunity to show "visionary leadership."

When managers are forced to evaluate someone in areas that they don't understand or can't have observed, or when they are unsure of what standards to use, the result is usually a "halo effect"—the candidate receives good or poor ratings in all areas. In general, we believe that nomination forms should focus on areas that are observable in most nominees' current jobs.

Ironically, many nomination processes concentrate on collecting and organizing detailed information about candidates' organizational knowledge and experiences. Great care often is taken to present detailed information on such things as functional roles they have filled, experience with key organizational processes, their complete career history within and outside the organization, and other knowledge- and experience-related items. While all these factors are relevant to one's future prospects, all are typically very developable—and are more appropriately considered when actually placing someone into a specific executive role. We argue that, given the need to build the supply of internal talent, these screening criteria unnecessarily restrict the amount and range of raw talent in the pool and significantly reduce the likelihood that an increase in supply will be realized. Figure 5-1 contrasts the criteria for nominating individuals for an Acceleration Pool with the criteria for diagnosing their development needs.

Figure 5-1: Contrasting Areas of Focus for Identifying High Potentials with Diagnosing Development Needs

Criteria	Identifying High Potentials	Diagnosing Development Needs
Support of Company Values • Behaves consistently with values. • Displays respect for others. • Is a good team player. • Identifies with management.	X	
Leadership Promise • Is motivated/eager to lead. • Accepts leadership responsibility. • Mobilizes resources/people to action. • Leads teams that have high morale/spirit.	X	
Interpersonal Skills • Communicates clearly and effectively. • Makes effective presentations. • Demonstrates interpersonal diplomacy. • Is trusted and respected.	X	
Demonstration of Results • Shows positive team/unit results. • Displays objective indicators of success (e.g., sales, productivity, profit, quality, etc.). • Accomplishes major assignments.	X	
Developmental Orientation • Has accurate self-insight. • Is coachable; accepts feedback. • Has history of learning from experiences. • Quickly learns new tasks in new situations. • Self-initiates development activities.	X	
Importance of Retention/Risk of Leaving • Has a unique or in-demand skill set. • Is a likely target of "poachers."	X	
Organizational Knowledge		X
Job Challenges		X
Competencies		X
Executive Derailers		X

The Form

Because the goal of the nomination process is to find—but not yet diagnose—talent, focusing on a small number of basic characteristics can yield an efficient process that casts a wide net through the organization. Given that the Executive Resource Board is the ultimate user of the nomination form, the board should be responsible for designing it.

The rating scale used on the nomination form should be very simple. We find that a three-point rating scale often is sufficient to capture the precision needed from the raters. For example:

- **Development Need**—Needs development in this area.

- **Proficient**—Would be expected to demonstrate an effective level of performance in this area.

- **Strength**—Would be expected to demonstrate significant strength in this area (i.e., better than most others).

It is important to remind raters that candidates are being rated against *a future standard* (e.g., general management level) so that the criteria are consistent. They also should have examples of the kind of behavioral support required to provide evidence for the ratings. Some organizations require nominators to support their ratings with specific written behavioral examples; others elect to merely ask them to come to Executive Resource Board meetings prepared to provide examples to the board (see The Meeting: Making Final Decisions later in this chapter). We see no major advantage in one approach over another, as long as observable behavioral examples are used in making a case.

Should Retention Be a Factor in Nominations?

We could argue that the nomination of people to an Acceleration Pool should be based on their potential long-term value to the organization rather than short-term rationale, such as the desire to retain a particular high flier. But in practice, retention is an extremely important issue in most organizations, and our experience has shown that an Acceleration Pool can be a major factor in retaining high-potential people. Thus, as part of the nomination process, companies often collect information about nominees' impact on company success and whether they are at risk of leaving. Such factors might lead an organization to give special consideration for nomination to the pool.

Key Considerations in Building a Fair, Efficient, and Effective Nomination Process

This section discusses some of the primary decisions that must be made about selecting candidates for an Acceleration Pool.

Sizing the Acceleration Pool

To begin the process of nominating people to the Acceleration Pool, it is first necessary to determine how many people to bring in. Acceleration Pool size depends on a variety of factors, including the organization's growth, expected retirements, the quality and number of current pool members, and the resources (e.g., mentors, training, rotational assignments, etc.) that can be dedicated to pool members' accelerated development. Usually, the number is not rigid and can be changed depending on circumstances, but some general target is necessary. In most Acceleration Pool organizations, the pool size ranges from 1 to 2 percent of the total population.

Clearly, organizations must think carefully about the appropriate size of the pool. For those wishing to include more people for retention purposes, there might be value in some pool stratification, differentiating a select few who seem to have the greatest near-term potential from others who might need longer-term development. We recognize that in many organizations, resources will be scarce, requiring difficult decisions about who will receive the most valuable forms of support (e.g., a senior executive mentor, special assignments, etc.); yet, we believe that the ongoing development and formal recognition of all key players is essential. Stratifying the Acceleration Pool allows for the organization to introduce multiple developmental strategies for members at different levels of potential. Pool members with the highest potential can be given access to the kinds of developmental assignments that will most quickly prepare them for a senior-level assignment, such as membership on an important task force. The development of those with less potential can take a slower, more economical route (e.g., on-the-job assignments, etc.).

Once overall size is determined, slots in the pool are allocated to various organizational units (e.g., business units, functions, countries, subsidiaries, etc.). In general, large units get more slots in the Acceleration Pool than smaller ones, although that need not be the case if a smaller unit has greater growth potential or has done a good job of cultivating talent. Like the overall target number, this allocation can be revisited once all nominations are in and the Executive Resource Board has had a chance to compare candidates from different units. It might be that Unit A has many strong candidates, while Unit B can't fill its allocated slots. In such a situation the board can change the allocation in favor of Unit A, while taking action to correct the problem in Unit B for the future.

Who Should Be Involved?

Many organizations have asked us how to determine the most qualified or appropriate nominators. The simple answer is that all current senior executives and major business heads should be asked to offer nominations. They do so by communicating to their people the criteria for selecting candidates into the pool and then getting their recommendations. Many types of nomination systems, from informal to formal, are used. Most managers communicate the criteria and solicit nominations at staff meetings. A few allow individuals to nominate themselves for pool membership.

What happens if an executive is not competent enough to be trusted to nominate high-potential individuals? In these cases the organization's firmly adhering to the established criteria and requiring behavioral evidence of potential are essential to ensure objectivity and accuracy. In nomination meetings other group members might ask questions to elicit data and calibrate the judgments of those whose initial nominations seem unjustified. These executives also can learn to become better nominators through their involvement in the process. Executives contributing to nomination discussions find that they learn to understand and speak a certain language for describing talent and discussing potential. Debates about the meaning of such terms as "results achieved" or "proficient" enhance the group's understanding about what is being evaluated and what is being sought in leaders. As these conversations mature, nominators speak the language more fluently and develop more reliability in their judgments. Thus, eliminating "problem executives" from the nomination process might only perpetuate the problem.

Finding Hidden Talent

Every organization will have its obvious high fliers—individuals who are widely recognized as the best and brightest. The challenge is to get nominators to identify unknown, and perhaps even unlikely, candidates. These are the people who might not fit the classic mold for success at the company but who nevertheless have shown an ability to take on larger challenges. Avoiding preconceptions and looking in new places for talented people who can contribute new perspectives almost always pay surprising dividends.

There are several actions that can ensure that a wide range of people are considered for entry into the Acceleration Pool:

- Begin by creating a list of all leaders who meet the organization's minimum requirements for the Acceleration Pool.

- Create another list of people who have completed educational programs (e.g., an evening MBA course) or in other ways have attracted positive attention (e.g., membership on teams that receive awards, leadership skills spontaneously mentioned by associates).

- Look at leaders from the organization's smaller divisions or staff functions rather than just in its core business areas.

- Consider people who have successfully led a task force or special committee.

- Ask managers which people in their units are the most requested for special assignments or projects.

- Consider people who are returning from special assignments (e.g., a virtual product-development team).

- Check on people in international assignments—even those who have never been to the headquarters office.

- Check on "hosted" people (i.e., those who work for one unit but are based in another), who often are left out of the process.

- Consider people who have mentioned a desire for senior management when completing their personal development plans.

To gauge how well an organization is doing in casting a wide net, we recommend that managers take a few minutes to compile simple but telling data, such as:

- Percentage of nominees whose primary strength is a particular technical skill or who have the same operational background.

- Percentage of nominees who are not trained or educated in the company's core technology.

- Percentage of nominees who represent ethnic minorities, other cultural backgrounds, or are female.

- Percentage of nominees who are located outside the corporate office.

The use of such data encourages expansive thinking about leadership potential. It also helps nominators gain perspective on the overall talent landscape being considered and avoid standards that are too high, too low, or too traditional (i.e., not future oriented).

Reinforcing "Talent Hunters"

Executives who show energy for and commitment to identifying talent should be recognized and encouraged. These "talent hunters" often are unsung heroes—and invaluable organizational assets. An effective tactic many senior managers use to encourage talent hunters and highlight their value is to make a point of telling their success stories regularly and publicly. Every organization has these tales of high performers who were found in unlikely places or had unusual backgrounds and rose to positions of great responsibility and influence. Several real-life examples spring to mind:

- A chief executive's former administrative assistant who moved on to become the manager of research and development.

- The CEO of a large Canadian manufacturing organization who failed two elementary school grades.

- A woman who took her vows to become a nun and then rose to become vice president of marketing and sales.

The point, of course, is that leaders can foster even more success stories by drawing attention to the achievements of such individuals—*and* to the importance of the people who spotted them and moved them along at key points in their careers.

Role of the Executive Resource Board

Ultimately, nominations are submitted to the Executive Resource Board, which can take a variety of approaches to finalize them. For example, a large multinational manufacturing organization with whom DDI consults has two major Acceleration Pools—each with a distinct identification process. The first pool, known as the Early Acceleration Pool, focuses on professionals who have potential for middle management or operational-leadership roles within a business unit. Information about candidates for this pool is processed primarily by the Human Resource group, which coordinates all the forms and materials, including folders with a brief personal history and the submitted recommendation forms. In addition, HR sometimes nominates other people for the pool and assembles similar folders of supporting information. Executive Resource Board meetings are brief, focusing on making final decisions. These decisions are essentially a "sanity check" and an opportunity for the board to confirm that the group of nominees has the appropriate composition and diversity and the desired representation in terms of product, function, or business unit.

The company's second pool is known as the Strategic Acceleration Pool, and it targets higher-level positions. Identification of members for this pool follows a more top-down approach. The COO and key SBU officers, who together compose the Executive Resource Board, drive the talent-selection meetings. Nominations are extremely selective, requiring much detail and justification. Final decisions are made in a focused (and sometimes heated) meeting of the board. Individuals who are selected to the Strategic Acceleration Pool are targeted for both specific key roles and general management potential. The HR department's primary role is to facilitate and document the process; nominations are clearly owned and sanctioned by top-management stakeholders.

Role of the Human Resource Department

At both the unit and overall organizational levels, the Human Resource department plays a pivotal role in identifying high-potential people. They make sure that the Executive Resource Board and other nominating executives understand and use the selection criteria correctly, including constructively challenging nominations and pointing out potential disconnects between nominations and other performance or talent-related data. HR representatives also ensure that forms are completed correctly, and they develop summary data that help the Executive Resource Board compare candidates and find "holes" in the candidate list. Usually, HR also is responsible for keeping diversity statistics so that the board always knows where it stands in that regard.

The Human Resource department should prepare a list of the candidates and their individual ratings in the nomination factors, as shown in Table 5-1.

Note that the table lists the candidates roughly in descending order of ratings. This makes it possible to examine an entire group of nominees relatively quickly. It can also give senior executives insight into the nomination process. For example, among a group of individuals with similar ratings, some will usually make it to the Acceleration Pool and some won't. A closer examination of those cases often will show that criteria beyond those on the form are being used in the nomination and selection processes. The Human Resource department can then either change the company's criteria or take steps to ensure that the "unofficial" criteria are no longer used.

Table 5-1: Candidates, Success Factors, and Ratings

Name	Support of Company Values	Leadership Promise	Interpersonal Skill	Results Achieved	Developmental Orientation	Retention Concerns
John Doe	S	S	S	P	S	High
Jane Do	S	S	P	P	S	High
Jim Doh	P	P	S	S	P	Med
Joan Dough	P	S	P	S	P	Med
Jack Doghue	P	P	P	P	S	Low
Jill Dohhe	D	P	P	P	P	Med

S = Strength, P = Proficient, D = Development Need

Tabular arrays of information also can facilitate the stratification of the Acceleration Pool members, as previously mentioned. Looking across individuals and criteria often can illuminate natural breaks between certain groups of individuals (e.g., high potential and very high potential). Whether stratification is intended or not, however, visual representation of the data always helps to confirm judgments and avoid major oversights or mistakes. We are not suggesting, however, that overall potential be reduced to a computational sum or average across the criteria for each individual. Two individuals can have the same number of S, P, and D ratings and have very different potential. Each person must be considered separately, and the·overall decision about inclusion in the Acceleration Pool must be made by a consensus judgment of the Executive Resource Board, which takes all the selection factors into account (a holistic view).

Overall, an effective Human Resource department can act as an independent source of information about possible nominees. And, because it has access to unique data from sources such as exit interviews and employee attitude surveys, it is in a good position to identify high-potential people who might have been overlooked in the nomination process. With the right relationship, HR can also effectively play the role of "sounding board" or "conscience" for senior executives facing difficult decisions.

The Meeting: Making Final Decisions

Final decisions on Acceleration Pool membership are made during a meeting of the Executive Resource Board, which works with background information and nomination forms that were compiled by the Human Resource department.

During the meeting nominations are reviewed, debated, and confirmed or denied. It is essential to have a strong, well-prepared, unbiased, credible facilitator who can keep the discussion focused on key selection criteria and behavioral evidence. The meeting can be conducted along the lines of this sample agenda, which should be shared with attendees in advance:

1. Review the agenda and desired outcomes (how many Acceleration Pool slots to fill).

2. Establish or reaffirm any meeting ground rules.

3. Review a draft list of candidates, and prioritize the discussion.

4. Conduct an in-depth discussion of individual candidates, and make a tentative decision as to their readiness for the pool.

5. Compile a tentative list of those accepted. Consider functional, cultural, geographic, and gender-related diversity as well as trends in pool makeup and common needs.

6. Finalize the Acceleration Pool slate, and document decisions.

7. Ensure that a strategy for communicating the decisions is in place.

Because so much depends on the success of these meetings, we'll expand on some agenda-related topics in the remainder of this chapter.

Managing Long Lists of Acceleration Pool Candidates— Prioritize the Discussion

Executive Resource Boards sometimes have too many candidates and issues to discuss in a limited time. However, cutting short meaningful discussions about key players is counterproductive. One way to sidestep this dilemma is to use pre-identified criteria to allocate differing amounts of discussion time to the various candidates (agenda item 3).

The discussion can be prioritized using this classification scheme:

• Obvious candidates

• Controversial and "dark horse" candidates

• Borderline candidates

• Unlikely candidates

Obviously, the unlikely candidates should be identified quickly so that any discussion devoted to them is limited. The most time should be allocated to clarifying the readiness of dark-horse and borderline candidates. The obvious candidates will get their due during the comparison review of all the prospects (agenda item 5).

Discussing Individual Candidates

Once the initial list is streamlined and prioritized, substantive discussion about individual candidate readiness begins (agenda item 4). At this point the purpose is to gauge each candidate's potential by considering nomination data as well as available performance and observational data. This discussion is the "meat and potatoes" of the nomination meeting.

The depth of discussion around individual candidates is critical. The structure of each discussion depends on available supporting data but generally includes these tasks:

- Review basic career history, including relevant education, experience, and HR file data.

- Confirm readiness and motivation for Acceleration Pool membership via discussion around the criteria determined by the Executive Resource Board and on which data are available for all candidates.

- Consider strategic role assignments or mentor matching. Concrete assignments will be made when development priorities are established (see Chapter 7), but briefly discussing possible prescriptions for perceived development needs at this time helps the board to be realistic about what can be done to help a prospective pool member.

If new Acceleration Pool members do not go through an Acceleration Center, the board should recommend additional in-depth assessment activities to further diagnose development opportunities.

Make a preliminary decision to accept the candidate into the Acceleration Pool (categorize candidates in terms of their appropriateness for the pool).

Finalize the Acceleration Pool Selections
After Considering Diversity Factors

Preliminary selection results should be displayed and decisions reviewed for accuracy, consistency, and cultural, gender, functional, and geographic diversity (agenda item 5). Look for strategic fit too. For example, an organization whose future relies on making the shift to e-commerce should nominate people who will be able to add value in that area.

Invariably, common themes and learning needs will emerge from the discussions. These themes often highlight larger intervention opportunities at the organizational level (e.g., a broad need to enhance the Global Acumen or Visionary Leadership competency or to conduct more negotiation skills training).

Confirm and Execute Communication Strategies

The Executive Resource Board's decisions must be communicated to the people who are chosen for the Acceleration Pool as well as to the people who will support them (agenda item 7). A board member (or the HR representative to the board) should be designated to invite each participant into the Acceleration Pool and outline the benefits, obligations, expectations, and next steps. In essence, the person communicating with the prospective pool member is charged with recruiting him or her into the Acceleration Pool. However, the recruiter should describe *realistic* expectations and not oversell the opportunity. And remember that people have the option of *not* joining the pool—without consequences to them. Once an individual decides to join the Acceleration Pool, the designated board representative also should inform the person's direct supervisor (unless the individual is to be moved fairly quickly). The supervisor will be a critical ally in speeding the pool member's development; therefore, getting the supervisor on board early and actively seeking his or her help make good sense.

Preparing for the Meeting

Clearly, Executive Resource Board members' preparation for the selection meeting is important in optimizing time and making the best decisions. All too often, however, such preparation never happens. Human Resource professionals often are reluctant to ask busy executives to do anything other than show up at the meetings; in fact, they often try to do the prep work for them. This doesn't work, of course. Although it is very appropriate for HR to assume responsibility for the critical steps of facilitating the process and preparing administratively, they cannot take on the role of deciding who has the greatest amount of potential.

We cannot overstate the importance of thoughtful preparation by all parties. Board members must re-familiarize themselves with the nominees, reviewing their career histories, available assessment and performance data, and the rationale and challenges associated with the nomination. When board members do their homework, they dramatically enhance the depth, candor, and efficiency of their discussions about nominees.

Preparing to Offer Acceleration Pool Membership

Communication to prospective Acceleration Pool members need not be complex, but it must be clear. The best way to prepare a thoughtful communication plan is to consider the questions that people will ask when they learn that they've been invited to join the pool, such as:

- How was I selected into the pool? What criteria were used?
- Who else was selected?
- Who knows about this? Who may I tell?
- What happens next? When?
- What am I responsible for at this point?
- How will I receive support in the process?
- What if I don't care to participate?
- How will my progress be tracked?
- If I begin a development plan, will I get support in my primary job?
- What role does my boss play?

The Executive Resource Board must be able to answer these questions (and plenty of others particular to your organization). Inconsistency will breed concern among pool members and might cause them to lose faith in the process. Core communication messages should be discussed and agreed upon by the Executive Resource Board at the close of the nomination meeting. Inevitably, while meeting with prospective pool members, questions will arise for which answers are not yet available. In these instances the worst approach is to make up an answer. Instead, offer to find out the information, and then be sure to follow through on your promise. HR plays a key role in ensuring that questions are addressed appropriately.

Second Chances

When someone who is nominated does not make it into the Acceleration Pool, it can actually lead to better things down the road. Managers are often prompted to focus on developing these individuals and gathering more data about them in order to make a stronger case for nominating them again at the next opportunity. For example, a manager might have the person attend a training program to calibrate his or her ability to learn or encourage the person to use multiple-perspective (360°) instruments to get feedback in behavioral areas. Most important, the process often encourages higher-level managers to directly observe individuals so that they can more accurately evaluate them.

Identification Is Not Enough

Of all the succession management components covered in this book, none captures more practical attention than the topic of identifying high-potential individuals. To varying degrees of sophistication, nearly every organization we encounter has some sort of talent identification process. Some spend weeks administering their processes, while others spend only minutes. Regardless of their names and features, however, these processes have one common objective: to find people with leadership talent from within the organization. Historically, identification systems were the most heavily emphasized element of annual replacement-planning programs. Once an effective nomination process was installed, most organizations believed that the succession management system was complete. They overemphasized nomination efforts under the faulty assumption that naming talent is equivalent to *developing* talent. Great succession management organizations see the nomination process as only the first step of a succession management system; they move quickly to the business of developing the right people into more agile leaders. The rest of this book covers the development of potential.

Appendix 5-1: Acceleration Centers as Nomination Tools

Acceleration Centers are modern-day assessment centers that use professional assessors, highly realistic job simulations, and a wide variety of other assessment methodologies (see Chapter 7). They are used by many organizations to screen nominees for an Acceleration Pool. Before their names are submitted to the Executive Resource Board, nominees go through a center so that the organization can get an accurate fix on their potential as well as their development needs. The Acceleration Center can confirm that the people nominated to join the Acceleration Pool do, in fact, have high potential by immersing them into a simulated business environment in which they must use senior executive leadership and management skills to perform effectively. Acceleration Centers provide holistic profiles of the behavior patterns, skills, and dispositions that are likely to help or hinder future leadership abilities. Although most organizations opt to reserve these in-depth assessments for those who have been accepted into the Acceleration Pool, others find that professional assessors and validated simulation technology offer invaluable insights earlier in the process—when the organization is making its initial decisions on Acceleration Pool membership.

When Acceleration Centers are not being used to identify candidates, we highly recommend that the organization have individuals complete an Acceleration Center immediately after they enter the Acceleration Pool (see Chapter 7). The resulting profile is a critical tool for establishing development priorities.

Relatively few organizations can put all their potential pool members through an Acceleration Center as part of a screening process, but for some organizations it is clearly the best alternative, as the following example illustrates.

Some organizations use Acceleration Centers as an optional screen, sending borderline or relatively unknown individuals through them. Meanwhile, when there is a volume of data available on a nominee, these companies are able to make a decision without Acceleration Center data and put people through the Acceleration Center after their acceptance. Because the U.S. Equal Employment Opportunity Commission (EEOC) requires that all candidates for positions be treated the same, this procedure must be handled carefully and decisions about candidates properly documented.

The Pros and Cons of Using an Acceleration Center to Screen Candidates for an Acceleration Pool

Pros:

- Proven accuracy and reliability.

- Outside professional assessors give an accurate, unbiased view of competencies and derailers that are important to future success but difficult to evaluate in the candidate's present position.

- High-potential people would go through an Acceleration Center anyway for a development-needs diagnosis after they have joined the Acceleration Pool. It doesn't cost any more to get this information before letting someone into the pool, so the organization can be more sure of its decision.

- Acceleration Centers provide development insights for those not accepted into the Acceleration Pool. Thus, people see it as a worthwhile time investment, whether or not they get in.

- Legal defensibility.

- Participants see the Acceleration Center as fair, job relevant, and accurate.

- Acceleration Centers allow for an accurate comparison of individuals across cultures and throughout the world.

Cons:

- The costs are relatively high in terms of time and money.

- Considerable time might be required to get all potential pool members through an Acceleration Center before a final decision on pool membership.

- People who don't get into the Acceleration Pool afterward might experience a drop in morale.

Using an Acceleration Center to Find Talent at the United States Postal Service

As one of the world's largest civilian employers, the United States Postal Service (USPS) has an enormous succession-planning challenge: Ten USPS geographic areas and six functions comb the ranks of some 800,000 employees to identify and recommend their own potential executives. These recommendations are reviewed by the Postmaster General as well as several high-level officers. The organization also faces extreme pressure to accelerate the development of its leaders because more than 60 percent of its incumbents are eligible for retirement in the next five years.

In response, USPS has implemented a customized, holistic assessment process that includes a highly customized Acceleration Center with simulations designed to mirror USPS' business, cultural, and leadership challenges. These simulations are complemented by inventories that offer insights into motivation, personality/style, and potential derailers.

High-potential people are first identified through a simple nomination form, completed by their manager, that focuses on predicted potential. Only those identified as potential executives are eligible for the Acceleration Center. Results from the Acceleration Center are considered in the advancement process. It is anticipated that high-potential candidates complete the assessment as a development experience several years before they are selected for an executive role.

One Area Resource Board recently began using Acceleration Center data in its talent-selection meetings. Although the organization clearly valued this information in making promotions and targeting training, center data had never before entered into Executive Resource Board discussions about high-potential candidates. In this new approach board members collaborate with experienced DDI assessors in a facilitated review of all the available candidate information. Each discussion begins with an overview of the candidate's career and educational history as well as internal observations (i.e., early, subjective executive opinions and anecdotal observations). The facilitator supports concise, but thorough, discussions of job history to ensure a sound context for the rest of the discussion. In addition, the facilitator sets the tone for a balanced discussion by probing for both positive and negative behavioral observations as well as biases or impressions that could cloud objectivity. This approach, which gets executive input on the table early, allows Executive Resource Board members to focus on other data without being distracted by individual points of view.

Next, results from the Acceleration Center's behavioral simulations are summarized, and trends in broad performance domains, such as interpersonal, leadership, and business skills, are identified. Finally, the motivation, personality, and derailer inventory data are interpreted against the emerging behavioral profile. Explanations for behavioral patterns often are discussed (e.g., conflict avoidance).

The final profile received by each USPS executive candidate represents a consensus of all the professional assessors involved in the formal Acceleration Center as well as the candidate's immediate supervisor, executives, and USPS Executive Resource Board members.

At that point the Executive Resource Board determines whether the individual is a likely executive "successor" and targets several areas for developmental focus. Development recommendations are fairly generic and assume that the successor will partner with his or her manager to tailor actions to the individual situation. The profiles also are used extensively to make strategic role assignments and developmental decisions.

Overall, this approach has integrated the perspective of USPS executives with behavioral assessment and personality insights—and has provided the Executive Resource Board members with the information, explanation, and guidance they need to make an informed decision. The board's confidence in its conclusions about development recommendations and strategic role assignments/promotions has soared. Board members have concluded that the use of integrated data has made them better observers as well as better coaches. And, based on this Area's experience, several other USPS geographic areas are implementing similar processes.

SECTION III

UNDERSTANDING ORGANIZATIONAL TALENT

This section defines the basic activities and best practices associated with diagnosing the development needs of high-potential pool members. First we describe the executive descriptors (i.e., organizational knowledge, job challenges, competencies, and derailers) that define successful executive performance and highlight an array of assessment tools/practices for supporting an in-depth diagnosis of development priorities. We then deal with the very important—and often neglected—issue of translating an individual's diagnosis into a commitment to action.

Chapter 6

Defining the Executive of the Future

"If you don't know what you're looking for, you'll never know when you find it."

This old saying certainly holds true for an Acceleration Pool system. If an organization doesn't have a well-defined profile of what it wants in its future senior leaders, there's no way it will be able to effectively develop people for senior management positions. Nor will it be able to accurately evaluate the readiness of high-potential individuals. It is extremely important, then, for an organization to carefully and accurately define the characteristics of the leaders who will carry it into the future.

At most organizations the challenges facing leaders have changed dramatically beginning with the last part of the 20th century. Table 6-1 shows how contemporary leadership compares with more traditional leadership roles. Leaders of today must embrace change, think globally, and more often than not, manage more people in less time with fewer resources. Their approach has to be one of focus, inspiration, and supporting people without removing responsibility. Quite a change from leaders of old.

denotes that information on this topic is available at the *Grow Your Own Leaders* web site (www.ddiworld.com/growyourownleaders).

Table 6-1: Contrasting the Traditional Leader with the Contemporary Leader

Traditional Leader	Contemporary Leader
Made all major decisions. Solved problems for the team; acted as the expert.	Shares responsibility with team members. Helps team solve problems.
Controlled the work flow; was responsible for work group's results.	Promotes self-management and responsibility as well as ownership of the task or process (e.g., direct reports measure own progress and take corrective action as necessary).
Gave the answers; played the "expert" role.	Asks the right questions; allows direct reports to be the experts.
Laid down the rules.	Articulates and rallies the troops around a vision and set of values.
Valued unanimity/conformity.	Values diverse perspectives.
Sought to eliminate conflict.	Sees conflict as an opportunity for synergy and enriched decision making.
Tended to be reactive; resisted change.	Is proactive; initiates change. Embraces change as necessary for organizational survival.
Focused on tasks, products, and technical skills.	Focuses on process and people.
Used linear, analytical thinking.	Uses nonlinear, holistic thinking (systems).
Sought to achieve functional, specialized expertise.	Seeks to achieve cross-functional and cross-cultural expertise.
Was concerned only about own area of responsibility.	Is concerned about the total organization; tries to be a good partner with other groups in the company.

Table 6-1: Contrasting the Traditional Leader with the Contemporary Leader (cont'd)	
Traditional Leader	**Contemporary Leader**
Was fiercely competitive.	Is still fiercely competitive, but must often partner with competitors, vendors, and customers.
Was concerned only with domestic operations.	Needs to be prepared to think on a larger, global scale.
Thought of people as interchangeable resources.	Thinks of people as the organization's most valuable resource and knows that they are difficult to replace.
Put the organization's needs before people's needs.	Works for a balance between the organization's and people's needs.
Avoided risks.	Takes risks.
Used a functional, short-term thought process.	Uses a systematic, long-term thought process.

Target Job Level

Before defining its "leader of the future," an organization must first choose the job level that it wants to target with the Acceleration Pool. Each organization's needs are unique. The appropriate target job level depends on the expected growth of the organization, projected executive turnover, organizational structure, and depth of management talent. Examples of target job levels include:

- **General manager and above.** A general manager is someone with responsibility for several parts of the organization, rather than one function or business unit.

- **Strategic leader.** This person maps out the high-level direction for the organization.

- **Plant manager.** As we mentioned in Chapter 2, we know of Acceleration Pools within manufacturing organizations that are aimed specifically at plant manager positions. This position is below general management and not highly strategic.

- **The level that reports to the chief executive.** Some large organizations aim their Acceleration Pools at this level, which is well above the first level of general management and is the first level where people must be strategic thinkers.

Defining What You Want

Ever since the first tribal chieftain arose among the Neolithic cave dwellers, people have been trying to pin down the characteristics that a good leader should have. These characteristics—or *executive descriptors*—have changed over time as leadership and organizational tasks have evolved and as professionals from various academic disciplines (i.e., historians, psychologists, sociologists, and economists) have tried to describe them.

In the 1990s various individuals, groups, and organizations have tried to portray leadership in terms of competencies, roles, experiences, tasks, personality traits, and values. For example, an Andersen Consulting study determined that a leader thinks globally, anticipates opportunity, creates a shared vision, develops and empowers people, appreciates cultural diversity, builds teamwork and partnerships, and embraces change. That leader also shows technological savvy, encourages constructive challenges, ensures customer satisfaction, achieves a competitive advantage, demonstrates personal mastery, shares leadership, and lives the values (Walt & Robertson [as cited in Stewart, 1999]).

While conducting more than 1,000 studies of supervisory, managerial, and executive positions, Development Dimensions International has explored a wide variety of methods to describe leadership attributes. We have found that it takes four types of information to develop a solid understanding of executive candidates' strengths and weaknesses:

- Job challenges/Preparatory experiences (what one has done).

- Organizational knowledge (what one knows).

- Behaviorally defined competencies (what one is capable of).

- Executive derailers and other personal attributes (who one is).

Job Challenges/Preparatory Experiences

Job challenges describe the kinds of situations that someone entering top management should have experienced or at least had some exposure to. Examples include:

- Carry an assignment from beginning to end.

- Become heavily involved with a merger, acquisition, strategic alliance, or partnership opportunity.

- Implement a companywide change.

- Develop and implement a plan to cut costs or control inventories.

- Negotiate agreements with other organizations.

- Operate in a high-pressure or high-visibility situation.

- Show entrepreneurial skills.

Appendix 6-1 provides a more complete list of common job challenges.

More than any other factor, it is lack of experience with critical job challenges that prevents high-potential people from achieving the promotions they seek. Many organizations won't entrust major assignments to people who haven't "been there, done that," thus significantly reducing opportunities for many excellent people. Without a succession management system to regulate the job challenges provided to candidates, promotions are largely in the hands of fate—lucky individuals getting the critical challenges and the subsequent promotions, while unfortunate others don't.

Obviously, there's a significant difference between situations in which executive candidates merely *observe* a challenge, such as a unionizing effort, and those in which they *play a key role,* such as managing a corporate defense to a unionizing effort. In reality there is a large gray area between these two extremes; therefore, in an Acceleration Pool system, the Executive Resource Board must determine the extent to which a pool member's experience meets a job challenge requirement. Considerable judgment is often required. The wording of the challenge can help by reflecting specific, required management responsibilities (e.g., "manage a high-growth operation" as opposed to "experience a high-growth operation").

Describing positions in terms of job challenges is preferable to merely listing required job titles because:

• Job titles often do not adequately describe the kinds of issues or problems a person confronts, particularly with today's fluid organizational structures and rapidly changing strategic directions.

• A person can confront several challenges in the same job. Thinking of development in terms of job challenges allows the Executive Resource Board to be more creative in finding or tailoring jobs to maximize pool members' growth (see Chapter 10).

Lists of challenges are unique to organizations and their particular strategy, but organizations often tend to produce lists that are far too long. If Acceleration Pool members were actually exposed to all the challenges on the initial lists developed by many senior executives, they would be 100 years old before they could ever land a significant management position. Thus, organizations must carefully identify the most important job challenges and then decide which ones an Acceleration Pool member *absolutely must* experience. Job challenges are relatively easy to evaluate through a behavioral interview (see Chapter 8).

Organizational Knowledge

Organizational knowledge refers to the degree of understanding that senior managers must have about how the organization operates. It includes areas such as:

• Functions (marketing, sales, production, domestic/international).

• Processes (core, business, support).

• Systems (long-range planning, budgeting, compensation).

• Products and services.

To develop into an effective general manager, an Acceleration Pool member needs to understand how the total organization functions and how its various functions interrelate. Appendix 6-2 lists some common knowledge areas divided into functions, processes, systems, and products/services. Thinking of organizational knowledge along these breakdowns helps the organization to avoid missing important knowledge. The breakdowns are generally not used in the final list of knowledge areas.

Some organizations go into great detail in listing the areas that pool members should be knowledgeable about, while others can be quite vague, requiring that pool members have exposure to only a certain number of areas. One organization defined minimal knowledge about its major product lines as "being able to hold a short business conversation about a product line with an important customer of that line." Traditionally, organizational knowledge was cultivated by assigning high potentials to various parts of the organization. In practice, however, such movement often didn't occur—and without that broader experience, individuals often carried a narrow functional view as they progressed in their careers. At one company we worked with, an excellent salesperson always stockpiled sales at the end of a year when he was over budget, so that he could get a good start on his goals for the following year. He used the same tactic when he was promoted to district sales manager and later to regional manager. When he used the same approach after being promoted to national sales manager, it nearly bankrupted the company: Because there were no reported sales, manufacturing virtually shut down. Not knowing how other parts of the company operated, the salesperson could not foresee the impact of his decision.

Determining an Acceleration Pool member's level of organizational knowledge is usually a fairly simple task—just look at past assignments. But it is also easy to underestimate someone's organizational knowledge. An Acceleration Pool member might have assimilated organizational knowledge from jobs in previous organizations, task force assignments, or possibly in discussions with coworkers, friends, or relatives. Thus, organizations should routinely ask for self-reports and interview pool members about knowledge areas.

Behaviorally Defined Competencies

Competencies (or as DDI calls them, dimensions) define clusters of behavior, knowledge, and motivations that are related to job success or failure and under which data on behavior, knowledge, and motivations can be reliably classified. The competencies that DDI has found to be commonly related to executive success fall into four domains: Interpersonal Skills, Leadership Skills, Business or Management Skills, and Personal Attributes. We list these competencies and domains on the next page.

Interpersonal Skills	Leadership Skills	Business or Management Skills	Personal Attributes
• Building Strategic Relationships	• Change Leadership	• Drive for Results	• Accurate Self-Insight
• Building Trust	• Coaching/ Teaching	• Economic Orientation	• Adaptability
• Communicating with Impact	• Delegation	• Establishing Strategic Direction	• Energy
• Cultural Interpersonal Effectiveness	• Developing Organizational Talent	• Global Acumen	• Executive Disposition
• Customer Orientation	• Empowerment	• Managing the Job	• Intellectual Capacity
• Persuasiveness/ Sales Ability	• Selling the Vision	• Marketing and Entrepreneurial Insight	• Learning Orientation
	• Team Development/ Team Leadership	• Mobilizing Resources	• Motivational Fit
		• Operational Decision Making	• Positive Disposition
			• Reading the Environment
			• Resilience
			• Technical/ Professional Knowledge and Skills

Appendix 6-3 lists some of DDI's commonly used executive competencies and their definitions. Obtaining an accurate list of competencies is vital to a succession management system because they provide a window into future behavior. Figure 6-1 illustrates the importance of competencies in an Acceleration Pool system. Competencies reflect the organization's vision, business strategy, goals, and values as well as the job and role requirements of the target level.

Competencies are especially useful as a means to distill the vision, values, strategy, and desired results into a common language that can be supported by key elements of a succession management system. Because

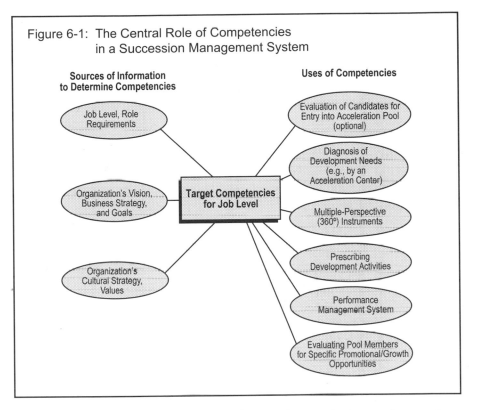

Figure 6-1: The Central Role of Competencies
in a Succession Management System

**Sources of Information
to Determine Competencies**

Uses of Competencies

Job Level, Role
Requirements

Organization's Vision,
Business Strategy,
and Goals

Organization's
Cultural Strategy,
Values

**Target Competencies
for Job Level**

Evaluation of Candidates for
Entry into Acceleration Pool
(optional)

Diagnosis of
Development Needs
(e.g., by an
Acceleration Center)

Multiple-Perspective
(360°) Instruments

Prescribing
Development Activities

Performance
Management System

Evaluating Pool Members
for Specific Promotional/Growth
Opportunities

it would be difficult to evaluate or train people on nebulous values such as "trust" or "customer service," we must break down those concepts into competencies that are defined by the behaviors a person would exhibit to demonstrate the value. We call these *behaviorally defined competencies.*

Simply defining competencies by behaviors is not enough; the definitions also must be tested for accuracy and reliability of understanding. This is important because all managers and executives must speak the same language and look for the same behaviors when considering candidates for open positions and promotion. When competencies are well defined and reliable, they can be a valuable leadership descriptor for an organization. Conversely, when executives work from vague or overlapping competency definitions, they waste valuable time debating a candidate's attributes. They might actually be in agreement about the candidate's abilities without realizing it because each person is interpreting competency definitions differently.

One Company Recognizes a Competency Weakness

A large "bricks and mortar" company wanted to become more of a "click and mortar" organization. To make this transition, it recognized that it needed significantly more strategic alliances and external business partnerships. However, the company could point to very few successful partnership relationships in the past. Executives would talk about the need for an alliance and start a discussion, but deals never came to fruition. The few alliances they tried failed. The company realized that most of its executives, who had grown up in a vertically integrated organization in which they did most things themselves, were weak on the competency *Building Partnerships and Customer Relationships*. To solve this problem, it made proficiency in this competency a criterion for hiring and promoting executives, provided skills training in this competency, and recognized its importance in the performance management system. To emphasize the importance of alliances, the company also rebuilt the training program that all Acceleration Pool members attended to include a simulation involving alliances. The strategy worked, and the company now has several successful alliances.

Poorly Defined Competencies

A common mistake is to create overlapping executive competency definitions. For example, we have seen organizations use definitions such as these within the same competency model:

People Development—Creating an environment that allows people to develop to their potential. Aligning organizational and people-development objectives and encouraging, supporting, and rewarding appropriate behaviors in peers and associates.

Leadership—Creating energy and rewarding and supporting behaviors that create shared vision and values and encourage people to perform effectively. Using a range of leadership styles and maintaining appropriate role models to build cohesive, independent, and effective teams and individuals.

Impact and Influence—Helping people and the business grow by removing impediments to improving performance and by using appropriate rewards and recognition. Overcoming impediments based on divergence of culture, values, and ideas.

Evaluators using these definitions would face a serious challenge. For example, they would have difficulty deciding where to classify observed behavior relative to reinforcing and rewarding appropriate direct reports. It could fall under any of the three competencies. When competencies are so broadly defined, providing feedback is far more complex (i.e., less precise) and difficult for people to understand. We call these complex, overlapping descriptions "kitchen sink" competencies because they include everything but the kitchen sink.

Well-Defined Competencies

Contrast those definitions with the following definition of the executive competency *Customer Orientation*. As you can see, this definition is thorough and specific, and it describes the key actions (behaviors) a person would exhibit when effectively displaying this competency.

Customer Orientation—Actively seeking input from internal and/or external customers to better understand customer needs, perceptions, etc.; making efforts to ensure that customer needs are listened to and understood by self and other team members, thus making customer focus a driving force behind program/project activities; placing high value on customer enthusiasm by exceeding customer expectations.

Facilitates open communication—States action-oriented purpose in customer meetings that focuses the discussion on the customer's needs; establishes rapport; uses effective questioning style and other procedural suggestions to facilitate discussion.

Clarifies mutual understanding of customer needs—Gains full understanding of the customer's position by seeking or confirming information and opinions; questions customer assumptions in such a way that hidden needs can be surfaced.

Maintains customer trust—Listens and responds with empathy to customer issues or ideas; acknowledges customer contributions to discussion in a manner that maintains esteem.

Develops ideas/solutions—Presents information relevant to solutions or alternatives; seeks customer's ideas and suggestions about solutions or alternatives.

Gains agreement—Gains agreement that proposed solutions or alternatives would successfully address the customer's issues or ideas; summarizes and clarifies potential solutions or alternatives in relation to customer's issues or ideas; checks for acceptance of solutions or alternatives; clarifies any needed follow-up actions.

Manages customer expectations—Avoids unreasonable commitments.

Follows up—Initiates appropriate actions based upon customer input.

How Many Competencies Are Needed?

Second in importance to having well-defined competencies is having a workable list—that is, a roster of competencies that is neither too long nor too short. A list that is too long will be impractical and essentially unused in today's frantic business world. On the other hand, if the list is too short, the organization will have an incomplete profile of the competencies that an executive candidate needs. Our experience has shown that, at the executive level, usually 10–18 competencies can adequately describe the target level. Some organizations are able to keep the list at 10 competencies because previous assessment and development efforts have given them a good fix on pool members' general leadership and management-level competencies. That is, they feel that earlier efforts have already ensured that those competencies are in place among Acceleration Pool members. However, many organizations are not so sure of their knowledge in these areas and need to work with a broader list of competencies.

Another way to shorten the list is to use categories, or domains, of related competencies. DDI research in addition to research done by Borman & Brush (1993) suggests four primary competency domains:

- **Interpersonal Skills**—Behaviors associated with interacting with others, such as *Communicating with Impact* and *Building Strategic Relationships*.

- **Leadership Skills**—Behaviors associated with leading others, such as *Delegation, Coaching,* or *Change Leadership*.

- **Business or Management Skills**—Behaviors associated with the business or technical aspects of one's role, such as *Establishing Strategic Direction, Global Acumen,* or *Operational Decision Making*.

- **Personal Attributes**—Stable individual attributes, abilities, or orientations, such as *Intellectual Capacity, Adaptability, Resilience,* or *Energy*.

No matter what structure is used, the competencies within each category must be related, should not overlap or straddle domains, and must prove to be evaluated consistently within a behavioral measurement system.

Competency Rating Scales

The rating scale used in evaluating competencies should also be carefully considered. It is possible to have a well-defined competency, but to then have its reliability diminished by a poorly defined rating scale. Figure 6-2 shows an example of a poorly constructed rating scale used by a large organization to evaluate high-potential candidates. This scale has no clear progression of increasing skill or difficulty from top to bottom; a pool member could demonstrate the behavior described at one level without demonstrating the behavior described at a lower level. For example, someone might demonstrate decisiveness in a crisis (scale point "3") but fail to persist in taking action when encountering resistance (scale point "1"). Moreover, some of the points on the scale are related to the characteristics of an assignment (e.g., "Acts 4–12 months ahead") and not the person being evaluated. In some positions an individual could not get the highest rating because the position does not allow demonstration of the behavior. A scale with these kinds of inconsistencies will serve only to confuse evaluators.

Figure 6-2: A Behaviorally Anchored Rating Scale with No Clear
Progression of Skill or Difficulty from the Bottom of the
Scale to the Top

Proactivity—A bias for taking action, independently doing things, and not simply thinking about actions.

0 **Not demonstrated:** This competency is not demonstrated.

1 **Shows persistence:** Persists; takes several steps to overcome obstacles. Does not give up easily when things go wrong.

2 **Deals with opportunities:** Recognizes and acts upon present opportunities or addresses present problems.

3 **Demonstrates decisiveness:** Acts quickly in a crisis or emergency situation.

4 **Acts 2–3 months ahead:** Creates opportunities or minimizes potential problems by making an extra effort (new program, special travel, etc.) within a two- or three-month time frame.

5 **Acts 4–12 months ahead:** Prepares for opportunities or problems that are not obvious to others. Takes action to create an opportunity or avoid a future crisis.

Developing clear, reliable, specific, and unidimensional behavior anchors to describe each point on the rating scale is a time-consuming task. It requires extensive research involving the senior executives who will ultimately be using the competencies. Their task is far more involved than simply writing down an example for each point on the scale.

Most organizations use the easier-to-develop, 1-to-5 Likert scale, which lets evaluators make judgments relative to the target level. An example of a scale used to evaluate individuals for general management positions is shown in Figure 6-3.

Figure 6-3: Likert Scale Used in Rating Competencies

5 Much more than acceptable. Significantly above criteria required at the general management level.*

4 More than acceptable. Generally exceeds criteria relative to quality and quantity of behavior required at the general management level.

3 Acceptable. Meets criteria relative to quality and quantity of behavior required at the general management level.

2 Less than acceptable. Generally does not meet criteria relative to quality and quantity of behavior required at the general management level.

1 Much less than acceptable. Significantly below criteria required for successful job performance at the general management level.

* Or whatever the target level is.

When properly developed, both the Likert scale and behaviorally anchored rating scales (BARS) are equally reliable. Both have advantages and disadvantages, which are discussed in DDI's Monograph XXV, *Using Competencies to Build a Successful Organization* (Byham & Moyer, 1996/1998). ☞ The monograph also presents a third type of scale, developed by DDI, that blends the best features of the Likert scale and BARS and focuses the rater's attention on the key actions associated with each competency. Figure 6-4 shows an example of this behaviorally anchored scale.

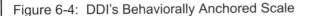

Figure 6-4: DDI's Behaviorally Anchored Scale

5 Excels in all key actions; full mastery of all aspects of this competency.

4 Excels in some but not all key actions; has no significant development needs in any key actions.

3 Performs well in the more important/critical key actions; needs development in at least one or more subtle or complex key actions.

2 Performs well in some key actions but has significant development needs in at least one key action.

1 Performs adequately in basic key actions but has significant development needs in several areas.

For more information on determining competencies, read DDI Monograph XI, *Understanding Job Analysis* (Hauenstein & Byham, 1989). Appendix 6-5 cites rationale for integrating all of an organization's executive-level resource systems around a common list of executive competencies. More information on this subject can be found in DDI Monograph XXIV, *Developing Dimension-/Competency-Based Human Resource Systems* (Byham, 1996).

Executive Derailers and Other Personal Attributes

Research by DDI, Hogan and Hogan, the Center for Creative Leadership, and others has isolated certain qualities and learned behaviors that often cause trouble for executives (Hogan, 2000; Hogan, Curphy, & Hogan, 1994; Hogan & Hogan, 1997; McCall & Lombardo, 1983). These qualities, which we will refer to as personal attributes, are not always directly observable like behavioral competencies, job challenges, and organizational knowledge. Nevertheless, it is essential to consider personal attributes as an individual rises to the executive ranks. Personal attributes include personality traits and dispositions (i.e., tendencies) that either facilitate executive success (i.e., enablers) or impede effective executive performance (i.e., derailers).

At the simplest level, personal attributes predict how a person is likely to behave in certain circumstances or, alternatively, explain why he or she behaved as observed or reported. Factors such as sociability, ambition, conscientiousness, and resilience represent the bright or positive side of a person's personality; a series of other factors represent the "dark side" tendencies that can cause otherwise capable leaders to fail (Harris & Hogan,

Using Competencies Rather Than Experience in Promotion Decisions

A large U.S. company purchased one of its main international competitors in Japan and was faced with sending a president to the newly acquired operation. The easy choice was the head of the company's small Japanese office—an American manager who had been successful at starting the office and growing it over four years. The Japanese office had about 250 employees, most of whom were involved in sales and service. The newly purchased company had about 5,000 employees and was mostly involved in manufacturing.

Although he was a proven market expert, an excellent marketing strategist, and knowledgeable about the company's technology, products, and customers, the new company president was deemed a failure within several months. The operation's productivity had declined precipitously, morale was at an all-time low, and even the much-touted Japanese quality had vanished.

While the initial selection to head the new Japanese acquisition was made quickly because the choice seemed so obvious, the replacement decision was made much more deliberately and with much greater consideration for what was really needed. The competencies defined for the position emphasized *Adaptability, Building Trust, Change Leadership, Communicating with Impact, Empowerment, Cultural Interpersonal Effectiveness, Selling the Vision, Mobilizing Resources,* and *Global Acumen.* A search within both organizations turned up a number of candidates, who then participated in an Acceleration Center to determine their appropriateness for the position. The individual selected to replace the organization's first choice was an employee of the acquired company. He had worked for an American business in the United States for 10 years and had proven himself as a manager in Japan.

The previous manager had shown good leadership skills, but the organization he built for the parent company in Japan was a model of the American organization. He never learned Japanese, and all the systems and procedures were basically Japanese translations of what was done in America. The new manager truly bridged the two cultures and had the newly acquired company back on track and thriving in nine months.

1992 [as cited in Hogan, Curphy et al., 1994]; Hogan & Hogan, 1997). As leaders move into positions of more responsibility, accountability, ambiguity, and pressure, these personal characteristics tend to make more of a difference in either supporting their success or impeding their effectiveness.

Derailers

The label *executive derailers* has come into common usage to describe the dysfunctional behaviors that individuals are predisposed to demonstrate because of underlying personality characteristics. Derailers are the executive's "Achilles' heel." They can lead to failure—even when a senior manager has the necessary competencies, job challenges, and organizational knowledge. Think of executives that you have known who have failed. You'd probably notice that simply having an abundance of competency gaps was not what hurt them. You would likely recall situations in which you witnessed their fateful downturn, including examples of defensiveness, volatility, impulsiveness, and arrogance. These descriptors reflect underlying tendencies that, under pressure, are behaviorally manifested in dysfunctional ways. They also represent classic executive derailers. Other common derailers include being aloof, distrustful, eccentric, overly cautious, and perfectionistic.

Appendix 6-4 lists executive derailers based on research covering a wide range of organizations.

Richard Nixon is a well-known example of a leader who was probably derailed by his own demons (i.e., personal attributes) as opposed to poor skills, knowledge, or abilities (i.e., competencies). Nixon was not forced to resign because of his poor negotiation skills or because he had a developmental need in building partnerships. He was a very intelligent politician who had excellent analysis and judgment in many legal and international forums. Arguably, Nixon's downfall was caused by a variety of actions and poor decisions driven by his own paranoia and emotional volatility rather than any analysis skill deficits.

Derailers often occur when an executive overuses a strength, such as when high standards shift to overcritical perfectionist behavior or when assertiveness crosses the line to being argumentative. Self-confidence is a positive personality characteristic that will help a person succeed, but taken to the extreme, it is seen as arrogance—especially when others' views are not considered or valued. The person who is determined to win at any cost, the selfless team player, the individual who always follows up and corrects all of her team's mistakes—all are exhibiting attributes that are positive at one level yet a potential source of problems at another, higher level.

For example, consider "Mary," who was a rising star in her organization. She did almost everything right, but her major strength was her ability to focus. When Mary took on an assignment, nothing got in her way. At lower levels in the organization, that focus worked well. To be sure, there were some negatives, particularly relative to her relationships with other departments and her image of selfishness at company meetings, but her bottom-line performance more than outweighed the negatives. Mary repeated the same behavior in each new position, and with each promotion the negative impact of her narrow focus increased. Because she was so intent on increasing sales, she cut R&D expenses, thereby impairing the long-term viability of her department. Later, not realizing the need to take a broader, organizational view of events as she rose in the company, she made decisions that had a short-term positive impact on her department but a larger, negative impact on the organization as a whole. Being myopic and highly focused was no longer appropriate behavior for Mary.

Or consider "Jerry," an adept corporate politician. He had a talent for rallying managers above his level to support his projects. When his projects were being considered for funding, Jerry always met individually with decision makers and persuaded them to take his side. Upon reaching higher management, he continued to display this same behavior—but at that level it was interpreted as being untrustworthy. In the eyes of those around him, Jerry was circumventing other managers and not confronting issues directly.

Sometimes derailers don't derive from strengths, but instead are slightly negative traits that are ignored at one level and then balloon into problems at the next. A good example is "Sam," an up-and-coming technical expert in one of his firm's major growth sectors. Throughout his career Sam seemed to be a little moody. His colleagues never knew quite what to expect from him. He'd be very positive about something one time, then completely change his position later. Most people who worked with Sam learned to live with his mood changes because they got the benefit of his technical skills. Also, he was funny, likable, and a very hard worker who got things done. When Sam was promoted to management, of course, the same moody behavior drove his direct reports to distraction. Every morning, the office would be filled with speculation about whether Sam would be in a good mood or a bad mood. Should they have a meeting with him or cancel it?

Enablers

Just as there are derailers that can cause executives to fail, there are also "enabling" personal attributes or tendencies that can act as catalysts for positive behavior. For example, Acceleration Pool members who are naturally risk oriented might be quicker to offer paradigm-breaking ideas in an assignment supporting a strategic organizational acquisition than would equally bright, analytical peers who are conservative and pragmatic by nature. Those who are naturally resilient and steady are more likely to focus their energy in the right places in the midst of stressful, ambiguous leadership challenges than those who are anxious and prone to second-guessing themselves. A good example is golf sensation Tiger Woods. As he matures, he complements his considerable physical talents with a calm, assured disposition that allows him incredible focus on every shot.

Awareness of enablers helps pool members identify ways to consciously leverage strengths and helps them to better understand behavior-based competency feedback.

How Can Personal Attributes Best Be Measured?

At DDI we have thought long and hard about how to reconcile the concept of personal attributes, whether derailers or enablers, with our firm belief that the bottom line for any leader's success is the *actual behavior* he or she demonstrates. Personal attributes are relevant only to the extent that they are manifested in positive or negative behaviors. These attributes, when measured through personality inventories as traits or dispositions, are one step removed from our desired level of measurement—behavior.

Therefore, when practical, organizations should define target positions or levels in competency terms. Enabling attributes (e.g., initiative) are relatively easy to define as behavioral competencies and can be measured primarily through behavioral assessment (discussed in Chapter 7). Personality inventories can and should provide complementary insight and support to behavioral evidence of enablers and key executive derailers. (Further discussion on effective and recommended uses of personality inventories can also be found in Chapter 7.)

Defining a Personal Attribute in Behavioral Terms

One of our favorite examples of how personal attributes can be translated into competencies is the trait of optimism. In the late '90s we were interviewing senior leaders in a multinational organization as part of a redesign of its global succession management system. We visited several sites in Europe and heard many common themes from those who were asked to identify behaviors essential for leaders of the future. However, a unique concept emerged from the interviews conducted at a manufacturing facility in Italy.

Each interviewee emphasized the importance of optimism and provided compelling examples of individuals with a "glass half full" approach to the world who were especially successful in their culture. We were intrigued by their examples and were able to relate their view to our own organization, where those with a can-do attitude are often the entrepreneurs and change agents who fuel DDI's growth.

Shortly thereafter, we defined the competency *Positive Disposition*. It was quickly validated as a key success factor in numerous client organizations as well as DDI, where it became a favorite competency of our COO. Today, we commonly use *Positive Disposition* in Targeted Selection (behavior-based) interviews with prospective DDI candidates.

Positive Disposition

Demonstrating high energy and positive attitude in the face of difficult or challenging situations; providing an uplifting (albeit realistic) outlook on what the future holds and the opportunities it might present.

Key Actions

- Demonstrates high energy.
- Champions the organization.
- Instills confidence.
- Provides a positive outlook.
- Uplifts spirits.

The other executive descriptors discussed in this chapter—behaviorally defined competencies, job challenges, and organizational knowledge—are customized to each organization's needs. Derailers, however, as attributes of people rather than a job, are usually not tailored.

Are Executive Derailers and Other Personal Attributes Developable?

Personal attributes generally become solidified by early adulthood, although they are not always so entrenched that later adjustments are impossible. Enhancing behavior associated with personal attributes requires extraordinary focus and motivation. It is a bit like breaking an extreme habit; the person must believe change is critical to leadership success and then work diligently and consistently on addressing the challenge presented by the personal attribute. For example, our professional coaches often hear executives (commonly from highly technical backgrounds) credit their improved social skills to a spouse who told them that they would never get ahead unless they learned to become more outgoing. These self-described introverts did not lose their natural shyness so much as they learned to demonstrate behaviors that enabled them to balance their technical acumen with the interpersonal competencies important to career progress.

In our chapter on executive coaching (Chapter 13), we deal further with strategies to avoid, and possibly correct, executive derailers.

Cognitive Ability and Motivation

In a broad sense, personal attributes also include the special categories of cognitive ability (i.e., intelligence) as well as motivations and values. Obviously, developmental implications associated with cognitive ability and motivation are quite different than those offered for executive derailers and enablers.

Unfortunately, improving raw cognitive ability is difficult; however, there are many examples of individuals who rise above ability constraints through sheer diligence or common sense. Therefore, while cognitive tests might be appropriate in certain applications (see Chapter 7), we prefer to describe cognitive ability in an applied sense, namely in terms of behaviors demonstrated in competencies such as *Judgment* or *Ability to Learn*. When we use cognitive ability tests in Acceleration Centers, it is to help us understand the behavior and decisions that we have observed in the simulation and have obtained from behavior-based interviews.

Motivation also represents another category of personal attributes that is best described in competency language. In Targeted Selection® behavior-based interviews, we seek examples of particularly satisfying or dissatisfying experiences that an interviewee experienced in a previous job or organization. Then we compare those experiences with the characteristics of the job or job level for which the person is applying. If a person worked hardest and felt most satisfied when he or she had plenty of time to think about decisions and study the pros and cons of issues, that individual would probably have a difficult time in a "ready-fire-aim" type of organization. This does not mean that the person is not motivated in a general sense; it simply means that he or she is not motivated by a specific characteristic found in the target organization. If several such mismatches are revealed, the individual would probably be unhappy in the position. Before a Targeted Selection interview, interviewees often are asked to complete a questionnaire in which they rate job and organization motivational facets. A computer quickly relates their ratings to the ratings of comparable facets found by research to be present (or not) in the target job or job level. The computer program provides interviewers with suggested behavioral follow-up questions to probe areas of potential mismatch.

DDI's Position on the Use of Personal Attributes in Assessment

Use only behaviorally defined competencies to make decisions when:

- The results will aid in selection decisions for employee, supervisory, and middle-management levels.
- The goal is to determine the development needs.

Combine inventory and behavioral measures of personal characteristics with competencies when:

- The results will be used to select executives (general managers and above).
- The goal is to determine the development needs of individuals being developed for executive positions.

When we use personality instruments, we use them to supplement and explain observed or reported behavior because we look for corroboration of data points to improve the accuracy of our assessments.

Determining Executive Descriptors

The process of determining the behaviorally defined competencies, job challenges, and organizational knowledge associated with executive success starts with individual interviews and group meetings with top management regarding their vision for the company.

We have found that a group visioning exercise is an excellent way to start the process. First, we ask executives to characterize the organization's specific future challenges and opportunities—things like new technology, changing government regulations, and competitive pressure. They then brainstorm the possible ramifications of these factors, the changes that will be needed for the organization to succeed, the special challenges leaders will face in this environment, and the skills required to address them. We then have the executives describe the kinds of leaders the organization will need to solve problems, overcome barriers, take advantage of anticipated opportunities, and manage the change that will inevitably occur.

We don't ask the executives to generate lists of competencies (otherwise, they will produce what we call "boy/girl scout lists"—meaningless, general descriptors, such as "hard working," "loyal," "proud," and "creative"). Instead, the senior managers' task is to define the roles of the executives of the future, the critical organizational tasks that must be accomplished, the values that must be in place, and the behaviors important for each role. We do ask the senior managers to suggest the categories of organizational knowledge required and define the job challenges that Acceleration Pool members should have faced before reaching the target job level.

We round out these views by interviewing executives at the target level about their jobs and how those jobs are changing. Then we take the information from all these sources and mold it into lists of behaviorally based competencies (using the DDI Taxonomy of Executive Competencies), job challenges, and organizational knowledge. We ask senior managers to edit a preliminary list of competencies to ensure that it represents key needs, contains compelling and clear language, and allows for ownership of the descriptors by the executive team. Finally, we give these lists to all executives at or above the target level, who rate, rank, and revise the items until final lists emerge.

As previously mentioned, the list of executive derailers comes from research into common derailers and usually doesn't need to be tailored to the organization.

Equal Employment Issues

Because executive descriptors are used as input for job-placement decisions, they come under the purview of fair employment legislation—and therefore must be legally defensible (i.e., the organization must be able to prove that the descriptors are truly related to job success at the target level).

If determined correctly, job challenges and organizational knowledge are job related. They are samples of job content thought to be important by management. Thus, it is unlikely that any Equal Employment Opportunity Commission (EEOC) issues will arise.

Considerable research supports the importance of executive derailers in a large variety of executive situations. If the derailers were evaluated by a professional who used them strictly as an aid in interpreting observed or reported behavior, rather than as rigid cutoffs, there would appear to be little chance of EEO concern. The United States EEOC has stayed away from any such case.

Competencies receive the most scrutiny in the United States and Europe. They are most directly related to selection and training decisions; thus, their job relatedness must be well documented. To ensure reliability of use, accuracy, and legality, the development of competency definitions and the selection of rating scales are best left to professionals who are knowledgeable in employment legislation, rating scale systems, and professional standards.

Summary

By now you are probably getting tired of us saying, "This is important" or "That is very important." The truth is that every step in the Acceleration Pool process is important. Missing just one step can cause the entire process to fail. Yet, we can't emphasize strongly enough the criticality of accurate, well-defined executive descriptors. Pool member assessment and development is built on the descriptors. Miss a critical descriptor, and an entire cadre of leaders will move into battle at the executive level with a hole in their armor.

Yet we know many organizations that take the process of defining descriptors very lightly—or worse yet, generate lists that might challenge Superman* himself and that might or might not relate to executive success. Having inaccurate descriptors wastes the time of all managers and executives who will use them.

* Superman is a registered trademark of D.C. Comics.

Toward Holistic Insights

It might seem from this chapter that we are proposing an atomistic view of leadership based on competency and derailer scores. Certainly, a good leader would demonstrate many competencies and few derailers. While examining these is important in choosing the right people for leadership positions, it is even more important to reach a *holistic insight,* which can be different than merely a sum of the parts.

The task of choosing the right people is similar to choosing a town in which to live. When a family is considering moving to a new location, it often develops a list of characteristics that are important, such as schools, recreational facilities, shopping, community spirit, and cultural activities. The family doesn't add up these factors; rather, it weighs various pieces of information relative to its unique situation. The family uses these characteristics to develop a holistic view of the town. The various characteristics of the town are of differing importance and are interrelated.

In using executive descriptors, we are doing exactly the same thing. Instead of lists of community attributes, we have competencies and derailers. People are not expected to rate high in all competencies and overcome all derailers. Instead, at the executive level we're trying to understand individuals by looking at "pieces"—the competencies and derailers. While the pieces are important, it is the insights into the whole individual that are the most important in placement and development.

An even bigger waste is having the descriptors defined in a manner that makes their use unreliable. Everyone involved (pool members, managers, Executive Resource Board members, etc.) must be able to use descriptors and their accompanying rating scale in an accurate, reliable manner. If the descriptors are neither well defined nor reliable, countless hours will be wasted discussing nuances of the definitions or the rating scale. If there ever was an example of "pay me now or pay me more later," this is it. A small investment up front in choosing and defining descriptors will save thousands of hours of valuable executive time.

Appendix 6-1: Job Challenges

Job challenges are descriptions of the kinds of situations that an individual entering top management should have experienced or at least had some exposure to. Examples include:

- Carry an assignment from beginning to end.

- Solve a difficult problem.

- Assume a significant leadership role.

- Build and lead a team.

- Follow through with a plan, product, process, or market start-up.

- Manage or become heavily involved with a merger, acquisition, strategic alliance, or partnership opportunity.

- Implement a companywide change.

- Complete an assignment with tight time and resource constraints (e.g., be first to market).

- Manage in an e-commerce environment.

- Assume responsibility for growing, downsizing, reorganizing, or shutting down a unit or operation.

- Handle an emergency situation.

- Build an entrepreneurial mind-set.

- Develop and implement a plan to cut costs or control inventories.

- Learn and apply skills quickly.

- Manage a union or nonunion operation.

- Be responsible for an operation in another country or in multiple countries.

- Take on an expatriate assignment.

- Deal with conflict, change, or hurt feelings.

- Build a new management team.

- Identify/Select talent.

- Without position power, lead a team or group through personal influence (e.g., project team, task force).

- Oversee a corporatewide process (e.g., new product development, hiring).
- Negotiate agreements with external organizations.
- Face a situation outside the individual's area of technical expertise, relying heavily on leadership skills.
- Deal with people from different disciplines, cultures, or countries who have diverse perspectives.
- Manage a geographically dispersed team.
- Operate in high-pressure or high-visibility situations.
- Manage in a fast-paced, hard-nosed business environment.
- Work with people outside the organization, such as government bureau representatives or special interest groups.
- Make presentations to senior managers or a board of directors.
- Develop others.
- Manage a quality improvement team or project.
- Manage a large-scale infrastructure project (e.g., build an office building).
- Lead a formal meeting where attendees compose different functions within the organization.
- Assume bottom-line responsibility for an operation.
- Interact directly with an external customer.
- Leverage technology into products or services.
- Create multi-organization relationships.
- Create a corporate culture.
- Develop or maintain alliances with external partners.
- Implement systems, processes, and strategic plans.
- Work in a line/staff position.
- Work in or with fast-, slow-, or hyper-growing organizations.
- Create a new product.
- Manage a group of consultants.

- Manage a large project.

- Manage a product.

- Manage a long- or short-cycle business.

- Create a breakthrough product or service (as opposed to incremental improvement).

- Control costs against a fixed budget.

- Manage "Generation Xers."

- Show entrepreneurial skills.

- Manage in a flat organization (e.g., many direct reports).

- Manage in a matrix organization.

- Manage a virtual team (e.g., direct reports in different locations).

Appendix 6-2: Organizational Knowledge Areas

Organizational knowledge refers to the understanding that senior managers have about how the various parts of the organization operate. There are four components of organizational knowledge: functions; processes; systems; and products, services, and technologies. Using this breakdown helps ensure that no important knowledge areas are left out. (There is some overlap in the areas.)

Functions

To perform effectively, an executive must have at least a working knowledge of the company's functions as well as how they interrelate. Examples of organizational functions include:

- Major Division or Group Office
- Field Operations or Field Office
- International Operations
- Research & Development
- Product Management or Brand Marketing

- Sales
- Distribution
- Finance & Accounting
- Human Resources
- Information Technology (e.g., MIS)
- Engineering

Processes

There are three types of processes to consider:

- **Core Business Process**—Activities that physically create a product or service that is of value to external customers. A key source of competitive advantage, core business processes interact with internal or external customers at the beginning and end of the process. For instance, the auto industry's core process might be new car design, manufacturing, distribution, sales, and service.

- **Enabling Business Process**—Produces outputs that act as the inputs to core processes. In other words, the enabling process gives the core process the materials needed to operate. Examples of the enabling business process include selection/recruitment (employee acquisition is the input to the core processes), financial reporting (provides "feedback" input to the core processes), sales training (sales representatives must obtain training to do their jobs well), and marketing (magazine and newspaper advertisements, television commercials, corporate sponsorships of events).

- **Support Process**—A pool of resources that is assigned to and shared by core and enabling processes. Examples of support processes include information technology management, financial management, employee orientation, and staff development.

Leaders need a thorough understanding of company processes to improve the efficiency, accuracy, productivity, and quality of products and services. Many leaders lack the process orientation or knowledge to be able to differentiate between process or system problems and people issues. Understanding these processes will help in that assessment.

Systems

The third component of organizational knowledge is systems knowledge—the degree to which a senior manager understands how the organization's internal systems work. Organizational systems include:

- Long-range planning.
- Budgeting.
- Staffing/Selection/Promotion.
- Performance management (performance appraisal).
- Succession management.
- Compensation.
- Training.

Because many systems support business processes, there can be overlaps in the lists (e.g., staffing/selection/promotion is both a process and a system).

Products, Services, and Technologies

The fourth component of organizational knowledge is familiarity with core products, services, and technologies. Because senior managers often must deal with issues that cut across the total organization, they need a working knowledge of these areas of the company.

Products, services, and technologies are unique to each organization. Following is an illustration of how they might break out for one company.

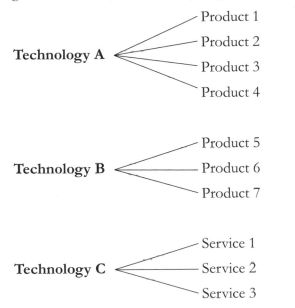

An effective senior manager in this company would be at least knowledgeable about all three technologies and ideally should have experience with several key products and services.

Appendix 6-3: Executive Competencies

You are probably familiar with the research that has sequenced and plotted the DNA of human beings. The hope is that once we can pinpoint the genes that trigger various diseases and maladies, someone will use the information to develop a remedy (e.g., a new drug) to prevent or cure them.

DNA research is analogous to what DDI has been trying to do with competencies. Since our company's inception in 1970, we have worked very hard to come up with a list of competencies that describe the knowledge, behavior, and motivations of individuals in all organizational levels. We call this the DDI Competency Taxonomy.

We're very proud of our taxonomy. We believe its research base, which involves hundreds of thousands of people and thousands of organizations, is unique. The competencies are also unique. There's no overlap across competencies in the behavioral descriptions, and assessors and assessees have molded the competency definitions over time to be very understandable.

Competencies (also known as dimensions) define clusters of behavior, knowledge, technical skills, and motivations that are important to job success. Here are some executive-level competencies used by DDI, along with their definitions:

• **Adaptability**—Maintaining effectiveness when experiencing major changes in work tasks or the work environment; adjusting effectively to work within new work structures, processes, requirements, or cultures.

• **Building Strategic Relationships**—Using appropriate interpersonal styles and communication methods to work effectively with others (e.g., peers, customers, functional partners, cross-sector partners, external vendors, etc.) to meet mutual goals and objectives; building networks to obtain cooperation without relying on authority.

• **Building Trust**—Developing other people's confidence in leadership through consistent action, values, and communications; setting an environment where employees can develop trust in one another through behaviors consistent with the Management Model and Concepts.

• **Change Leadership**—Continuously seeking (or encouraging others to seek) opportunities for different and innovative approaches to addressing problems and opportunities; facilitating the use of knowledge or help from outside the workplace (from the larger organization or outside the organization) to identify potential problems or improvement opportunities; advocating the need for self or others to seek a better way to address work process issues.

- **Coaching/Teaching**—Using appropriate interpersonal styles to inspire and guide direct reports to action; supporting and facilitating the development of the knowledge and skills of individual work team members; providing timely feedback, guidance, mentoring, and training to help individuals reach goals; sharing information on individual performance relative to expected standards; facilitating discussion of improvement strategies.

- **Communicating with Impact**—Expressing thoughts, feelings, and ideas effectively in individual and group situations (including nonverbal communication); presenting ideas effectively (including use of visual aids); clearly expressing ideas in memoranda, letters, or reports that have appropriate organization and structure, correct grammar, and language and terminology; adjusting language to the characteristics and needs of the audience.

- **Cultural Interpersonal Effectiveness**—Demonstrating understanding and effective adaptation to varying interpersonal styles and norms across cultures.

- **Customer Orientation**—Actively seeking input from internal and/or external customers to better understand customer needs, perceptions, etc.; making efforts to ensure that customer needs are listened to and understood by self and other team members, thus making customer focus a driving force behind program/project activities; placing high value on customer enthusiasm by exceeding customer expectations.

- **Delegation**—Using appropriate information (e.g., skill level, experience, knowledge, etc.) to transfer decision-making and task responsibility to individuals; establishing procedures to monitor the results or transfer of responsibility or authority, assignments, or projects.

- **Developing Organizational Talent**—Creating a learning environment that ensures associates realize their highest potential, allowing the organization as a whole to meet future challenges.

- **Drive for Results**—Setting high goals for personal and group accomplishment; tenaciously working to meet or exceed those goals while deriving satisfaction from process goal achievement and continuous improvement.

- **Economic Orientation**—Analyzing, integrating, and utilizing financial data to accurately diagnose business realities, identify key issues, and develop strategies and plans.

- **Empowerment**—Creating a sense of ownership and encouraging individuals to stretch beyond their own capabilities.

- **Energy**—Demonstrating the physical and mental stamina to meet the challenges of a demanding schedule.

- **Establishing Strategic Direction**—Securing information and identifying key issues and relationships relevant to achieving a long-range goal or vision; establishing and committing to a course of action to accomplish a long-range goal or vision after developing alternative courses of action based on logical assumptions and factual information and taking into consideration resources, constraints, and organizational values.

- **Global Acumen**—Maintaining and fostering in others an understanding of the competitive global business environment as well as an awareness of economic, social, and political trends that may impact the business environment.

- **Learning Orientation**—Actively identifying new areas for learning; regularly creating and taking advantage of formal and informal learning opportunities; using newly gained knowledge and skills on the job and learning through their application.

- **Managing the Job**—Effectively controlling one's job by planning time on priority goals, requirements, and areas of opportunity.

- **Marketing and Entrepreneurial Insight**—Keeping abreast of market trends and competition to create and seize opportunities to increase current business and/or expand into new markets; encouraging innovation and risk taking.

- **Mobilizing Resources**—Managing staff and resources consistent with organizational goals; proactively negotiating and accessing resources outside of one's immediate domain when necessary.

- **Operational Decision Making**—Relating and comparing; securing relevant information and identifying key issues; committing to an action after developing alternative courses of action that take into consideration resources, constraints, and organizational values.

- **Persuasiveness/Sales Ability**—Persuading or influencing other people to accept a point of view, to adopt a specific agenda, or to take a specific course of action.

- **Positive Disposition**—Demonstrating a positive attitude in the face of difficult or challenging situations; providing an uplifting (albeit realistic) outlook on what the future holds and the opportunities it may present.

- **Selling the Vision**—Creating a clear view of the future state; helping others understand and feel how things will be different when the future state is achieved.

- **Team Development/Team Leadership**—Using appropriate methods and interpersonal style to develop, motivate, and guide a team toward success of a program/project.

Appendix 6-4: Executive Derailers

Executive derailers are personal attributes that can cause executives to fail even when they have all the other necessary descriptors. DDI generally uses derailer definitions and labels recommended by Hogan and Hogan (1997) and by Hogan (2000) in its executive acceleration practice.

Aloof

This derailer describes executives who are generally imperceptive and not naturally inclined to read others' behavior, intent, and motivations. They might not understand others' reactions to their own behavior and are likely to have poor personal insight because they are not introspective or are self-doubting. These executives might derail because they lack self-awareness; might misread or misunderstand others' behaviors, intentions, or reactions to their own behavior; and might not pick up on social/political cues.

Arrogant

This derailer applies to executives who are overly self-assured or confident. They might overestimate their own abilities, seem self-absorbed or inconsiderate (perhaps bruising the egos of others), or be perceived as too independent (i.e., not needing or valuing others). These executives might derail because others see them as condescending, promoting their own career over others', not accepting feedback as valid, and attributing little value to others' points of view.

Cautious

Executives with this derailer are described as indecisive, too deliberate, risk averse, or reluctant to take unusual or unconventional actions. They also might fear change. These executives might derail because they miss opportunities to capitalize on good ideas. They are seen as being reactive (versus proactive), unwilling to work outside their comfort zone, and requiring predictability.

Dependent

Executives with this derailer seek and need praise or reassurance from others, particularly from people higher in the organization. They also might be compliant and conforming. These executives might derail because they are not willing to "rock the boat," and they avoid confrontation or taking unpopular stands (particularly with senior management). They also might miss opportunities to stand up for their team if an issue is controversial.

Distrustful

Executives with this derailer might be described as argumentative, skeptical, tense, paranoid, suspicious, focused on protecting their own interests, and likely to resist coaching and feedback (perhaps because they are easily hurt by criticism). They might derail because they are difficult to coach and manage. Many acquire the label of "high maintenance" because they tend to challenge authority or supervision. People with this derailer generally feel mistreated, perhaps because they take criticism personally.

Eccentric

Executives with this derailer often are described as creative and, accordingly, different from others, perhaps to the point of being unorthodox or even odd. Because their ideas are perceived as "strange" or unfamiliar, they can derail when their judgment is questioned.

Low Tolerance for Ambiguity*

This derailer describes executives who are focused tactically or operationally rather than strategically. While accomplished at implementing others' ideas or strategies, they might have difficulty stepping up to increased complexity or ambiguity as well as focusing on the future versus the present.

Melodramatic

Executives having this derailer are described as gregarious, charming, and persuasive—perhaps excessively so—as well as attention seeking and self-serving. They might find (sometimes shrewd) ways of diverting attention or credit from others to themselves. These individuals might derail because peers and direct reports resent their tendency to monopolize attention or take credit for others' contributions. They might have manipulative ways to articulate or demonstrate that they are special or unique; they might be seen as narcissistic.

Mischievous

This derailer describes executives who are impulsive, impatient, unpredictable, and even overly imaginative. Although they are "original" thinkers, they lack common sense. Their approach is "ready, aim, fire!" While energetic and intelligent, executives with this derailer are unable to learn from mistakes and might be prone to taking ill-advised risks.

Passive Aggressive

Individuals with this derailer are typically seen as overtly calm and cooperative, but tend to be privately irritable, resentful, stubborn, or uncooperative. Those with this derailer are also sometimes described as procrastinators.

Perfectionistic

Executives with this derailer are often described as micro-managers, perfectionists, controlling, and demanding of others. Their results orientation and cautiousness might render them controlling and get them overly involved in the activities of their direct reports. These executives might derail because people resent their level of meddling and detail orientation. They might miss opportunities to become more strategic because they get caught up in tactical details. When priorities change, they resist changing course accordingly.

Volatile

This derailer describes executives who have difficulty controlling their emotions, are moody, and erupt quickly in anger. They might also be characterized as having short attention spans, frequently changing interests and enthusiasms, and "taking a roller-coaster ride through life." These individuals might derail because others see them as too moody, they have a history of unstable job relationships, and they fail to express emotions appropriately.

* Low Tolerance for Ambiguity was added by DDI. The other derailers in this appendix were identified by Hogan and Hogan.

Appendix 6-5: Linking Human Resource Systems Through Competencies

A company's selection, performance management (appraisal), training, career planning, succession management, and promotion systems for a position or organizational level all can be based on a uniform set of well-defined competencies that accurately reflect position requirements (see Figure 6-5). However, many organizations' HR systems are not linked through a set of common competencies, resulting in wasted time and money and even possible litigation if the company is challenged to defend one or more of its systems.

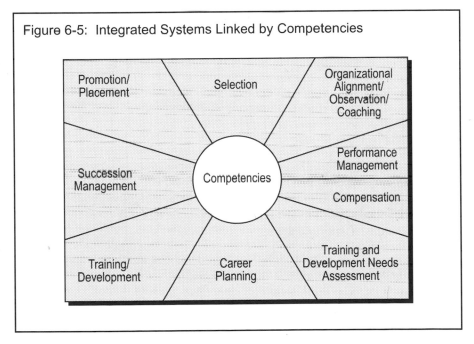

Figure 6-5: Integrated Systems Linked by Competencies

- Promotion/ Placement
- Selection
- Organizational Alignment/ Observation/ Coaching
- Succession Management
- Competencies
- Performance Management
- Compensation
- Training/ Development
- Career Planning
- Training and Development Needs Assessment

More specifically, there are six reasons why an organization should integrate its HR systems around a common set of competencies:

- **It makes sense to the systems' users.** It is difficult to explain why an individual is selected on one set of competencies, trained relative to another set, and appraised based on a third.

- **Working from the same competencies reduces time spent on communication, training, and administration.** Executives and managers need to learn only one set of competencies and definitions.

Less training time is needed to install or learn each new system because the competencies are understood and major concepts, such as focusing on behavior and organizing behavior into competencies, are used throughout.

- **Systems build on one another.** If an Acceleration Pool member has been diagnosed with a developmental need in a competency, prescribing the appropriate training program is much easier when both systems use the same set of competencies. Also, information from different sources can be compared, and data from one component can be used to validate the effectiveness of the others. For example, performance review ratings can be used to validate the effectiveness of a selection or training system.

- **Systems reinforce one another.** The use of one system supports the use of others. Using the definitions and rating scales successfully in one subsystem reminds managers of the importance of using them in other activities. For example, successfully using a performance management system organized around competencies reinforces using a succession management system organized around the same competencies.

- **All the systems can be validated at the same time using a content-oriented validation strategy** (i.e., the competencies can be related to defined job requirements). For most organizations with operations in the United States, this is the only way they can meet EEOC guidelines, and the only way that companies with operations in the U.K. and E.U. can meet Equal Opportunities Commission (EOC) and Commission for Racial Equality (CRE) guidelines.

- **It ensures all HR systems are focused on the right competencies and thereby will have the highest return on the investment for the organization.**

For more information on linking HR systems through competencies, we recommend DDI Monograph XXIV, *Developing Dimension-/Competency-Based Human Resource Systems* (Byham, 1996). ☞

Chapter 7

Diagnosing Strengths and Development Needs

(Competencies and Derailers)

*"It is a poor doctor who starts treatment
before knowing what the problem is."*

Once an organization has identified its high-potential leaders, the next
step is to diagnose their strengths and development needs. When
that is done, they can get the training and coaching they need to take
advantage of their strengths and to fill any development gaps. The
targeted, deliberate acquisition of new skills is essential if *high potential* is to
blossom into executive success.

This chapter outlines the tools used in assessing executive-level
competencies and derailers and how those tools can be applied in a
succession management system. In Chapter 8 we'll cover diagnosing
development needs relative to job challenges and organizational knowledge
as well as communicating to pool members about the assessment of all four
executive descriptor areas.

Why Is Assessment Needed?

One thing is certain: The targeted development of high-potential people
won't happen if they are simply left to their own devices. The best and
brightest generally know they're good, as do the executives who've
identified them. Thus, "leadership development" is often perceived as a
more or less automatic rite of passage rather than an opportunity to learn
important new skills.

denotes that information on this topic is available at the *Grow Your Own Leaders* web site
(www.ddiworld.com/growyourownleaders).

Many succession management systems fall apart once the high potentials have been identified. The recognition of *potential* typically is more successful than the acceleration of readiness. Consider the following example.

"Jose," a senior manager in the customer service unit of a major Silicon Valley corporation, was identified as a rising star. His record was replete with successful implementations and outstanding "numbers," such as profit-and-loss data and customer satisfaction metrics. Direct reports respected and admired Jose, and his peers offered glowing evaluations. The succession management review panel uniformly agreed that he was ready to take on an executive role overseeing a much larger proportion of the unit's operations.

About a year after Jose's promotion, his reputation had changed quite a bit. Direct reports complained of his micromanagement and unclear objectives and goals. Peers reported a lack of flexibility and cooperation in cross-functional problem solving. Newly launched initiatives faltered under his direction. In just 12 months a highly successful manager had become a failing executive.

Hoping to find a cause for Jose's poor performance, senior management hired an outside consultant to conduct a comprehensive assessment. The consultant used multiple methods, including leadership simulations, several inventories and tests, an interview, and a multiple-perspective (360°) survey, to explore Jose's executive competencies and derailers. The assessment process revealed that Jose lacked strategic-planning skills. In the discussions preceding his promotion, executives had suggested that such planning was actually one of his strengths; but as they looked more deeply at the assessment results, they could see the problem. They had mistaken implementation planning for strategic planning. They also agreed that Jose had been put at a disadvantage by not receiving any preparation for his new strategic role. Clearly, some level of developmental intervention, such as basic coaching from a skilled internal strategist, would have helped Jose do a far better job in his executive position.

Jose's story is not uncommon. We have found that such cases are typically based on two faulty assumptions:

Faulty Assumption 1: Having a rigorous process for identifying Acceleration Pool members is enough to improve leadership depth. From that point development will happen "naturally."

Faulty Assumption 2: The identification process provides the information needed to formulate people's accelerated-development plans.

The reality, of course, is that identifying individuals with senior management potential is only the first step in building bench strength. Before effective, in-depth action plans can be tailored to each individual, a comprehensive, holistic assessment is needed to pinpoint specific areas that need to be developed related to executive success.

What an Assessment Does

Executive assessment serves three essential functions in a succession management system:

- **Confirms potential.** Although a sound nomination process will tell you who has talent, a good assessment process will tell you *what kind of talent* you have identified. The nomination process provides preliminary judgments of potential based on past performance in lower-level roles. Follow-up assessment provides analysis needed to confirm that Acceleration Pool members actually have the skills required for higher-level jobs.

- **Helps target development.** Understanding the relationship between individual capabilities and the company's business objectives is essential to making an Acceleration Pool work. Ideally, high-potential leaders will be developed in ways that help them as individuals while also contributing to the success of the business. To achieve both goals, a fairly deep assessment is needed to provide more *diagnostic granularity*, or detailed information, so that developmental efforts can be targeted most accurately. We frequently see talented leaders being thrust into roles without regard for their personal development needs. The standard training options or university-based executive education curricula rarely address individuals' specific needs. A full assessment makes it possible to determine a more customized solution.

- **Guides placement decisions.** An assessment provides critical data that can be used in making placement decisions. The most successful decisions rely on matching an individual to an assignment using an integration of objective assessment data, developmental progress information, and job performance reports. This combined information can reveal insights into people's characteristics relative to specific positions (e.g., job challenges, amount of support, positive models, time, and other pressure). These insights then help ensure that selected individuals will succeed in the job.

In short, an effective assessment system can give an organization accurate diagnostic data that helps it focus on the right people, target their development most effectively, and ensure that they are placed in roles that take advantage of their strengths and minimize their weaknesses.

The Assessment Tools

The most accurate way to predict executive success is to use *multiple measures* to learn about executive competencies and derailers. To understand why, imagine a totally dark room. Seeing only blackness, you have no concept of the size of the room or its contents. Then, a spotlight switches on, shedding light on one simple object—a yellow square that seems to hang in midair, surrounded by blackness. Just as the image of the square becomes clear, a second light coming from a different angle reveals that the yellow square is actually a box or cube. Yet another light comes on, revealing that the box is resting atop a small stool. As each light illuminated the scene from a different angle, you were able to perceive more information about the true nature of the subject—and that your original interpretation was well off the mark.

This analogy holds true for executive assessment. When several complementary assessment tools are used to measure the various aspects of leadership potential, you are in a far better position to predict whether a person will succeed as a leader because you will better understand the person. The more complex (i.e., high level) the job, the more important it is to use multiple assessment methods.

Research and practice have led to the development of many tools for executive-level assessment. The primary categories of tools are:

- **Simulations**—Professional evaluations of executive competencies and derailers gained by observing behavior in simulated leadership situations.

- **Multiple-perspective (360°) surveys**—Comparison of a person's self-perceptions with the perceptions of others who are familiar with his or her behavior relative to target competencies and derailers. Paper-and-pencil or web-based questionnaires are used to collect the perceptions. Results are provided on an anonymous basis.

- **Multiple-perspective (360°) interviews**—A systematic means of gathering interview-based competency and derailer information from a number of people who work with the person being assessed. This approach is similar to the one used in multiple-perspective surveys, but it is conducted via interview rather than questionnaire.

- **Personality inventories**—Objective measurements of underlying personality characteristics (e.g., sociability, adjustment, etc.) relative to derailers.

- **Cognitive ability tests**—Basic measures of intelligence, which is a component of some competencies.

- **Behavior-based interviews**—Interviews that investigate how past work experiences relate to executive descriptors (competencies, derailers, challenges, and organizational knowledge).

- **Clinical psychologists**—Licensed professionals who conduct psychological assessments to aid in the development or selection of specific individuals. Assessments are typically done through personality inventories and clinical interviews.

As explained above, any of these methods, if used alone, would fail to provide a comprehensive evaluation of an individual's strengths and weaknesses. Because each measure offers a different perspective, the secret lies in knowing how to assemble a battery of assessment tools to achieve maximum insight. Table 7-1 illustrates how the tools compare in terms of their ability to measure the four categories of executive descriptors (competencies, job challenges, organizational knowledge, and derailers).

Table 7-1: Quantity and Quality of Assessment Information Provided by Assessment Methodologies				
(Note: The Xs denote quantity and quality of information; the more Xs, the greater the quantity and quality of information. Clinical psychologists are discussed separately because they cannot be considered assessment tools, per se.)				
Assessment Tool	**Competencies**	**Challenges**	**Knowledge**	**Derailers**
Simulations*	XXX			XX
Multiple-Perspective (360°) Surveys*	XX			X
Multiple-Perspective (360°) Interviews	XX	XX	XX	XX
Personality Inventories*	X			XX
Cognitive Ability Tests*	X			
Behavior-Based Interviews*	XX	XX	XX	

* Often incorporated as a component of an Acceleration Center.

As Table 7-1 illustrates, each tool measures competencies at some level but differs substantially in the nature and quality of the information gathered. Simulations, for example, provide the most in-depth and direct competency information because they allow experts to *observe* an individual's behavior relative to specific competencies, much like an audition or tryout. On the other hand, personality and cognitive ability (intelligence) tests are aimed at gathering underlying trait-type data that would add to the understanding of competencies; however, this information is not as directly related to future job performance. As a result, these are important elements of a larger assessment system but of limited value if used alone. We recommend that personality and cognitive ability tests be used *in conjunction* with other behavioral measures.

The assessment tools that are usually included in an executive Acceleration Center are simulations, personality inventories, cognitive ability inventories, and behavior-based interviews. Multiple-perspective (360°) interviews are used only in special cases, usually for high-level executives. Written (or electronic) 360° surveys are often administered separately from Acceleration Centers, but the data are integrated in the final diagnostic discussions.

We next will discuss each of the assessment tools in more detail.

Simulations

When designed and administered effectively, simulations in an Acceleration Center are like flight simulators for pilots. They realistically present the decisions, interactions, and strategic challenges that executives face, and they reflect the ambiguous environment in which top-level leaders must operate. Simulations provide insight into a candidate's ability to address executive-level challenges that require competencies such as *Establishing Strategic Direction, Global Acumen,* and *Change Leadership.* Most high-potential individuals lack experience with these types of challenges, so without the simulation, information on their abilities would be unavailable.

Today's Acceleration Center simulations are a far cry from the assessment center developed nearly 50 years ago by AT&T for the Bell operating companies. The most striking enhancements include:

• The use of outside professional assessors rather than a company's middle managers.

- The use of computer-based technology, which speeds and enhances the process.

- The use of video to record interactions so assessors have more time to study behavior.

- The strategic high-level nature of the simulations, which are integrated to simulate a day in the life of an executive.

- The availability of facilities built specifically to conduct the assessment, thus adding to the realism and reliability of the simulation.

Acceleration Center simulations help define specific individual development needs and assist organizations in estimating how far and fast candidates will progress. They look beyond resumes and current performance and help predict a person's potential to help the company meet future objectives. Moreover, Acceleration Centers can fairly and accurately compare the potential of employees in corporate locations around the world, allowing the organization to fully tap into its global talent.

In an Acceleration Center the prospective Acceleration Pool member assumes the role of a senior leader in a simulated business environment. This person must craft strategic plans using various sources of information (e.g., financial data, customer surveys, competitor analyses, production data), meet with internal partners, coach direct reports, build alliances with other companies, and maintain operational stability. Well-designed simulations place participants in an office environment with all the technology needed to operate effectively (e.g., voice mail, e-mail, personal computer, fax). Professional assessors play roles, such as coworkers, direct reports, vendors, customers, a television reporter, or managers, and interact with the participant. These meetings are recorded for review and evaluation after the event. Overall, the Acceleration Center simulation is a carefully crafted web of activities, each targeted at measuring specific descriptors (i.e., organization-specific competencies and derailers).

A Day and a Half in the Life
of an Acceleration Center Participant

Acceleration Centers allow participants to try on senior roles, accountabilities, and activities in a relatively risk-free, simulated environment. Participants usually find that these "stretch" experiences deliver important self-insights and give them realistic job previews. Here's an example, as seen through the eyes of a participating manager:

> If you're being perfectly honest with yourself, you're a little nervous—perhaps more than a little. You've gotten a thick folder of information (via the Web or the mail—your choice) about ABC Corporation, your hypothetical company. You've read that you're the new vice president, and you're preparing for a busy day on the job. The CEO is traveling and unavailable for the next few days. It's 7:30 a.m. You face a dizzying collection of e-mails and voice mails that demand replies and a stack of notes and memos in your in-basket. If that isn't enough, you have a very full schedule of meetings and your boss needs a strategic plan from you by tomorrow.

> Welcome to the deep end of the pool!

- You dig in, establishing priorities for everything and organizing your time. You meet with Dana Wright, a peer who's upset about one of your staff—and who once held the job you hold now.

- You get three more e-mails.

- You meet with Chris Jackson, who's been late filing for FCC compliance for your company's make-or-break new product.

- You have a working lunch to begin creating your strategic plan.

- You meet with Ronnie Hightower, whose company could be a profitable strategic partner. But now Ronnie wants to buy your company's technology outright.

- You review new in-basket items.

- You meet with an irate customer who's ready to jump ship.

- You do a live interview with a local TV reporter who has heard rumors that health hazards might be linked to your products and is digging for an exposé.

- You leave the office after a long day and, that night, prepare for your presentation.

- You arrive early the next morning to add some final touches to your strategic plan, which you will present to a group of vice presidents. And you review your speech, which you hope will motivate and inspire a heretofore lackluster workforce.

- Your presentation and speech, except for a few minor glitches, go better than expected. It's around 1 p.m. on the second day. The whirlwind is over. You've made it through.

It's been a demanding 36 hours. You've solved strategic problems, tested your vision, and addressed vendor problems, personnel matters, thorny diversity issues, and professional jealousies. You've smoothed ruffled feathers, averted disasters, built trust, demonstrated leadership, delegated, and established a strategic direction. You feel tired but good.

The deep end of the pool isn't so bad after all.

During the Acceleration Center simulation, the task of evaluating each part of the simulation is assigned to different professional assessors. Using several assessors to evaluate an individual helps to eliminate unintended biases (e.g., if a person did well in one part of the simulation, there might be the expectation of similar good performance in some other, unrelated part). Multiple assessors also provide different viewpoints on the observed behavior, thereby increasing fairness and objectivity. After each assessor has written a report on his or her assigned portion of the simulation, the assessor team meets to discuss each participant. This discussion process, called *data integration,* is the nucleus of the Acceleration Center method.

During data integration each assessor presents the observed behavior (what the participant said or did) relative to the targeted competencies and derailers. Using preestablished criteria identified in the competency analysis for the organization, assessors challenge one another to provide behavioral evidence of their conclusions. In time the team reaches consensus and rates the participant's performance against the organization's specific executive criteria. Trends and interrelationships of competencies and derailers are documented, and the assessor team often brainstorms development actions appropriate for the participant's diagnosed needs.

The following excerpts from a sample assessment report illustrate the type of data derived from an Acceleration Center. Note that the observations made by the professional assessor team are descriptions of *behavior patterns,* observed in multiple, integrated simulations by multiple assessors. Results are used for diagnostic purposes.

Following are excerpts from an executive summary of the relative strengths and developmental opportunities that were observed by assessors at an Acceleration Center. Included is an overall summary page, which presents individual competency ratings and a summary of competency "clusters," or domain trends. Each competency measured in the assessment is explored in depth in the body of the report (not shown in the summary). Specific examples are cited to illustrate and support the overall competency ratings.

Assessment Summary for: A. Candidate

	Strength	Proficient	Developmental Opportunity	Domain-Level Comments
Interpersonal Skills				
■ Building Business Partnerships			✓	Strong focus on building lasting customer relationships; missed opportunities to collaborate with internal partners.
■ Customer Orientation	✓			
■ Communication		✓		
Leadership Skills				
■ Selling the Vision			✓	Could be more inspirational with direct reports; somewhat directive in coaching situations; devised effective change initiatives.
■ Coaching/Teaching			✓	
■ Change Leadership		✓		
Business/Management				
■ Economic Orientation	✓			Demonstrated strong business judgment at an operational level; effective, strategic recommendations.
■ Establishing Strategic Direction	✓			
■ Operational Decision Making	✓			
■ Managing the Job		✓		
Personal Attributes				
■ Drive for Results		✓		Diplomatic and even-keeled manner; could have demonstrated greater command presence in formal presentations.
■ Executive Disposition		✓		

STRENGTHS TO LEVERAGE

- **Economic Orientation:** This represented your area of greatest strength. Throughout the assessment simulations you showed a strong propensity to analyze and use financial data and business indicators to drive your plans. Your strategic plan for the business reflected an in-depth understanding of the key market drivers and a focus on creating capability to respond to emerging market demands. For example, your plans to create a European Brand Team to support your "Go Global" strategy was well aligned with an emerging demand and customer buying trends (as Indicated in the market research data). The multiple-perspective (360°) survey also indicated that your colleagues view you to be highly effective in competencies including Strategic Thinking and Execution, Operational Decision Making, and Business Acumen.

- **Customer Orientation:** In your dealings with customers, you clearly sought to build long-term strategic partnerships. For example, in the meeting with Marty Morris from Alpha Technologies, you spent considerable time gathering Marty's ideas on how your unit could support his business objectives. You used diplomacy and built trust by assuring Marty of the importance of the Alpha contract. You also shared your plans about the Alpha strategic plan with your staff. This competency was the most highly rated in the multiple-perspective (360°) survey, as indicated by such items as "Seeks to Understand Customer Needs," and "Ensures Alignment of Strategies and Plans to Meet Customer Goals."

SUGGESTED AREAS FOR DEVELOPMENT

- **Selling the Vision:** In your presentation to the entire business unit to unveil your market vision, you used a highly logical, rational approach, outlining a series of troubling financial indicators (e.g., the unit's profit margins in the last four years). While your emphasis on the "financial realities" of the business was convincing, your presentation lacked clarity and focus. It was clear that you were not satisfied with the current return on investment; however, it was not clear how you hoped to change that situation or how you envisioned the future. Additionally, your demeanor was unenthusiastic and generally lacked energy. You could have enhanced your performance by focusing your presentation around a simple, memorable image of how you saw the future being different and by conveying excitement and passion for your vision.

- **Building Business Partnerships:** You missed a series of opportunities to build lasting partnerships with your colleagues. For example, you started your meeting with Dana Kupp by informing her that you had no

Validity and Fairness of Assessment Centers

Research in applied selection and assessment has shown assessment center methodology (on which Acceleration Centers are built) to be one of the most valid and reliable predictors of leadership success. Its reliability stems from the trained assessors who observe the participants' behavior in job-related leadership situations. When data on this observed behavior are combined with information on past behavior gleaned from behavior-based interviews, personality, and cognitive instruments, the result is a complete profile of an individual's behavioral strengths and weaknesses.

Originally developed as a tool to screen military intelligence officials, assessment centers were researched and validated for some time before they were popularized for use in business. Research using business subjects began in the 1950s at AT&T, where Dr. Douglas Bray conducted the Management Progress Study that defined modern assessment center methods (Bray, Campbell, & Grant, 1974). Bray's research included more than 400 AT&T managers who participated in an assessment center. Ratings of potential were made based on participants' performance in the center, and then their careers were tracked over the next 25 years. The results showed that the original ratings of potential were valid, long-term predictors of managerial advancement (Howard & Bray, 1988).

Since then, many researchers and practitioners have extended that research. Reviews of accumulated studies (Gatewood & Feild, 1987/1990; Gaugler, Rosenthal, Thornton, & Bentson, 1987; Guion, 1998; Hunter & Hunter, 1984; Landy, Shankster, & Kohler, 1994; Schmidt, Ones, & Hunter, 1992) suggest that more than 250 studies of the assessment center method have been conducted. When summarized, these studies point convincingly to the validity of the methodology as a predictor of managerial and executive success.

An Acceleration Center is a more realistic and sophisticated version of an assessment center. It retains all the salient features of the traditional assessment center (i.e., multiple trained assessors, multiple simulations that bring out behaviors at the target level, use of appropriate tests and self-report instruments, behavior-based interviews, and structured data integration). At the same time it uses electronic and video technology to record behavior and unique executive challenges integrated in a day-in-the-life experience to make the Acceleration Center more engaging, challenging, and realistic.

intention of compromising your unit's operations to accommodate her wishes. When Dana attempted to explain her position, you repeated your statement and prevented further conversation about the topic. You could have improved your performance by more collaboratively discussing the situation and by working with Dana to reach mutual agreement on a solution.

- **Coaching/Teaching:** In meetings with your direct reports, your approach was pleasant yet highly directive. In both of your coaching meetings with Terry and Jill, you asked few questions to learn about the true nature of the situations and moved immediately to prescribe remedies to the issues at hand. Had you taken more opportunity to probe into the issues and solicit the input of your direct reports, you might have more readily gained their commitment to improvement.

For the organization Acceleration Centers represent an opportunity to gauge how talented managers will respond when placed in challenging business situations—and what that might mean for future development and placement decisions. For participants the Acceleration Center offers an opportunity to gain firsthand experience with the challenges facing the organization and to learn which of their behaviors will help or hinder them in such situations. From both perspectives the outcome of the assessment process is a solid foundation from which effective development can be launched. Following is a process flow for a typical Acceleration Center:

Sample Acceleration Center Process Flow

Step 1: Participants are invited to participate in the Acceleration Center. The process, purpose, and importance are fully explained.

Step 2: Participants complete prework materials (online or via mail). Prework includes background information on the fictitious company, organization charts, agenda, etc.

Step 3: The Acceleration Center event is conducted. Professional assessors and roleplayers administer exercises and meetings in a day-in-the-life format. Participants do not interact with other people being assessed at the same time; they deal only with the roleplayers. Behavioral information is captured via audio, video, electronic data, written memos, etc.

Step 4: Professional assessors are assigned to different portions of the simulated day to evaluate participants (e.g., a discussion with an unhappy client). They review the information independently, organize it by target competencies and derailers, and then evaluate it.

Step 5: Professional assessors perform data integration. They share and discuss findings to arrive at consensus about final assessment conclusions.

Step 6: The assessment report is written to summarize behavioral trends.

Step 7: The assessment report is delivered to the participant in a feedback and coaching session where trends are reviewed, additional information is considered, and a Development Priority List is generated (see Chapter 8).

Step 8: As determined by the organization's Acceleration Pool system, an executive summary of assessment results can be shared with the Executive Resource Board to help crystallize development plans and initiate action. This information also might be shared with the participant's immediate manager and the mentor. In many organizations the Executive Resource Board receives only the Development Priority List (See Chapter 8).

Multiple-Perspective (360°) Instruments

Perhaps the most widely used diagnostic methodology is the multiple-perspective (360°) instrument. It begins with a set of evaluation criteria—typically, competencies or behaviors that relate to competencies. An individual rates his or her own effectiveness, while coworkers rate the person on the same criteria. The self-perceptions are then compared with the perceptions of the others—hence the label *multiple perspective*. The results show individuals how they are perceived in the work environment by providing insights into specific strengths and development needs as judged by work colleagues, supervisors, direct reports, and customers. Figure 7-1 shows a sample multiple-perspective survey report.

Figure 7-1: Multiple-Perspective Survey Report—Competency Summary

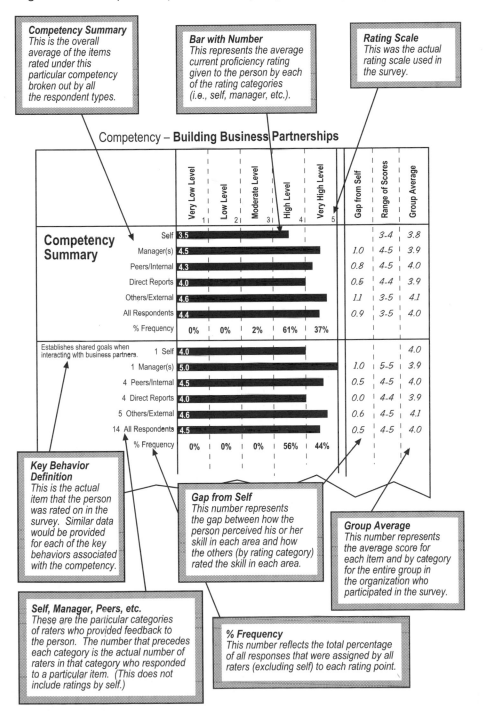

Competency Summary
This is the overall average of the items rated under this particular competency broken out by all the respondent types.

Bar with Number
This represents the average current proficiency rating given to the person by each of the rating categories (i.e., self, manager, etc.).

Rating Scale
This was the actual rating scale used in the survey.

Competency – **Building Business Partnerships**

Competency Summary

	Self	Gap from Self	Range of Scores	Group Average
Self	3.5		3-4	3.8
Manager(s)	4.5	1.0	4-5	3.9
Peers/Internal	4.3	0.8	4-5	4.0
Direct Reports	4.0	0.5	4-4	3.9
Others/External	4.6	1.1	3-5	4.1
All Respondents	4.4	0.9	3-5	4.0
% Frequency	0% 0% 2% 61% 37%			

Establishes shared goals when interacting with business partners.

	Self	Gap from Self	Range of Scores	Group Average
1 Self	4.0			4.0
1 Manager(s)	5.0	1.0	5-5	3.9
4 Peers/Internal	4.5	0.5	4-5	4.0
4 Direct Reports	4.0	0.0	4-4	3.9
5 Others/External	4.6	0.6	4-5	4.1
14 All Respondents	4.5	0.5	4-5	4.0
% Frequency	0% 0% 0% 56% 44%			

(Rating scale: Very Low Level 1, Low Level 2, Moderate Level 3, High Level 4, Very High Level 5)

Key Behavior Definition
This is the actual item that the person was rated on in the survey. Similar data would be provided for each of the key behaviors associated with the competency.

Gap from Self
This number represents the gap between how the person perceived his or her skill in each area and how the others (by rating category) rated the skill in each area.

Group Average
This number represents the average score for each item and by category for the entire group in the organization who participated in the survey.

Self, Manager, Peers, etc.
These are the particular categories of raters who provided feedback to the person. The number that precedes each category is the actual number of raters in that category who responded to a particular item. (This does not include ratings by self.)

% Frequency
This number reflects the total percentage of all responses that were assigned by all raters (excluding self) to each rating point.

Although the value of such feedback is clear, there are a number of issues to keep in mind with the multiple-perspective methodology:

- One must consider who completes the forms. In most organizations the person being evaluated chooses the "others." This is fine if that person sees the positive development implications of the process and wants to get the most accurate feedback possible. However, if the individual foresees negative consequences, then it is quite easy to send the forms only to friends or people with whom he or she has had positive interactions. (Many organizations make this a non-issue by deciding who completes the forms.)

- Raters are not trained behavioral assessors; therefore, the feedback is subject to biases. Also, they might not understand the competencies or the rating scale being used and, thus, fail to differentiate among the competencies (e.g., having a strong feeling about one competency might influence the ratings on others, avoiding extremes on the rating scale). Rating patterns also have been shown to change based on the purpose of the assessment (e.g., evaluation results are often higher when a promotion is involved).

- Not all raters have equal opportunities to observe the target individual on the factors to be rated. For example, peers might not know how to evaluate the target's coaching behaviors; similarly, direct reports might not be qualified to rate partnership behaviors.

- Perhaps most important, accurately rating certain competencies might be impossible because the individual being evaluated has never had an opportunity to exhibit them. This is especially true with many of the executive competencies and derailers that might be targeted in succession management programs. For example, a middle manager possibly would never have had the opportunity to do long-range planning.

We have found that multiple-perspective feedback can be a highly valuable developmental tool because it can help people see themselves through others' eyes, thereby revealing blind spots. It can be especially powerful when combined with other objective behavioral measures (e.g., simulations used in Acceleration Centers or personality inventories) that allow the 360° information to be seen in a larger context. Having multiple perspectives can also create acceptance (buy-in) of developmental needs when someone is defensive about accepting assessment insights from other tools. Because of its inherent limitations, be careful in using multiple-perspective feedback in succession management systems. We do not recommend using multiple-perspective tools in making selection or placement decisions.

How *Not* to Use 360° Surveys

Multiple-perspective feedback is the most widely used assessment tool, but we believe that it is also the most widely *misused* method. Some of the most common mistakes include:

- **Inadequate communication about the purpose, importance, and uses of multiple-perspective feedback.** Without clear communication people will reach all possible conclusions about the purpose of the assessment tool, and the most negative interpretations will spread most quickly. Based on our experience, overcommunicating the purpose of the multiple-perspective process is impossible. More information might raise more questions, but it also will enhance people's trust in the process, thereby yielding more productive, honest feedback about performance.

- **Lack of top-management support.** Top management must provide strong, visible encouragement to everyone involved in filling out the questionnaires by encouraging them to give honest and direct feedback.

- **Use of multiple-perspective data to make hiring, promotion, or compensation decisions.** We firmly believe that multiple-perspective data are not appropriate for such decision-making purposes. On numerous occasions we have seen organizations suffer through the fairly useless "popularity contests" that emerge when people know that multi-perspective ratings will determine promotion decisions. In such cases, of course, popular individuals receive high ratings, while others, who might have greater potential but fewer friends and allies, receive less-favorable feedback.

- **Insufficient quality feedback and support in interpreting results.** A written report of results is seldom enough to help someone fully process and use multiple-perspective results. If they are obtained, respondents' comments (beyond their multiple-choice answers) are often recorded verbatim, so the feedback can be harsh and, at times, unrelated to specific skills or competencies. Support in understanding results, linking results to the job, and planning developmental actions will help maximize the value of the feedback.

- **Inadequate follow-up, support, and accountability in planning and implementing developmental actions.** Producing a diagnosis of development needs without providing appropriate prescriptions, encouragement, and accountability usually leads to ineffective development actions (see Chapter 8).

> • **Using multiple-perspective feedback without complementary tools.** Methods that rely on others' perceptions to drive performance evaluations are only as accurate as the perspectives of those making the evaluations. This, in itself, does not mean that these tools lack value, but it does suggest that the results must be used carefully. In addition, multiple-perspective methods look at past experiences in situations people have already faced and do not necessarily speak to their potential in future settings.

Multiple-Perspective (360°) Interviews

In some cases one-on-one interviews with people's coworkers, direct reports, and supervisors can be conducted to gather competency or derailer information. This 360° interview approach yields contextual information to supplement the static performance ratings and brief written comments from anonymous parties in 360° questionnaires. A major advantage is that the interviewer can change the interview questions as themes emerge and need follow-up. Even the list of planned interviewees can change if a name comes up frequently in early interviews. Usually, the target manager is the last to be interviewed so that the questioning can focus on issues that arose in the earlier interviews, such as self-perceptions of interpersonal or business relationships. These self-perceptions can be related to the descriptions provided by others, and thus an indication of accuracy of self-insight can be obtained.

All 360° interviews must preserve confidentiality. An interviewer compiles the results and distills outputs into a smaller set of core themes that are fed back to the individual (and/or the organization). Because it is fairly labor intensive, this approach generally is used only in the following situations:

- **Very important placement/promotion decisions, particularly when doubts exist about whether an individual is in sync with the organization's vision or values.** Sometimes the usual sources of information are not enough and special efforts are needed. Live 360° information can help address lingering questions and doubts. (The use of diagnostic tools in making promotion decisions is discussed further later in this chapter.)

- **Expatriate assignments.** Interviews with colleagues and family members are conducted to gather performance, motivational, and cultural fit data about an individual being considered for an assignment in a different culture.

- **Senior-level executive coaching.** For senior executives facing unique, critical challenges, often the first step for an executive coach is to gather live 360° data. These data are used to help the executive craft an accelerated development plan that can help him or her deal with a crisis, prepare for a major change, or provide assistance to a struggling unit or business (see Chapter 13).

Personality Inventories

Personality inventories are self-report questionnaires that measure underlying traits—such as ambition, sociability, and interpersonal sensitivity—and potential derailers—such as arrogance, volatility, micro-management, and approval dependence. When interpreted by trained practitioners, these inventories provide important insights into personality characteristics that become increasingly important as a person moves up and his or her personality affects a broader portion of the organization.

For example, a senior vice president of human resources at a large consumer-products manufacturer was known for his autocratic, intimidating style. Assessment showed that, on the positive side, his personality was characterized by high ambition, sociability, and creativity. On the negative side intense arrogance, interpersonal detachment, and emotional volatility emerged when the pressure was on. The negatives affected the vice president's performance—the HR department was in disarray, with profound discontentment among his staff. Perhaps more troubling, his direct reports had begun exhibiting many of the same dysfunctional behaviors, especially in his presence. His negative side was, in a sense, spreading into the organization.

With the appropriate personality inventories and professional interpretation (in conjunction with simulations and other assessment tools), this executive might have been made aware of the behaviors that emerged from his derailing characteristics. He then could have avoided them and tried to leverage the more positive aspects of his personality.

Cognitive Ability Tests

Cognitive ability tests are essentially intelligence tests. They measure critical thinking, situational judgment, etc. They tell us about others' intellectual "horsepower"—their ability to process complex information quickly, understand relationships among various sources of information, and arrive at accurate judgments based on their analyses. Cognitive ability has been shown during many years of research (Gottfredson, 1986;

Hunter & Hunter, 1984; Landy et al., 1994; Schmidt et al., 1992) to be one of the strongest single predictors of managerial success. But as we all know, the smartest people are not necessarily the best leaders.

As with other assessment tools, organizations should bear a number of caveats in mind when considering the value of cognitive ability tests:

- Because there are many types of tests to measure cognitive ability, the particular characteristics of the test being used must be known to properly interpret the results. For example, some tests employ arithmetic, while others don't. Some deal with abstract issues, while others are very down-to-earth and practical.

- Is the test timed? This is important because in real life executives work at high speeds, but they also take time to think about important issues. Thus, time-sensitive tests are not very appropriate for executives because they don't realistically mirror the target job.

- Some people freeze up or have other problems in testing situations, rendering their scores unreliable. For example, Winston Churchill was known as a notoriously poor test taker (Leonhardt, 2000).

- The correlation between cognitive ability and job success is far from perfect. We all know highly intelligent people who are not successful as well as people of average intelligence who are. Executives need certain minimal-level skills, but in many cases other competencies—including the ability and willingness to perform good, old-fashioned hard work— are more important than cognitive ability.

Again, the lesson here is that cognitive inventories are best used in conjunction with behavioral measures of leadership potential. Ideally, you should measure cognitive ability and observe how an individual *applies* that ability.

Finally, because of the great potential for misusing cognitive measures, we believe that cognitive ability tests should be chosen and administered only by professionals. We have seen many organizations make arbitrary and limiting decisions concerning cutoff scores (e.g., "people must be above the 85th percentile on a cognitive test to move into an executive position"). Others have mistakenly related high cognitive scores to competencies such as *Planning* or even *Leadership*—an inaccurate approach that only clouds the picture.

Behavior-Based Interviews

Behavior-based interviews gather specific examples of past job experiences that relate to future job responsibilities. The methodology is based on the tenet that interviewers who are trained to collect and evaluate job-relevant behavior in a standardized fashion are more accurate in their evaluations (Campion, Campion, & Hudson, 1994; Campion, Palmer, & Campion, 1998; Janz, 1982; Orpen, 1985; Wright, Lichtenfels, & Pursell, 1989).

There are many variations on behavior-based interviewing. The most popular method is Targeted Selection® (TS), developed by Development Dimensions International in 1970 and used by thousands of organizations throughout the world. As far as we know, TS was the first behavior-based interviewing system. Its effectiveness is well documented, including the following DDI research studies: Targeted Selection Evaluation Summary (1999), Baptist Health System, Inc. (1997), Equate Petrochemical Corporation (1997), MediaOne Group (1999), Oracle (1999), Kraft Foods (2000), and Targeted Selection (Return on Investment [1998]).

In a TS interviewing system, each interviewer has an interview guide with suggested behavior-based questions for each competency to be evaluated. The target competencies are divided among the interviewers. When more than one interviewer is assigned the same competency, the suggested questions are different. Candidates are typically asked to describe situations in which they used behaviors that will be required in the target job or job level. For example, to learn about coaching behavior, the interviewer might say, "Tell me about a time when you had to work with an employee to help that person improve performance." Interviewers are trained to ask follow-up questions designed to yield highly specific information about the interviewee's role, his or her specific actions, and the results obtained from those actions. Several behavioral examples are collected for each competency.

Interviewers are trained to conduct efficient, effective, esteem-enhancing interviews, integrate their findings, and make a final decision. A data integration system is used, much like the one described in the "Simulations" section earlier in this chapter. During data integration the interviewers share their behavioral evidence on each competency and arrive at consensus judgments about each candidate.

Behavior-based interviewing has traditionally been used mostly as a tool for selecting individuals for jobs. In an Acceleration Pool system, this approach is also commonly used in conjunction with an Acceleration Center that uses other evaluation methods as well.

Clinical Psychologists

Many organizations have access to a trusted staff psychologist (either in-house or through a consulting or contract arrangement) who senior leaders can approach for help in a variety of situations. These professionals often are used in executive development, coaching, selection, and hiring situations. To perform assessments, most rely heavily on psychological testing (e.g., personality and cognitive inventories) in conjunction with in-depth clinical interviewing.

A caution: Clinical psychologists' services might not be linked to an organization's competencies and might, in fact, have no competency structure to them at all, making it difficult to link or contrast their findings with those of an Acceleration Center or 360° instruments. However, psychologists undoubtedly add value at the individual level through their unique insights. They can be effective in coaching executives and can play a key role in supporting the ongoing development of high-potential leaders. When clinical psychologists are used, organizations often restrict this relatively expensive and labor-intense method to a small number of very high-level incumbent executives.

Integrating Multiple Assessment Tools into a System

As we have pointed out several times, the best assessment approaches rely on the use of multiple, complementary tools to provide different perspectives on an individual's potential. The key is to use the right mix of tools and bring them together into a structured system.

In determining which assessment tools to use, consider the following:

• Current job performance (e.g., accomplishments, achievements).

• Past examples of relevant behaviors.

• Behaviors demonstrated in future-focused simulations.

• Personal characteristics, such as cognitive ability and personality test results, that will help explain behavioral findings and suggest possible executive derailers.

Figures 7-2 and 7-2a show how various assessment tools map to these four sources of assessment information. The figures underscore that each tool offers a unique perspective on potential and plays an important role in the overall assessment process. For example, an assessment that does not include simulations will fall short in evaluating a person's behavior in "stretch" roles—an important consideration in evaluating executive candidates. Similarly, processes that omit personality inventories and tests will fail to measure key personal characteristics that can enhance or inhibit potential.

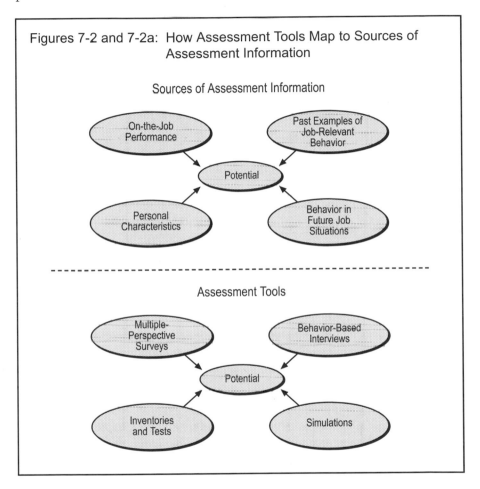

Figures 7-2 and 7-2a: How Assessment Tools Map to Sources of Assessment Information

Sources of Assessment Information

Assessment Tools

There is a guiding principle to remember when trying to determine the right mix of assessment tools: **Ensure that some level of behavioral measurement is combined with measurements of personal characteristics, such as cognitive ability, motivation, and personality.** Unlike *behaviors,* which we can observe, change, and control, personal characteristics are more "fixed" and are fairly difficult to observe directly. Simply put, behaviors represent *what we see,* while personal characteristics help to explain *why we see what we see.*

The consideration of both types of information makes for a deeper, more comprehensive assessment. Entrepreneurial qualities, for example, might be identified by examining past situations in which a person had opportunities to build new business. However, knowing about the person's creativity and propensity for risk taking will provide a more complete picture of entrepreneurial potential over the long term.

Using our guiding principle, numerous combinations of tools are possible for a more holistic process, depending on resources, time, and patience. Some executive assessment systems incorporate personality and cognitive ability tests, multiple-perspective inventories, and behavior-based interviews in two-day Acceleration Centers comprising 10 to 15 short, integrated simulations. Others take a more streamlined approach, using fewer simulations—perhaps 2 to 5—in combination with one or two tests and one behavior-based interview or multiple-perspective survey.

How streamlined can you get? Some organizations will forego simulations entirely and rely only on maybe a multiple-perspective inventory—but that is not a solution that we recommend. These shortcut solutions can be tempting, given that an in-depth approach can cost $5,000–$10,000 per assessment. But in light of the sacrifices they require in terms of thoroughness and accuracy—coupled with the importance of the positions being filled—any cost savings might not be realized in the long run.

Succession Management Practices Can Help in Mergers/Acquisitions

A major high-tech company came to DDI after acquiring a division of another large high-tech organization. The $3 billion acquisition created some leadership redundancy as well as new leadership opportunities. The CEO, unsure which leaders to place in the various new positions of the new organization, called DDI for help. Essentially, a short-term succession management process ensued in which leadership talent had to be identified, diagnosed, and deployed into new positions.

We quickly worked through the CEO's vision for the new organization and designed a customized Acceleration Center process, which highlighted many of the challenges associated with integrating the two organizations. Then the CEO and his steering team successfully pilot tested the Acceleration Center process themselves. Using his knowledge of and confidence in this process, the CEO conducted small-group orientation sessions with all 165 executives from the two organizations, explaining the value of the assessment process that would be used to help determine leaders for the new organization.

Participants began by completing a Career Achievement Portfolio (CAP) in which they documented their crowning leadership accomplishments. The CAP provided leaders with an opportunity to "present themselves" using behavioral examples of their choosing. Each leader then participated in the Acceleration Center process. The CAP and Acceleration Center results were reported back to the organization in sessions designed to review the participants against roles in the new organization.

A cascading review and decision-making process ensued. The process began with a review of the CEO's Acceleration Center results, so that he fully understood the information that would be used to discuss all other assessees. Next, top candidates for the Chairman's Council were discussed by presenting Acceleration Center results and integrating them with career achievement information. Through a two-day review and discussion, the CEO painstakingly selected his staff.

Several days later, the CEO returned with his newly appointed staff to work through the same process to fill the leadership positions in their respective units. While the process involved several very long days, the Chairman's Council reported enormous confidence and satisfaction in the quality of the decision-making process, contending that better decisions emerged from the use of objective, comprehensive information about leadership strengths and development needs than could have been made without it.

Following the complete staffing of the new organization, the Chairman's Council worked with DDI to initiate its own individual and team development strategies. All other leaders received feedback and developmental coaching from DDI and worked to implement developmental strategies that would facilitate personal growth and enhance the quality of the integration of the two companies. The assessment and placement process was reported by most to have boosted their confidence in the quality and fairness of the staffing process. The CEO, having agonized over numerous difficult decisions regarding his own staff, reported that the assessment process was pivotal in assuring himself that he was making the right decisions.

A year and a half after the acquisition, the CEO maintained that position, as did his staff, and shareholders enjoyed a stock price that grew 1,000 percent since the merger.

How Acceleration Centers Measure EQ

In Acceleration Centers individuals are confronted with situations similar to those they would face on a new job. For example, the person being assessed might be asked to handle a difficult interpersonal situation with a "direct report," whom he would meet with while a trained assessor would evaluate the demonstrated behaviors.

In another common situation the assessee becomes part of a small group that must solve a difficult problem and then present its recommendations to higher management. *Interpersonal Skills, Persuasion, Leadership,* and other competencies important to leadership are evaluated.

How a person handles these and other exercises is a direct result of his or her emotional intelligence, or EQ. An Acceleration Center measures the output or use of a person's emotional intelligence—which is what a business really wants to know. If an organization requires a measure of emotional intelligence, an Acceleration Center can obtain this data by assessing all the competencies that make up EQ (i.e., *Self-Awareness, Risk Taking, Stress-Tolerance, Adaptability, Initiating Action, Positive Disposition,* and *Interpersonal Awareness*). ☞

The "Buyer's Guide"

Table 7-2 depicts a "Buyer's Guide," which describes the various assessment tools available today, along with some comments on when to use them and why they are effective.

Table 7-2: A "Buyer's Guide" to Diagnostic Tools

Diagnostic Tool	Description	What It Measures	When to Use It	Features of an Effective Tool
Acceleration Center (simulations, tests, inventories)	• An organized set of work simulations that systematically measure key competencies associated with success in a specific role or job family. • Often administered as a day in the life of a leader. • Might include multimedia decision challenges, role plays, strategy exercises, market-vision simulations, or other executive-level challenges. • Usually includes a professionally conducted, behavior-based interview process, such as Targeted Selection. • Might also incorporate tests and inventories as an adjunct measure to amplify simulation results (see the following pages).	• Behavior patterns across work situations. • Interpersonal competencies. • Leadership competencies. • Business competencies. • Personal characteristics. • Can be customized to measure specific competencies required by an organization.	• To identify and diagnose Acceleration Pool members' development needs. • To establish a baseline for developmental action. • As a key data point in making executive-selection decisions (i.e., placing Acceleration Pool members into roles).	• Futuristic. • Realistic. • Challenging. • Customized to reflect your business challenges. • Uses multiple tools to collect data. • Uses professional assessors. • Group assessment approach (data integration) to avoid personal biases. • Executive-level facilities. • Global consistency of facilities and quality of assessment. • Clear orientation to the process prior to participation. • Accompanied by professional feedback and coaching after the event. • Supported by sound validation research.

Table 7-2: A "Buyer's Guide" to Diagnostic Tools (cont'd)

Diagnostic Tool	Description	What It Measures	When to Use It	Features of an Effective Tool
Multiple-Perspective (360°) Survey	• Behavioral survey administered to an individual and a number of people with whom he or she works. • Typically designed to measure perceived performance against key competencies. • Feedback sources can include self, direct reports, peers, supervisors, and customers. • Feedback report provides comparison of self-perceptions with perceptions of other groups. • Ratings and comments are made anonymously to promote candor.	• Almost any behavioral competency that can be observed by respondents.	• For personal development. • As a key source of input to Acceleration Pool members' development-planning efforts. • To provide a measurable follow-up to development actions—prove that the individual has truly changed his or her behavior. • **Should not** be used to make selection or promotion decisions.	• Simple administration options (e.g.; Web-based, PC-based). • Clear, understandable feedback reports. • Comprehensive representation of observable leadership competencies. • Validation data for standardized scales. • Clear, frequent communications about the purpose, importance, and use of results in the process. • Strong, visible encouragement from the top to give others honest, open feedback for use in personal development. *(Continued on next page.)*

Table 7-2: A "Buyer's Guide" to Diagnostic Tools (cont'd)

Diagnostic Tool	Description	What It Measures	When to Use It	Features of an Effective Tool
Multiple-Perspective (360°) Survey (cont'd)				• Public guarantees that honest feedback will be properly processed (i.e., not used to promote or demote people). • Follow-up and support in interpreting the results, planning development, and implementing developmental actions.
Multiple-Perspective (360°) Interview	• One-on-one interview to gather input from people who work with a target individual.	• Individual performance patterns. • Contextual information surrounding an individual's approach to work.	• Filling expatriate positions. • Filling critical high-level positions. • Specialized high-potential coaching. • High-level executive coaching. • Convincing an individual of the need to change—more evidence required.	• Competency- and derailer-based approach. • Standardized interview and coaching protocol (used flexibly). • Qualified, trained assessors. • Documentation of data gathered, actions taken, and progress made against developmental objectives.

Table 7-2: A "Buyer's Guide" to Diagnostic Tools (cont'd)

Diagnostic Tool	Description	What It Measures	When to Use It	Features of an Effective Tool
Personality Inventory	• Self-report measures of stable, underlying traits. • Typically multiple-choice format; takes 30–60 minutes to complete.	• Positive personality traits, such as: – Adjustment. – Ambition. – Sociability. – Interpersonal sensitivity. • Executive derailers, such as: – Volatile. – Arrogant. – Eccentric. – Distrustful.	• To complement behavioral information (e.g., Acceleration Centers) in development and selection situations. • For added insight into the underlying explanations for observed behavioral trends. • When professional interpretation is provided.	• Has research and validation support. • Has relevant norm samples to which individuals and groups can be compared. • Has business-oriented validity evidence. • Produces clear, understandable reports. • Can be related to target competencies and derailers. • Does not ask embarrassing questions.
Cognitive Ability Inventory	• Tests measuring a variety of cognitive abilities. • Multiple administration methods employed but most often multiple-choice and/or fill-in-the-blank.	• General measures of intelligence, such as: – Critical thinking. – Numerical reasoning. – Reading comprehension. – Analytical reasoning. – Spatial relations. *(Continued on next page.)*	• Becomes more predictive as jobs become more complex; therefore, highly useful in executive settings. • To complement behavioral information (e.g., Acceleration Centers). *(Continued on next page.)*	• Heavily researched and validated. • Relevant norm samples to which individuals and groups can be compared. • Business-oriented validity evidence. *(Continued on next page.)*

Table 7-2: A "Buyer's Guide" to Diagnostic Tools (cont'd)

Diagnostic Tool	Description	What It Measures	When to Use It	Features of an Effective Tool
Cognitive Ability Inventory (cont'd)		• Provides insight into ability to process information efficiently and accurately.	• More useful for selection than development because results are difficult to act upon (i.e., difficult to develop). • When professional interpretation is provided.	• Clear, understandable reports. • Items that are appropriate for an executive—not elementary or "schoolish."
Targeted Selection Behavior-Based Interview	• Interviewing technique that probes into past experiences and accomplishments as they pertain to future role assignments. • Standardized training, interview guides, interview questions, and evaluation approaches are incorporated.	• Almost any behavioral competency. • Limited when interviewees do not have experience in the competencies being targeted.	• To complement an Acceleration Center process. • In selection systems (e.g., support hiring decisions).	• Heavily researched and validated. • Standardized training and certification methodology available in multiple training modes (e.g., classroom, online, self-study, etc.). • User-friendly interview guides. • Software support systems. • Customizable to organization-specific competencies.

Table 7-2: A "Buyer's Guide" to Diagnostic Tools (cont'd)

Diagnostic Tool	Description	What It Measures	When to Use It	Features of an Effective Tool
Clinical Psychologists	• Individual or small-practice consulting units supporting executive coaching, executive development, and staffing initiatives. • Wide variance in the range and quality of services.	• Customized batteries of inventories, tests, and (sometimes) focused simulations. • Sometimes can be customized to company competencies.	• Individual coaching and development endeavors. • In support of larger initiatives in which additional coaching might be needed.	• Experience, track record. • Proven results with executives. • Use of well-researched, proven methodologies and tools.

Appendix 7-1: Assessment Data Security

Many problems can arise if assessment reports from Acceleration Centers, 360° instruments, tests, personality profiles, and behavior-based interview reports are misused. An individual's career can be ruined if an executive misinterprets a report or overgeneralizes its findings. Assessments can also affect the atmosphere in an organization when a manager knows that a person did well and begins treating him or her better than others. This might cause some tension within the workforce. Thus, it is important that organizations using assessment instruments create standards relative to their use. Each organization needs to identify and adhere to standards that address these questions:

- Who will have access to the summary report and instrument reports? What are the training requirements for interpreting reports?

- Where will reports and other data be stored? How will they be protected from unauthorized access? How long will reports and data be kept on file?

- Will individuals have the opportunity to file an objection to their reports?

Often it is useful to draw a grid that delineates who is permitted to have access to which data. Table 7-3 on the next page provides an example.

For organizations using Acceleration Centers, we advise following the guidelines of the International Congress on Assessment Center Methods (http://www.assessmentcenters.org).

For organizations operating in European Union countries, we recommend following the E.U. guidelines on handling data and local statutory acts (e.g., the Data Protection Act in the U.K.). See Chapter 16 for more information on the European Union Data Protection Act of 1998, or contact the DDI Resource Center at ddiresctr@ddiworld.com.

In some countries special professional and legal conditions apply to the use of psychometric tests and inventories. Readers are advised to consult the relevant professional associations to determine if local restrictions apply.

Table 7-3: Simple Data-Sharing Matrix

	Executive Summary	Full Assessment Report	Personality Inventories*	Development Priority List	Development Action Forms
Pool Member	X	X	X	X	X
Human Resources	X	X	O	X	X
Manager	X	O	O	X	X
Mentor	X	O	O	X	X
Executive Resource Board	X	X	O	X	X
Executive Coach	X	X	X	X	X
Manager Considering Individual for Promotion	O	O	O	X	X

X = Data shared automatically as part of process.

O = Optional—Data not shared automatically. Participant may share data if he or she chooses to do so.

* With respect to personality inventories, we advise that raw profiles be shared only with trained professionals. Narrative summaries might be shared as shown on this chart.

Chapter 8

Understanding and Prioritizing Development Needs

(Job Challenges, Organizational Knowledge, Competencies, and Derailers)

"Know thyself."

—The Seven Sages
Inscription at the Delphic Oracle

The assessment of development needs described in Chapter 7 produces a great deal of data. Frequently, the meaning and value of these data won't be readily apparent to Acceleration Pool members. So, before they can target any development activities, members must have a firm grasp of what these data are telling them. That is, they must form a solid understanding of the areas in which they have strengths and those that they need to develop as well as how their development efforts should be prioritized.

To put their assessment results to work, pool members must accomplish six tasks:

1. Understand the organization's executive descriptors (in the four categories of job challenges, organizational knowledge, competencies, and executive derailers) and why they are important to the target organizational level.

2. Understand the findings from the assessment activities as they relate to the executive descriptors.

☞ denotes that information on this topic is available at the *Grow Your Own Leaders* web site (www.ddiworld.com/growyourownleaders).

3. Consider how the assessment results relate to past feedback from 360° instruments, performance appraisal discussions, and comments from friends, family, and coworkers.

4. Develop a list of strengths and development needs in each of the four executive descriptor categories.

5. Recognize how the executive descriptor data fit together. For example, an individual needs to know how his or her competencies and derailers have related to one another in the past and how they might relate at higher-level positions. Also, there often is a relationship among different areas of development need that must be considered in development planning. For example, a person might be weak in the competency *Marketing and Entrepreneurial Insight* and also lack exposure to the organization's marketing activities, a knowledge area. In such situations it would be efficient to work on developing both at the same time.

6. Prioritize development needs in each of the four executive descriptor categories.

These six tasks might sound simple enough, but getting through them actually presents a major hurdle for pool members; in most cases they will need some help. Because the person giving the Acceleration Center feedback (competencies and derailers) often does not know enough about the organization to accurately evaluate the company-oriented descriptors, many organizations divide the discussion of descriptors into two parts: 1) the "personal" arena of competencies and derailers, and 2) the "company-oriented" descriptors of job challenges and organizational knowledge. One professional usually works with the pool member on the first area, while another professional or a member of the Executive Resource Board focuses on the second. However, one professional can cover all four descriptor areas if qualified to do so.

Understanding Competencies and Derailers

Many rising leaders have strong opinions about how to succeed in business and can be reluctant to accept the notion that they have development needs. Their egos and successful track records can also stand in the way of making a personal commitment to change.

The key to overcoming those roadblocks is to provide feedback from an honest, credible source. The best source that we know of is an Acceleration Center professional. The professional can help pool members understand their behaviors relative to the organization's competencies and derailers, and integrate behavioral observations and indications with personal characteristics that have been determined by a variety of pencil-and-paper and self-report instruments (see Chapter 7). Pool members need to see how competencies and derailers interact; that is, being strong in one competency (e.g., *Decisiveness*) can magnify the impact of another (e.g., *Low Judgment*). Also, the professional can help pool members integrate information from 360° feedback and other sources to provide holistic insights that are compelling and challenging.

Acceleration Center professionals who provide feedback about competencies and derailers do so through high-level themes that pull together certain competencies and derailers. They cite specific behavioral examples of what the individual said or did in the simulation to support their observations.

Acceleration Pool members often will have multiple-perspective data from previous jobs or applications in their current organization. Multiple-perspective (360°) instruments are so prevalent today that it's not unusual for a pool member to have data from four or five of them. Pool members should be encouraged to bring in that information for their discussion of development needs. At the very least they should be prompted to recall the results of previous 360° instruments when considering their current data. It's also a good idea for pool members to bring performance appraisals or other performance-related forms to the discussion because they can be helpful in identifying behavioral trends or issues.

The more sources of available information, the better pool members will be able to understand their situation and pinpoint the implications of their data. For example, an Acceleration Center found one person to be weak in planning, although 360° data indicated that she had no problem in this area. During the discussion with the assessment professional, the pool member explained that her direct reports respected her planning skills because she delegated almost all the planning tasks. This insight explained the apparent disparity and confirmed the Acceleration Center's judgment that the pool member was strong in delegation. It also prompted the pool member to think about how her deficiencies in planning skills might affect her performance at higher organizational levels.

In another situation the Acceleration Center evaluated a manager as adequate in judgment, while his direct reports rated him as weak. Discussions revealed that the Acceleration Center had focused primarily on financial and other data-driven judgments, which were, in fact, a strength. In areas concerning the deployment of people, the Acceleration Center found his judgment to be average at best. Obviously, this was the aspect of judgment being rated by his direct reports in the 360° survey.

Overall, the discussion of competencies and derailers usually lasts several hours, including time for the final prioritization of development needs. Discussions should be held face-to-face if possible; a videoconference is usually the next best alternative. A phone conference is the least desirable option, but it can be effective if the pool member receives an Acceleration Center report and discussion questions in advance.

When an Acceleration Center professional is not available, other people can help pool members integrate data and prioritize development needs. These people include:

- **An executive coach.** A coach must understand the pool member's competency and derailer development priorities and the thinking behind prioritizing them; therefore, it would be sensible and efficient to pair the coach with his or her charge when needs are being identified and prioritized. To provide professional-level feedback, the coach must be trained in how the Acceleration Center operates.

- **A psychologist.** When an Acceleration Center is not used, some organizations use a psychologist to administer tests and interview pool members to identify enablers and derailers. When psychologists are used for this purpose, they should give their interpretive feedback directly to the pool members and help them to prioritize derailers.

- **An HR specialist.** This could be someone within the organization who specializes in executive development or succession management.

It's Not Easy . . .

Providing feedback about Acceleration Center results can be a very intimidating task because of the personal impact that such data can have and because the people receiving the feedback are such high-powered individuals.

For example, not long ago a highly regarded executive (a member of the chairman's committee) at a major automotive manufacturer participated in an in-depth Acceleration Center assessment. This executive received a descriptive report in preparation for a coaching session with an assessor, one of the authors of this book. Upon arriving at the session, the assessor was met with a gruff greeting and escorted to a large conference table.

The executive began by dropping his assessment report onto the table with a resounding slap and taking a seat—hands behind his head, feet up on the polished mahogany table. Obviously annoyed, he said, "I just want you to know right now that I ain't changin' one damn iota based on this stuff."

The "feedback and coaching" session that followed took on a life of its own, but not the planned one. A series of questions and answers confirmed the assessment results, which identified profound strengths as well as equally profound development needs. But the conversation quickly moved away from diagnosis and into the fundamental value of assessment and diagnosis. "Why even do this?" the executive asked, as he insisted that change was neither necessary nor possible.

Still, there were the assessment results, which the executive wholeheartedly acknowledged as accurate—and amusing. He was characterized by intense volatility, impatience, and work practices that, at times, bordered on the despotic. Ironically, he was regarded as one of the most inspirational and visionary leaders in the organization's history. He was feared and loathed by some, yet loved and revered by others. This bipolar persona required reconciliation. He explained that passion, love of the business, insistence on high performance, and the desire to win were behind his behavior. His pride in success and in having survived many corporate catastrophes led him to conclude that his style worked.

However, the conversation took a different turn when the auto executive was asked whether he would recommend his style to emerging leaders in the organization. Although he had quickly touted his style's merits in his own case, he said that he regarded its proliferation in the organization as a potential poison. Slowly, after many probing questions about the relationship of his style and the emerging leadership trends within the organization, he began to articulate a different opinion about his willingness to act on the assessment results. He ultimately acknowledged responsibility for making his organization aware that his style was generally ineffective in today's leadership environment. He also conceded that he would be unlikely to succeed with this style if he were starting his career today. In the end the executive pointed out—accurately—that the power of the assessment process was not in the diagnosis, but in the discussion of the diagnosis.

This example underscores a lesson that we have learned through years of providing feedback to thousands of executives worldwide. Even the most accurate, comprehensive assessment will be meaningless unless the person being assessed recognizes the accuracy and value of the data and accepts the diagnosed development needs. One of the main advantages of using simulations in Acceleration Centers is the availability of specific observations and descriptions of actions. Those observed behavioral data—coupled with other behavioral data from the background interview and multiple-perspective (360°) instruments and augmented by interpretive insights from self-report instruments—are usually enough to convince people that they need to change. Usually—but not always.

When a doubting individual needs to be further convinced that he or she needs development (or when there is a need to check the accuracy of a diagnosis), an organization has several alternatives:

- **Multiple-perspective (360°) instruments.** If the competency or derailer can be observed in the person's current job, 360° feedback from direct reports, peers, and managers can add persuasive information.

- **Live multiple-perspective (360°) interviews.** These can be even more persuasive because they provide behavioral examples gathered in interviews with appropriate peers or direct reports. They are particularly effective in obtaining targeted data to convince individuals already in or near the executive level.

- **An assignment in which the competency or derailer can be observed and appropriate feedback provided.** This provides a real-world setting in which the person is challenged to show that the diagnosed problem does not exist.

- **An additional assessment center experience focusing on self-awareness in the competency or derailer being discussed.** The Center for Creative Leadership and other organizations offer public self-awareness assessment centers that can provide a second opinion about the competencies and derailers in question.

- **Attendance at a training program that provides self-insights as well as skill development.** For example, several organizations use a training program, titled Strategic Leadership Experience[SM], that involves a four-day, computer-based business simulation. Participants are required to display a number of competencies related to nine strategic leadership roles and then receive feedback on them. They also receive feedback on derailers. (See Chapter 12 for a description of this program.)

Understanding Job Challenges and Organizational Knowledge

Compared to dealing with the more personal issues of competencies and derailers, it is relatively easy to diagnose and prioritize development needs in the areas of job challenges and organizational knowledge. Most Acceleration Pool members have fairly accurate insights about what they know and what they need to learn, and they are less sensitive about admitting that they might have a weakness in these areas. However, to ensure accurate ratings, the person counseling the pool member should closely review the self-report data provided on the target area and ask questions about any job or organizational insights gained, any skills developed, and the person's ease (or difficulty) of learning new skills and adapting to the new situation. For example, a pool member who reports experience in a new plant start-up might have been only peripherally involved in the effort and, therefore, learned relatively little about the trials and tribulations that it involved. A few targeted questions can usually prompt realistic self-evaluations of such experiences.

The HR representative who works with the Executive Resource Board usually discusses job challenges and organizational knowledge with pool members. The representative will understand the board's standards relative to the job challenges and knowledge and thus be able to ask questions that reflect its concerns. As in competency and derailer discussions, a face-to-face meeting is best, but if that is not practical, the discussion can be held over the phone. These discussions usually last one to two hours, depending on the number of job challenges, volume of organizational knowledge required, and whether the pool member had been asked to provide examples of experiences that relate to the targeted challenges and organizational knowledge.

While an HR representative usually holds these discussions, another excellent alternative is to have a member of the Executive Resource Board discuss job challenges and organizational knowledge with the pool member. A senior executive can bring a wealth of insights about the board's standards—as well as the prestige of the position—to such a meeting. To the pool member, this involvement is yet another indication of the importance of being in the Acceleration Pool.

During these meetings the pool member should be asked about any personal or retention issues that would affect assignments or learning. Possible responses might include family constraints (e.g., a strong desire not to be moved until a child graduates high school), education plans (e.g., one year left to finish a Ph.D.), or geographic preferences (e.g., hates cold climates). The organization's representative needs to probe for the criticality of these issues. Would an issue be so strong that ignoring it would propel the person to seek a recruiter? Such personal retention needs should be communicated to the Executive Resource Board.

We have found that clients usually have two basic questions about these discussions:

- **Why doesn't the organization just accept pool members' evaluations of job challenges and organizational knowledge?** Before they meet with the HR representative or Executive Resource Board member, most Acceleration Pool members are unclear about the requirements around job challenges and organizational knowledge. Discussing these topics with someone who is well versed in them and who asks penetrating questions will crystallize understanding, generate realistic expectations, and establish a more common evaluation standard.

- **Why aren't the ratings on job challenges and organizational knowledge checked with the managers in the pool member's work area?** There's no reason that they can't be checked, but doing so will add time and administrative work to the process. Most organizations are satisfied with the information they get from prospective pool members, so they don't bother. Most pool members realize that they are hurting only themselves if they exaggerate the breadth and depth of their experiences. Also, because they know that senior executives will see their lists, they don't want to be embarrassed by false claims.

Creating the Development Priority List

Figure 8-1 depicts an example Development Priority List completed by a first-level manager. The pool member has received Acceleration Center feedback and 360° feedback on competencies and derailers from peers and direct reports and has also discussed job challenges and organizational knowledge with a member or representative of top management. The Development Priority List shows that the pool member has chosen and prioritized the competencies, job challenges, organizational knowledge, and derailers that she needs to develop. Some descriptor categories have more areas to develop than others. The development targets in each

Figure 8-1: Example of a Development Priority List

Name: "Noni Collins"   **Date:** December 2000

Development Priorities

I. Competencies

   A. Empowerment/Delegation—major problem is following up on delegated tasks.

   B. Selling the Vision—not speech-making (a strength), more one-on-one.

   C. Economic Orientation—not acumen (more of not thinking of economic consequences).

   D. Adaptability—to sudden changes in work pace.

II. Job Challenges

   A. Responsibility for bottom-line results.

   B. Negotiating agreements.

   C. Determining pricing/sales strategy.

III. Organizational Knowledge Areas

   A. Accountability System—performance appraisal/management system.

   B. Company electronic development and delivery process.

   C. International operations.

   D. Company product development process.

IV. Derailers

   A. Self-promoting (melodramatic)—particularly in meetings.

   B. Impulsive (mischievous).

---

category are listed in order of importance or need. To increase the precision of the diagnosis, the manager has noted unique information or clarification in a number of areas. This information came out of her discussion about her Acceleration Center results.

There are many variations of Development Priority Lists. For example, an organization often will provide Acceleration Pool members with a preprinted form that lists all or some of the company's executive descriptors (see Appendix 8-1 on the next page). Organizations use a variety of scales to evaluate development priorities, but most methods are quite similar. The choice of a rating scale should be based on the organization's culture and past practices.

Some Development Priority Lists include space for pool members to note progress and change ratings after they have completed an assignment or training program. This not only helps people feel good about the progress they are making, but it also provides useful information for the Executive Resource Board.

The Executive Resource Board's Role

Pool members send completed Development Priority Lists to the Executive Resource Board for approval. The board's review and approval are important for several reasons:

- To show top management's support for the Acceleration Pool system.

- To make sure each pool member has a completed Development Priority List. (The pool member has a deadline for submitting the list to the board.)

- To ensure that each Development Priority List reflects the findings of the Acceleration Center and any other objective input.

- To make sure the priorities are in line with the organization's business strategy (i.e., the Acceleration Pool member will be developing skills deemed most necessary to keep the organization moving in its chosen direction).

- To prompt a meaningful discussion of each pool member and his or her development. Such discussions are an important part of the process of the Executive Resource Board getting to know Acceleration Pool members.

The Executive Resource Board usually accepts each pool member's Development Priority List at face value, although there are occasions when the board will revise it. Any revisions must be explained to the pool member.

Appendix 8-1

(Formatted form for typed entry by user; would be tailored to each organization.)

DEVELOPMENT PRIORITY LIST

Name: _____   Location: _____

Organizational Knowledge

The following is a list of organizational knowledge areas identified as important to executive success. Ideally, you should be knowledgeable in all the areas before reaching senior management. Place one check mark next to the knowledge areas in which you have adequate knowledge and two check marks next to areas in which you have expert knowledge. Use the space after each knowledge area to provide clarifying information. For example, you might note that you have knowledge in an area from other companies but none from your current organization. If you need to develop a knowledge area not on the list, list it and explain why.

☐ ☐ International

☐ ☐ Research

☐ ☐ Sales

☐ ☐ Finance

☐ ☐ Human Resources (staffing, selection, promotion, compensation)

☐ ☐ Accounting/Budgeting

☐ ☐ Information Technology

☐ ☐ Long-Range Planning

☐ ☐ Compensation

Job Challenges

The following is a list of job challenges identified by the organization as important to executive success. Ideally, you should experience all these challenges before reaching senior management. Place one check mark next to the challenges you have met once and two check marks next to those you have met more than once. Use the space after each challenge area to provide clarifying information. For example, you might write, "Although I worked in the marketing department for two years, I didn't learn anything about marketing because I was totally involved in bringing in new technology."

☐ ☐ Solve a difficult problem.

☐ ☐ Become heavily involved with a merger, acquisition, strategic alliance, or partnership opportunity.

☐ ☐ Complete an assignment with tight time or resource constraints (e.g., be first to market).

☐ ☐ Assume responsibility for growing, downsizing, reorganizing, or shutting down a unit or operation.

☐ ☐ Develop and implement a plan to cut costs or control inventories.

☐ ☐ Be responsible for an operation in another country.

☐ ☐ Deal with conflict and change.

☐ ☐ Develop or maintain alliances with external partners.

☐ ☐ Implement systems, processes, and strategic plans.

☐ ☐ Create a new product.

☐ ☐ Manage long-cycle or short-cycle business.

Competencies

Based on the feedback you've been given, list the competencies that need development. You might be weak in the competency or need to practice it because you were not required to use it in past jobs. List the competencies in rough order of importance, starting with the one in most need of development. Provide clarifying information that will further your understanding of the targeted competencies. For example, you might list the competency *Delegation* and note that your development need is "following up on delegations." The more specific you can be, the better.

Derailers

Based on the feedback you've been given, list the derailers that you would like to overcome or avoid. List them in rough order of importance, starting with the most important. Provide clarifying information that will enhance your understanding of these targets. For example, if you listed the derailer *Perfectionistic,* you might write, "Sometimes I'm overly critical. I need to enhance my empowering style."

SECTION IV

STRATEGIES FOR ACCELERATING DEVELOPMENT

The first chapter in this section overviews development strategies available to fill pool members' development gaps, with emphasis on developing competencies. These four strategies for facilitating pool member growth and development (assignments, short-term experiences, training/executive education experiences, and professional growth through short-/long-term coaching) are discussed at greater length in Chapters 10 through 13.

- Chapter 9   Development Options
- Chapter 10 Growth Through Assignments
- Chapter 11 Growth Through Short-Term Experiences
- Chapter 12 Growth Through Training/Executive Education
- Chapter 13 Growth Through Professional Coaching

Chapter 9

Development Options

"Being ignorant is not so much a shame as being unwilling to learn."

—Benjamin Franklin, U.S. Founding Father,
Diplomat, Author, and Philosopher

Armed with their understanding of the development priorities, the Executive Resource Board, the Acceleration Pool member, and the people supporting the pool member's growth must weigh the development options and choose those that best fit the individual's needs in the areas of competencies, job challenges, organizational knowledge, and executive derailers. Developmental assignments, short-term experiences, training, professional coaching, and reconfigured existing responsibilities can all serve as vehicles for pool member development. In the brief description of the development options that follows, we have provided examples and noted the chapters in which you can find more information about each.

Assignments (Chapter 10)

Assignments are significant responsibilities given to the pool member. They usually take the form of a job or a position on a task force and can span a significant amount of time (e.g., a two-year full-time job assignment or a one-year part-time task force assignment). An assignment is chosen because it offers the pool member an opportunity to meet a combination of development needs. Some examples of assignments might include:

 denotes that information on this topic is available at the *Grow Your Own Leaders* web site (www.ddiworld.com/growyourownleaders).

- Responsibility for a complex project.

- Significant task force assignments (at least part time).

- Expatriate assignments.

- Responsibility for a major project (e.g., choosing the location of a new facility, the start-up of a new plant).

- Working in a supplier or customer organization.

Short-Term Experiences (Chapter 11)

Short-term experiences can provide a number of development opportunities for Acceleration Pool members. A member might:

- Observe a unique role model (e.g., an excellent presenter).

- Obtain different perspectives (e.g., participate with competitors in a discussion of R&D strategy at an industry convention).

- Obtain new information (e.g., listen to an expert's presentation of new ways to align an organization behind a strategy).

- Understand a country or a culture (e.g., interact with a team of people from another country).

- Try out leadership skills (e.g., lead a committee).

- Learn how a different part of the organization operates (e.g., serve on a cross-organizational committee).

In addition, short-term experiences can vastly expand an individual's network of internal contacts—often an important factor in future success.

Short-term experiences are particularly helpful in building organizational knowledge, but they also can provide job challenges or an opportunity to work on a competency or derailer. Experiences are usually part-time and of limited duration. If being on a task force is a full-time job for a pool member, then it is considered to be an assignment. Possible experiences include:

- Attending a technical convention.

- Helping an outside consultant gather data on employee attitudes.

- Joining or leading a task force (e.g., a task force to recommend the purchase of major equipment).

- Serving on an organizational committee (e.g., a safety committee).
- Hosting someone from another country.
- Explaining the organization's vision and values to new employees.
- Helping a community organization develop a vision statement.

Training/Executive Education (Chapter 12)

Training to develop competencies, provide organizational knowledge, and prepare people for some job challenges can take a variety of forms:

- One-on-one training on a new company appraisal system.
- Behavior modeling-based leadership training modules (conducted one or two days each month for 10 months).
- A one-week action learning event for Acceleration Pool members.
- Self-directed modules on team skills—each usually 10 to 20 minutes and available as needed on the Internet or the organization's intranet.
- A one-day management game that teaches basic accounting concepts.
- Two days of presentation skills training.
- A seven-week, university-sponsored executive development program.
- A three-hour, self-directed program on customer service skills (via CD-ROM or web-based training).
- Two weeks of one-on-one immersion-language training.
- Four half-day sessions of computer skills training.

Professional Executive Coaching (Chapter 13)

Professional executive coaching involves one-to-one meetings between a pool member and a skilled, experienced advisor. The coaching generally focuses on one or two of these five broad areas:

- Competencies, derailers, and other personal characteristics (also known as *soft skills*).
- Organizational strategy.
- Day-to-day tactics.
- Helping executives through difficult assignments.

- Helping newly assigned executives socialize or assimilate their work styles into new work environments (sometimes called *on-boarding*).

Counseling in *all* these areas can benefit Acceleration Pool members, depending on their individual needs. The number of coaching sessions a pool member needs also varies from person to person.

Matching Development to Needs

Table 9-1 shows the most common prescriptions for Acceleration Pool members' development objectives. Of course, there are many exceptions and combinations of answers for any given individual.

Table 9-1: Relationship of Development Objectives to Development Prescriptions	
Development Objective	**Development Prescriptions**
Job challenges	Assignments
Organizational knowledge	Experiences, assignments (training)
Competencies	Training and an opportunity to practice, as described in the next section
Derailers	Professional executive coaching (training)
( ) denotes a less common prescription	

Each of the development options—assignments, experiences, training, and coaching—can play a role in addressing competencies, executive derailers, job challenges, and organizational knowledge. The most complicated relationship involves the development of competencies, which is discussed in the remainder of this chapter.

Developing Competencies

One might argue that, given enough time and money, all competencies can be developed, but in reality, organizations have a finite supply of both resources. The fact is that some competencies are so difficult to develop that an organization's efforts might best be directed at other competencies that are more easily improved. Table 9-2 shows a list of competencies from the DDI taxonomy along with a five-point scale describing each competency's ease of development (a "1" rating means very difficult to develop; "5" means relatively easy to develop). This is a rough and generalized rating based on our experience with helping organizations plan and implement prescriptive development actions, but it provides some guidance in determining where to focus development efforts for a given Acceleration Pool member.

In systems used to *select* individuals for participation in an Acceleration Pool, difficult-to-develop competencies are usually given more weight because people with major development needs in such hard-to-address areas are less likely to improve while in an Acceleration Pool.

A prime consideration in determining how easily a competency can be developed is the pool member's willingness to work on improving it. This greatly reflects the importance of the competency as perceived by the pool member. If pool members give a competency a low priority, they won't put forth the effort for improvement.

Also, competencies such as *Learning Orientation, Adaptability,* and *Accurate Self-Insight* can point to the likelihood for success in developing other competencies. If pool members haven't shown the ability to respond well to change or to accept and succeed in new learning situations, they will probably struggle with difficult-to-develop competencies. On the other hand, people who are strong in these three competencies often beat the odds and improve even the difficult-to-develop competencies.

Many people, including Morgan McCall, author of *High Flyers,* and Daniel Goleman, author of *Emotional Intelligence,* believe that *Accurate Self-Insight* is a critical executive competency. It measures the degree to which a person can sense his or her own strengths and weaknesses and how accurately he or she can evaluate an interaction while it is progressing (Goleman, 1995; McCall, 1997). There's a big difference between giving feedback to someone who is self-aware and someone who isn't—the person who lacks self-awareness needs more data to accept a diagnosis. Also, people with low self-awareness might need more time to fully accept their development needs as valid. In extreme cases these individuals might be described as not recognizing their own reflections in a mirror. At the least, when unaware of key development needs, they generally require additional time to reflect on the issue and think about on-the-job situations where the competency has affected work.

The third column of Table 9-2 reflects our recommendation of the most effective ways to develop each competency. Again, these are rough groupings, and there are many exceptions to what is presented. Most competencies are developed through multiple methods over several years (e.g., the cognitive part of a competency often can be learned best in a training program, while the skill part is best addressed through an assignment).

Table 9-2: Ease of Development and the Most Effective Methods for Developing Key Competencies		
Competencies (An organization would use only a subset of these competencies)	**Ease of Development (Scale 1–5, with 1 = Very Difficult to Develop and 5 = Relatively Easy to Develop)**	**Development Prescription**
Interpersonal Skills		
Building Strategic Relationships	5	Training with Assignments and/or Experiences
Building Trust with Assignments	3	Training and/or Coaching
Communicating with Impact	5	Training and/or Coaching with Experiences
Cultural Interpersonal Effectiveness	4	Assignments and/or Experience with Coaching
Customer Orientation	4	Training with Assignments and/or Experiences
Persuasiveness/Sales Ability	4	Training with Assignments and/or Experiences
Leadership Skills		
Change Leadership	3	Training and/or Coaching with Assignments and/or Experiences
Coaching/Teaching	4	Training with Assignments and/or Experiences
Delegation	5	Training and/or Coaching with Assignments and/or Experiences
Developing Organizational Talent	5	Training and/or Coaching with Assignments and/or Experiences
Empowerment	5	Training and/or Coaching with Assignments and/or Experiences

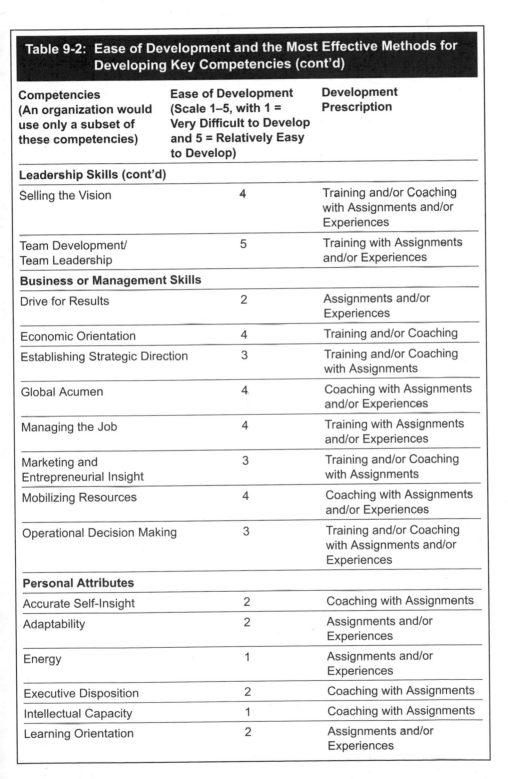

Table 9-2: Ease of Development and the Most Effective Methods for Developing Key Competencies (cont'd)		
Competencies (An organization would use only a subset of these competencies)	**Ease of Development (Scale 1–5, with 1 = Very Difficult to Develop and 5 = Relatively Easy to Develop)**	**Development Prescription**
Leadership Skills (cont'd)		
Selling the Vision	4	Training and/or Coaching with Assignments and/or Experiences
Team Development/ Team Leadership	5	Training with Assignments and/or Experiences
Business or Management Skills		
Drive for Results	2	Assignments and/or Experiences
Economic Orientation	4	Training and/or Coaching
Establishing Strategic Direction	3	Training and/or Coaching with Assignments
Global Acumen	4	Coaching with Assignments and/or Experiences
Managing the Job	4	Training with Assignments and/or Experiences
Marketing and Entrepreneurial Insight	3	Training and/or Coaching with Assignments
Mobilizing Resources	4	Coaching with Assignments and/or Experiences
Operational Decision Making	3	Training and/or Coaching with Assignments and/or Experiences
Personal Attributes		
Accurate Self-Insight	2	Coaching with Assignments
Adaptability	2	Assignments and/or Experiences
Energy	1	Assignments and/or Experiences
Executive Disposition	2	Coaching with Assignments
Intellectual Capacity	1	Coaching with Assignments
Learning Orientation	2	Assignments and/or Experiences

Table 9-2: Ease of Development and the Most Effective Methods for Developing Key Competencies (cont'd)

Competencies (An organization would use only a subset of these competencies)	Ease of Development (Scale 1–5, with 1 = Very Difficult to Develop and 5 = Relatively Easy to Develop)	Development Prescription
Personal Attributes (cont'd)		
Motivational Fit	1	Assignments
Positive Disposition	1	Coaching with Assignments and/or Experiences
Reading the Environment	2	Assignments and/or Experience
Technical/Professional Knowledge and Skills	5	Training with Assignments and/or Experiences

Developing Competencies Through Training and Assignments

Over the years, we have asked thousands of executives a basic question: "Thinking back on your business life, where did you get the competencies that have helped you succeed?" The answer is almost always the same: Their competencies were developed when they took on difficult assignments.

Assignments can indeed be very effective in developing competencies. A good assignment will push the individual slightly beyond his or her level of confidence and comfort. It will give the person considerable authority and responsibility and allow him or her to have a clear goal and a method for measuring progress. Often, a good coach or role model will be available to help the person's growth.

The effectiveness of assignments does not mean that training is irrelevant. In fact, training is clearly a viable way to accelerate the development of competencies in assignments. In fact, the best approach usually involves a combination of training and developmental assignments. If delivered correctly, each will reinforce the other. An assignment gives people an opportunity to apply their training immediately. Leading a task force, for example, offers a chance to practice team leadership skills in a situation where the person would normally have no position power.

The right balance between training and assignments varies with the organizational level involved. As Figure 9-1 shows, formal training plays a role at all levels, but its importance decreases as individuals climb the organizational ladder. The difficult challenge of making training acceptable to executives is discussed in Chapter 12.

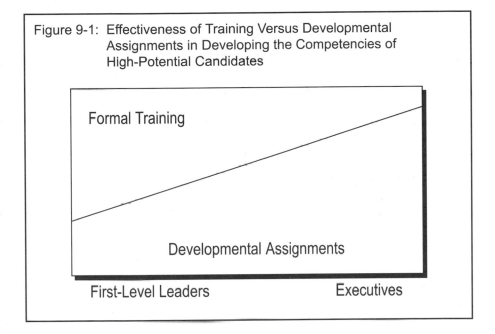

Figure 9-1: Effectiveness of Training Versus Developmental Assignments in Developing the Competencies of High-Potential Candidates

Formal Training

Developmental Assignments

First-Level Leaders   Executives

Developing Competencies Through Short-Term Experiences

Taking on special projects, serving on committees, and other short-term experiences can be excellent vehicles for developing certain targeted competencies. For example, someone with no real background in or understanding of computer technology might be assigned to a committee charged with selecting a new corporate software package. That person would naturally need to learn about the software to make an intelligent decision. (Ideally, he or she would have a coach to provide assistance.) As a rule, a pool member in this situation would be highly motivated because he or she could use the learning immediately.

Developing competencies through meaningful experiences is a necessity for most organizations. These companies usually have no other realistic way for their people to reach all their development targets.

Developing Competencies Through Coaching

As we discuss further in Chapter 13, executive coaches are used to develop a number of competencies, with the most common being those involved in building trust, communicating, selling an idea, and winning over a new group of direct reports.

Handling Difficult-to-Develop Competencies

Remember that some competencies are especially difficult to develop. When an Acceleration Pool member is weak in one of these difficult areas, managers need to work with or coach the person. Here are some suggestions for handling such situations:

- Discuss how strengths in other competencies can overcome relative weakness in another. For example, a strength in *Delegation* can compensate for relatively poor *Innovation* skills. A manager can help a pool member understand that it might be better at times to give responsibility for driving creative ideas to others.

- Assign the person to positions that minimize competency weaknesses while accentuating the positives. The person would not be in the Acceleration Pool if he or she were not strong in many competencies. At the same time, the pool member should have the opportunity to develop in his or her weak areas.

- Assign two people with counterbalancing strengths and weaknesses to a job in which their combined skills are needed to succeed. This gives them an opportunity to learn from one another.

- Make recommendations on self-development. While the challenge is great and the chance of achieving a dramatic change is small, it's still possible to build skills in difficult-to-develop competencies.

- Bring in a professional coach to help the person implement the previous suggestions.

We have seen all these approaches work, particularly with individuals who realize that a derailer or weakness in a competency is all that is keeping them from the senior management position they have always wanted. A good example is "Serge," who was blocked on his way to a senior vice president position of a large transportation company because he was widely perceived as lacking creativity. The company needed new ideas and directions, but Serge was not seen as someone who could deliver in these areas. However, he was extremely hard working and tenacious. After getting his Acceleration Center and 360° feedback, Serge enthusiastically accepted an executive coach to help him work on his creativity. They took a behavioral approach to the situation and together identified behaviors that would make Serge appear to others as creative and innovative, including: generating at least one new idea at every staff meeting (solicited from his staff), enthusiastically reinforcing people's creative ideas and offering to help implement them, and mentioning the need for "out of the box" thinking to solve problems. In hopes of presenting a more innovative image, Serge even altered his style of dress. Within one year his corporate image had changed, and so had his lack of creativity. As he did the things that creative people do, he became more creative in his thinking and in his judgment of others' ideas. Serge got the position he wanted and proceeded to lead the organization to some of the most innovative changes it had ever experienced.

In practice many managers find it effective to try multiple ways of helping pool members bolster a difficult-to-develop competency. In general, however, the focus should remain on the more easily developed competencies, where the payoff is more certain.

Developing Competencies Takes Time

Sound competency development takes place through a variety of methods. However, whether the goal is to provide insight into a particular country's culture, to enhance skills such as financial analysis or leadership, or to change attitudes, the process takes time. As you will see in the next four chapters, there are strategies that speed learning and technologies that can deliver information or training on a highly effective, just-in-time basis. But don't expect immediate improvement. People will improve at their own speed, and that will depend on their motivation, the time they have to devote to development, how difficult the competency is to develop, and their personal life situations. Overnight miracles are unlikely—look instead for steady progress. And remember that this is a long-term effort.

Chapter 10

Growth Through Assignments

"I hear and I forget. I see and I remember. I do and I understand."

—Confucius,
Ancient Chinese Philosopher

Jobs, task force memberships, and other long-term assignments offer opportunities for people to satisfy several development objectives at the same time (e.g., two challenges, two knowledge areas, one competency, and one derailer). Individuals will typically be on an assignment anywhere from two months to two years. A person who is in an Acceleration Pool for 10 years might have only six assignments or fewer; a 5-year member might have only two or three. Each assignment, therefore, plays a significant role in the individual's development.

In making assignments the Executive Resource Board should consider several key questions:

1. **Will the assignment provide one or more challenges that the Acceleration Pool member needs to master to function effectively at the general manager level or above?**

   The number and diversity of the challenges presented determine the quality of any assignment. The opportunity to experience specific challenges might be inherent in an assignment, or opportunities might easily be created as part of it. For example, new responsibilities might

☞⌐ denotes that information on this topic is available at the *Grow Your Own Leaders* web site (www.ddiworld.com/growyourownleaders).

be added to a job, essentially enlarging it so that the individual has a chance to address development issues that might not otherwise be covered.

2. **Will the assignment develop one or more key competencies needed by the individual?**

A number of factors can help determine the potential for competency development in a particular assignment:

- Is there an effective model of the desired behavior available? This model can be a person (usually the leader), other executives, or a person or group outside the organization with whom the pool member will interact, perhaps an especially effective salesperson or negotiator. It's often impossible to find a perfect role model, and it's not uncommon to find that a person who is an excellent role model for a competency will also exhibit other behaviors that the organization does not want the pool member to adopt. This problem can be overcome by positioning the learner to see the positive impact of the competency to be developed while also observing the negative impact of the poor behavior. Research by McCall, Lombardo, and Morrison (1988) has found that negative role models can stimulate learning as long as the learner sees and understands the adverse impact of the behavior. The Development Action Form ensures that the individual has clear learning objectives.

- Will the leader or model disclose his or her thinking, planning, and strategy so that the pool member can understand the reasons behind observed behavior? Often just observing behavior doesn't provide the insights required for learning; explanations from the leader or model are required for the pool member to get a deeper understanding of the reasons behind the behavior.

- Will the pool member have a chance to actually use the competency being developed (e.g., to make speeches or perform a technical analysis)?

- Will the pool member get effective feedback, support, and coaching?

- Is the importance of the desired competency obvious in the assignment? That is, does success in the position clearly require using the targeted competency, thereby providing an incentive to learn it?

3. **Will the assignment provide insights into specific personality traits that might derail the individual's climb to an executive position or provide an opportunity to practice new behaviors that will keep the pool member on track?**

If an executive derailer has been observed in an Acceleration Center and the diagnosis is accepted by the pool member, the appropriate sequence of events is to provide coaching (see Chapter 13) and then put the pool member in an assignment where he or she can practice the behavior that will minimize the derailer. The following example illustrates this process.

A pool member, "Kathy," is a highly gifted technologist and has excellent business acumen. Many executives see her as being able to make a major contribution to the business. However, on-the-job feedback and Acceleration Center results show that she demonstrates arrogance and a lack of interpersonal sensitivity when dealing with direct reports. The Executive Resource Board worries that if those tendencies are not corrected, they could cause a problem in a major executive role. Kathy accepts the center's findings and agrees with their assessment. An appropriate assignment might focus on driving a cultural change in a customer-service unit that is suffering from poor morale and high turnover. In carrying out the assignment, Kathy would find it essential to work past her natural tendencies in order to be effective.

If Kathy did not accept the diagnosis, it would be appropriate to put her in an assignment that would bring out the derailer and, at the same time, provide considerable accurate feedback. The right assignment will, of course, depend on the derailer being evaluated. The key is to give people a chance to recognize when they are at risk of demonstrating derailment behaviors.

There is risk in doing this because it could result in significant damage to the business. Thus, the situation needs to be monitored very closely. We recommend that the Acceleration Pool member be told about the derailment concern and challenged to prove in a particular assignment that the derailer, or any other negative personality factor, is not going to adversely affect performance. The approach obviously requires close monitoring and feedback by the assigned manager or executive coach.

4. Will the assignment provide experience in different organizational areas (e.g., different product areas)?

Increasingly, people who can bridge fields and organizational functions are those most in demand to fill high-level jobs. Companies believe that these people can best integrate functions and systems and establish value-creating synergy. For this reason pool members should routinely be considered for positions outside of their organizational "silos."

5. Will the assignment provide a realistic preview of executive life?

Not everyone is attracted to life in the fast lane, so it is far better for people to learn early on whether they are cut out for an executive position. The best way to orient an Acceleration Pool member to the rigors of executive life is to have the person observe senior executives firsthand or talk with them about their jobs. An aspiring executive's orientation to senior management once came in the form of "assistant to" and similar jobs that put the person in close daily contact with a top-level leader. For the most part, assistant positions have long since been eliminated; yet the need for them is still there. Positions still exist that allow Acceleration Pool members to get an early taste of executive life by requiring them to travel with, prepare briefings for, and otherwise work closely with senior managers.

6. Will the assignment provide exposure to potential long-term mentors, organizational leaders, or other talented professionals who have unique skills or knowledge to share?

Will pool members encounter others who might be instrumental in helping them identify or meet career goals? An assignment can be a good vehicle for testing "interpersonal chemistry" before making a formal mentoring arrangement.

7. Will the assignment give senior executives a chance to observe the pool member?

To be effective in nurturing future leaders, top management must get to know Acceleration Pool members and see them in action. An ideal assignment provides opportunities for pool members to work in positions where senior executives can observe them. For their part, pool members usually enjoy these assignments because they like the idea of being able to show senior managers what they can do.

8. Does the assignment fit the individual's personal and family needs?

Assignments must be strategically crafted and timed to fit with contemporary personal and social realities. Pool members need to be consulted about assignments in light of their family situations. Both the organization and the individual need to be flexible in this area. By joining the Acceleration Pool, high-potential people have indicated their interest in skill growth and advancement as well as their willingness to make sacrifices to reach goals they see as meaningful and important. But they also expect to be included in discussions about assignments and to have some degree of choice when personal or family needs conflict with those assignments.

The Development Life Cycle

There are no hard-and-fast rules about the order of development assignments because there are simply too many variables. However, many organizations pursue a more or less planned progression in making assignments, such as:

1. Meaningful, measurable assignment as soon as possible after starting with the organization.

2. International assignment early.

3. Task force assignment after a few years.

4. Merger/Acquisition assignment in the middle of a career.

5. Small-scale general management "starter" assignment (often a small international operation).

6. Large-scale general management assignment.

Finding Assignment Opportunities

Finding assignments that meet several development goals is always difficult, and it hasn't been made any easier by the flattening of organizations, the elimination of many executive-assistant positions, and frequent changes to organization charts. Thus, executives making assignments often must be creative in their search for development opportunities. Following are some possibilities:

- Lateral moves
- Expanded current assignments
- Task force assignments
- Create a new job

- Virtual assignments
- Customer and vendor assignments
- Interim assignments
- Job trades

Lateral Moves

Today it is rare for a person to be promoted every time assignments change. Lateral moves often are necessary to meet special organizational needs, and without lateral moves it is almost impossible to give an Acceleration Pool member the desired breadth of organizational exposure. Fortunately, the lateral move has lost much of its traditional negative connotation as organizational levels have merged into fewer but broader bands (which tends to make lateral moves more common and less obvious) and as expectations about constant promotions have changed.

Task Force Assignments

A task force assignment can offer outstanding developmental opportunities for pool members. Companies use task forces to help resolve corporate issues, make organizational decisions, establish effective systems, and perform research. A task force assignment might last a number of months or even years. It is usually a full-time—or at least half-time—assignment. (In Chapter 11 we discuss part-time task force assignments as short-term experiences.)

A full- or part-time task force can generate effective developmental opportunities for a number of reasons:

- The relative short-term nature of task forces, compared to job assignments, makes it possible for Acceleration Pool members to develop important skills without forcing them to relocate their families.

- Task force assignments can be excellent vehicles for enhancing a pool member's international sophistication. Because task forces often include people from various countries, the experience can expose pool members to an international perspective or business issue they might not have otherwise encountered. Some assignments actually require members to spend considerable time in different countries as the task force does its research.

- Task forces often are microcosms of the organization, drawing members from various functions and processes. Thus, task force members can gain broad organizational knowledge that they might be able to use later.

- People on a task force often get the opportunity to see the organizational "big picture" because they must address issues and interpret data while considering all areas of the organization.

- A task force assignment can provide a unique opportunity for its members to try new roles (e.g., group leadership) or develop specific competencies (e.g., financial or analytical skills).

- A task force serves as an excellent vehicle for exposing pool members to others in the organization who are strong positive models of executive competencies as well as to people who might offer coaching or mentoring. Long-term friendships can blossom as people work and travel together.

To get all they can from a task force assignment, pool members need to clearly understand what they are to learn from it (see Chapter 8). Without that up-front understanding, people who join a task force will naturally tend to play on their existing strengths instead of using the task force as a laboratory to develop new skills. For example, if good at research, a person will be drawn to a research-related activity rather than one that requires him or her to focus on development, possibly negotiating with business partners or making presentations. If building presentation skills is a development goal, the individual must be encouraged to step out of the "comfort zone" and stretch his or her skills; otherwise, the pool member won't achieve maximum development in the targeted competency. Of course, placing people in these stretch assignments puts the success of the task force and the pool members themselves at some risk, but such risks are usually minor compared to the potential learning to be gained. On a well-conceived task force, other members skilled in the competency being developed will help or coach the pool member. And, because everyone on the task force wants the group to achieve its goals, members are usually motivated to help others who are struggling with assignments.

Virtual Assignments

Organizations with international operations usually feel that at least one international assignment early in a person's career is very important and that a second assignment at mid-career is advisable, if it can be arranged. However, a problem often occurs when an individual has children in school. Relocating the family to a different country is difficult and also can be expensive. Supporting a mid-level executive can cost an organization $300,000–$1 million a year (Black & Gregerson, 1999).

Recognizing the difficulty and expense of relocating people, more and more organizations have gone to short-term, "virtual" assignments. Acceleration Pool members assigned to a particular country are given explicit goals, such as "introduce a new technology" or "align the international affiliate's accounting system with the rest of the company." They might spend three weeks at a time in the assigned country, returning home for one week a month to be with their family. During the assignment they take an apartment or stay in a residence hotel, and essentially live like the locals. The pool members get the same language and cultural orientations as anyone who takes a traditional overseas assignment. Many organizations encourage pool members to invite family members to their assigned location for a visit when the children are out of school or at other convenient times. After completing the virtual assignment, they often supplement their learning by taking more-frequent business trips to that area of the world.

It's important to contrast these virtual assignments with traditional business trips, during which individuals are met at their plane by a company representative; stay in business-class, western-style hotels; are escorted to and from meetings; and dine only in finer restaurants. In such traditional trips the traveling executive is largely insulated from the local scene and gets very little feel for the country or its people.

Customer and Vendor Assignments

Customer or vendor organizations also can be a source of assignment opportunities. We know of one organization that wanted a future executive to gain experience in running a manufacturing organization in China because it had plans to open several plants there. There was one significant dilemma: The company did not yet have any operations in China where its people could develop the desired skills and knowledge. So, the company offered to "loan" its executive to a Chinese vendor for a one-year assignment. The effort was a great success—not only did the executive learn about doing business in China, but she also learned about the vendor's operations. This broadened her appreciation of the total manufacturing process and of the relationship between her company and the vendor. In return the vendor benefited from the executive's work during the assignment and gained a better understanding of an important customer's needs.

Another company assigned an executive to a customer's new-product task force—a move that was an experiment for both organizations. The host organization felt that the supplier would be able to ramp up more quickly to meet its needs if it were involved in the product development process from the beginning. The vendor organization saw a golden opportunity to gain insight into a customer's needs. The experiment was a success—both organizations got what they wanted. And it proved to be an excellent learning opportunity for the executive who had the assignment. He was able to get valuable, firsthand knowledge by studying the needs of the ultimate consumer—the buyer of the equipment made of materials provided by his company.

Expanded Current Assignments

It's not always necessary to move people into a new job to accomplish certain learning objectives. It's sometimes possible to get results by changing the scope, responsibilities, and direction of an individual's current job. For example, a pool member might assume responsibility for sales in a region of the world, and thus develop international knowledge. Or, the person might take on employee development or other personnel functions, thereby getting exposure to staff work. Expanding current assignments can reduce the number of relocations the individual has to make—a very desirable outcome.

Create a New Job

Sometimes organizations cannot find opportunities that meet an Acceleration Pool member's unique mix of development needs. This is often the case when people are about to be promoted to higher-level positions and need a quick dose of development in several competencies and organizational knowledge areas. In such situations we advise creating a job that fits the bill by pulling various areas of responsibility from other jobs and giving them to the pool member. For example, we know of a company that wanted to promote a fast-rising executive to manager of international operations. There were a few barriers to overcome: The executive had spent very little time abroad and had no sales experience—and sales was a major component of the new job. So the company created a new position: international sales manager. During his one-year assignment, the executive reported to the U.S. sales manager, who was an excellent coach and developer of people. The development of competencies associated with sales management, combined with the exposure to worldwide markets and personnel policies, equipped the executive with the additional skills he would need as manager of international operations.

Acceleration Pool members also can be placed in a newly created position parallel to a solid, tenured (but perhaps topped out) incumbent. For example, we know of a company that on two occasions created temporary "operating" positions that reported to business unit heads. These were analogous to a COO position. The incumbents were being groomed to take on strategic business unit (SBU) assignments. This approach works particularly well in rapidly growing businesses and offers a safety net for making high-risk or large "stretch" moves.

Interim Assignments

Having a job vacancy in a key management position is a problem for any organization. However, it can be a development opportunity for someone who needs to learn about that particular unit. A short-term assignment as a manager allows that person to become well grounded in the unit's operations without the stress that comes with a full-time assignment. The people who deal with the interim manager know that it is a short-term assignment and consider that in their expectations of performance. The individual has an opportunity to shine and exceed performance expectations while learning a great deal and becoming more valuable to the organization.

We've seen these developmental interim assignments work very well on a number of occasions. Each time, the organization put people into assignments that were extreme stretches of their knowledge and skills, but in every case the individuals succeeded. In two cases the interim managers were permanently assigned to the job; in other cases they learned a great deal and enhanced their reputation in the organization.

Job Trades

Companies can create development opportunities by having executives trade job responsibilities. For example, a marketing manager and a sales manager might switch roles, as might an R&D manager and the head of a customer service group. This strategy is usually employed when no physical move beyond changing offices is required. Such an approach can revitalize both people by giving them new challenges and allowing them to develop additional or existing competencies. Just as important, trading jobs builds a more rounded, in-depth understanding of the organization, making the individuals more effective if and when they return to their former units.

Early General Management Experience

Acceleration Pools are usually charged with producing general managers and executives who will someday have responsibility for a broad range of organization functions, such as R&D, manufacturing, sales, customer service, human resource management, and finance. However, few organizations have "starter" general management positions where individuals can oversee small-scale operations that entail a full range of general management challenges. Most starter assignments are likely to be found in international assignments in relatively small markets. These starter assignments let pool members try their skills before taking on a major assignment in their home country or another large market. Organizations need to recognize the importance of these positions and keep them open for the people who are being groomed for future leadership—Acceleration Pool members.

We know of a CEO who believes that the best way to develop his vice presidents is to have them trade jobs every three years. He feels that doing this helps them bring new perspectives to their new positions and re-energizes them. He also says that it makes people less competitive because they realize that they could be in the other person's shoes someday.

How Long Should an Assignment Be?

Acceleration Pool members should remain in assignments long enough to achieve measurable results or to learn what they need to learn, and no longer—something that's easier said than done. The appropriate assignment length varies, based on the nature of the assignment, the competencies being developed, the learner's ability, the support required and given, and the business results to be achieved. Assignments that are too short can keep people from experiencing the full range of responsibilities and learning opportunities. For example, prematurely removing someone from a retail-sales management position might mean that the person will miss the rich experience of the Christmas rush in a retail environment. Often the most valuable learning insights come from seeing one's own mistakes and having to act to remedy consequences. When an assignment is too short, people might miss out on these prime learning opportunities because they move on before the consequences of their mistakes become clear. Also, the individual might not feel as accountable for results.

On the other hand, keeping people in assignments too long is a waste of time for them and the organization. When confined to one job, a pool member might miss other valuable assignments, and the company is not going to get all it can out of the individual either. In fact, being kept in assignments too long is a major source of dissatisfaction among pool members. When people feel that their learning is being limited, they start thinking about jobs outside the organization and become highly vulnerable to the lure of corporate headhunters. The remedy, then, is to have an assignment last just long enough for the person to learn whatever there is to learn and to achieve measurable results, but not so long that the job becomes routine or easy.

People often adjust their learning to fit the time available—a concept illustrated in the old story about the Pope talking with two visitors to the Vatican. One visitor says that he'll be in Rome for a week, and the Pope responds, "That's wonderful! You'll get to see almost all of our beautiful city and appreciate our heritage." The second visitor explains that he is moving to Rome for two years, and the Pope replies, "Too bad, you won't really ever get to see all of our city." The point: If you know you have unlimited time, you probably won't push yourself as hard to get out and see the sights as you would with only a short window of opportunity. Similarly, if people assigned to a position for development know they are going to be there for only a limited time, and if they have clearly defined learning objectives, they will get busy and learn. They will seek out situations in which they can develop and use new skills and will be sure to observe, experience, and absorb as much as possible.

Learning tension—that is, the motivation and urge to learn—builds when people are challenged to show what they can do within a specific time. People continually cite their roles in new start-up operations or sweeping organizational changes as great learning experiences primarily because of this tension. A manager can create learning tension in any assignment by setting tight but realistic time frames and by helping the learner set measurable stretch targets.

In general, we tell executives that an assignment should typically range from a few months to two years, which represents what we believe to be a realistic "learning window." There are exceptions, of course, but overall an assignment that exceeds two years seems to fall short of the notion of "acceleration," and assignments of less than two or three months seem unlikely to yield meaningful results.

Stretch Assignments: How Much Is Too Much?

In placing Acceleration Pool members in jobs, a general rule of thumb is, The greater the change in responsibility, the greater the learning. Here's another: The larger the scope of responsibility of the position, the more learning. The underlying assumption for both axioms is that the most effective assignments challenge people's abilities and force them to use new, untested skills. However, stretching someone is a good strategy *only* if the person does not break—that is, if he or she doesn't completely fail in the assignment. Thus, the question is, How much stretch is appropriate?

It's impossible to generalize on that point. Obviously, it depends on the people, the organization's needs, available support mechanisms, etc. Some organizations have tried to quantify the amount of risk they are prepared to take. In the 1990s, for example, Citicorp announced that it was willing to promote people who were only 60–70 percent prepared for the new position (Clark & Lyness [as cited in Ohlott, 1998]). Of course, this edict wasn't meant to be taken literally; rather, it was merely a communication to managers about what to expect from these individuals.

To have the prepared, capable candidates they need to fill senior executive positions, most companies today have no choice but to stretch pool members considerably. This is especially evident in cases where an Acceleration Pool member is being considered for a "double jump"—a promotion two levels higher in the organization. Moving up so quickly leaves these high fliers without the support of their former peers or the guidance of their former leaders, who now, consequently, become their direct reports. Suddenly, they must learn to understand and fit into entirely new organizational and social structures.

We believe that a principal factor in determining the degree of stretch should be the pool member's level of proficiency in the targeted executive competencies. We have seen successful double—and sometimes triple—jumps when the pool member showed outstanding proficiency in leadership and management competencies. That's because in stretch assignments, new leaders must rely heavily on those leadership skills, but they typically won't have sufficient technical and professional skills or perhaps even organizational knowledge. So, if an organization is thinking about moving an Acceleration Pool member to a position for which he or she lacks considerable background, we advise conducting a comprehensive competency assessment, coupled with a thorough review of the person's background and motivations, before making the final decision.

Knowledge of an individual's strengths and development needs points specifically to those areas in which he or she might excel or struggle, and it gives the organization a chance to do something about them. For example, at a medical diagnostics company, a vice president of a regional sales unit was planning to place a budding manager into a senior sales leadership position as part of the manager's development plan. The assignment represented a major step up, but the Acceleration Center data showed that the manager's business and strategic abilities could be expected to be problem areas. Essentially, the manager was well versed in the technology, completely understood the sales process, and showed outstanding leadership skills, but did not yet understand the more complex business variables or show the level of strategic insight that the vice president might have hoped. After reviewing the data the vice president acknowledged that the assignment might be too much of a stretch; however, he also recognized that if significant coaching and support (far more than originally anticipated) could be applied, the assignment could yield major long-term benefits. Ultimately, the decision was made to move forward with the assignment, and the vice president provided heavy coaching and guidance. In the end the manager proved to be highly successful in the new role, and the decision to move ahead with the assignment is seen as having been a wise long-term investment. However, both the senior manager and the vice president acknowledge that the assignment might have been a disaster without the additional coaching element.

An Even-Faster Fast Track

In today's business world almost all development must be high speed. But increasingly there are situations in which "hyperspeed" is required. This is often the case when the organization finds itself with only one backup for a high-level position, and that person is still far from being ready. The challenge then is to help the individual to accumulate the wide range of job challenges, organizational knowledge, and competencies that will lead to success at the higher level—and to do so in a matter of months. The task becomes even more difficult if the person needs development in several competencies or has a potential derailer.

Such situations call for creativity. Usually, the organization needs to look at a combination of short-term and virtual assignments. It might also be possible to assign an advisor who is familiar with the day-to-day operation of the individual's new assignment to provide counseling as needed or even assume some responsibilities of the new position, thereby enabling the new executive to devote more time to personal development in the early days on the job.

Sometimes short-term assignments can be created to provide learning opportunities. For example, a pool member might be assigned to do a compensation survey of the people he or she eventually will be leading. This forces the pool member to delve deeply into the department before formally assuming the new position.

Summary

Assignments must be filled carefully because they are a valuable and limited resource. Creativity is needed in choosing and structuring positions so that organizations get the most "bang for their buck" (i.e., make a significant impact on job challenges and competencies). Also, senior management must be sure that Development Action Forms are completed for each assignment. The forms have the biggest payoff relative to assignments. Far too many people waste valuable development opportunities in assignments because they don't know what they are to learn, practice, or change and because they don't have their support lined up to help them accomplish their goals. Development Action Forms can remedy those problems.

Appendix 10-1: Assignments and Culture Change

One of the most important steps in achieving cultural change is to get an organization's managers to believe in and adopt the new culture and direction. Well-planned job assignments can help make that happen. Here is an example of how General Motors successfully changed its manufacturing culture and improved the quality of its products.

In the early 1970s, GM executives recognized that the company needed to drastically change its approach to building cars. They also saw that to make any new methods work, they would need employees who were quality oriented, empowered, attuned to continuous improvement, and willing to work in teams. Because they did not have a plant to use as a model of their new direction, GM senior managers were forced to look elsewhere. Ironically, their search led them to a major competitor: Toyota. GM established a joint venture with Toyota in 1984, centering on an antiquated, underachieving, former GM plant outside Oakland, California. Toyota managers essentially took over the facility, which had been closed due to poor performance, and rehired many of the former employees. Almost miraculously, they transformed it into one of GM's most productive plants, producing the highest-quality products.

Following the success in California, GM opened a greenfield joint-venture plant outside Toronto, Canada, this time with Suzuki as a partner. As in California, the Japanese managers ran the plant, bringing their values, manufacturing systems, and team organization structure. General Motors sent some of its best and brightest manufacturing executives to the Oakland and Toronto plants for two-year assignments, in which they were exposed to the new systems and the supporting culture. These managers then were assigned to significant GM operations throughout the world. The manufacturing manager of the Suzuki/GM facility in Canada, for example, moved to head up a new plant in East Germany, which soon became one of GM's most productive, highest-quality facilities. GM assigned more managers to its second-generation plants to absorb the new culture and manufacturing methods. In turn these managers traveled to other plants to spread the word. Meanwhile, the original managers of the joint venture plants moved up in the General Motors organization, ensuring that the new approaches would get the appropriate support from top management.

New technology, new organizational structures, and better-trained employees all were key factors in the changing culture at General Motors. GM had installed new methodologies and restructured its organization before, but with little success. Clearly, using assignments to get managers to absorb and support the new vision, values, and culture made a big difference.

Appendix 10-2: Managing Expatriates' Development

Managing the Acceleration Pool process for an international or global company presents a unique set of challenges. One of the most critical is establishing an infrastructure to effectively support "nondomestic" employees and their families. There are a number of special considerations. For instance, the HR planning process needs to ensure that international assignees and domestic expatriates are actively considered and brokered back into meaningful developmental assignments after their international assignments are completed. The assignment should leverage the learning that occurred while the pool member was on foreign duty and send a positive message to the organization on the value of taking an international assignment. Companies need to ensure that expatriates don't fall prey to the "out-of-sight, out-of-mind" syndrome. Maintaining active involvement with a "back-home" sponsor will help avoid this.

In managing the Acceleration Pool process for international assignees, companies must have an overall game plan to ensure all their key markets have pool members targeted for assignment. This plan must ensure that the organization's highest-potential people—both domestic and those from other countries—are identified and effectively rotated through assignments to leverage their development and maximize the business value to the company. Assignments should be long enough to allow pool members to transition to the foreign country and make a significant business contribution (typically two to three years), then return to the home country and apply what they have learned.

After accepting a foreign assignment, a pool member should go through a cultural orientation for the target country just before leaving. This should also include his or her spouse and older children, if there are any. We know of several professional organizations that specialize in these orientations, which are very effective in increasing the likelihood that the assignment will be a success.

Many failures of expatriate assignments are the direct result of the family's inability to adjust. In addition to the business expense of failed assignments, the emotional and career costs to employees and their families are considerable (Brake, Walker, & Walker, 1995). Because of the impact that foreign assignments have on the entire family, many companies have had success using both individual and family-oriented self-selection instruments. ☞ These self-administered questionnaires provide a realistic framework for helping the family to evaluate the impact of an expatriate assignment. Also, many organizations arrange for returning expatriate families to meet with prospective expatriate families to share their experiences and talk about the realities of the foreign assignment.

Another issue that must be addressed in many expatriate assignments—and one that can make or break the assignment—is the dual-career family. This is not only a very real professional issue for the "trailing spouse," but it can be a significant source of stress on the expatriate as well. Where feasible, the HR group managing the Acceleration Pool process will network to find career opportunities "in-country" for the spouse. Where this is not possible, an in-country spousal support system can help address the transition from an emotional and social perspective. Many companies with several expatriate families in the same location have established structured informal support programs for expatriate spouses and families, even where there are no dual-career issues. These programs can help facilitate adjustment to living in a foreign country. In addition to providing a social support network, they can be very effective in helping family members learn their way around in the new environment.

Ensuring that high potentials remain "connected" back home while on foreign assignment is especially critical for the success of expatriate Acceleration Pool members. Senior managers should make a point of seeking them out when visiting or traveling to the expatriate's country. This will help them gauge the pool member's progress and help keep the person connected to important business issues back home. Because of the unique experience that expatriates gain while on assignment, they should also be actively recruited for special projects or task forces (even while on assignment) that will take advantage of what they've learned and keep them committed.

Another critical element of managing the development of Acceleration Pool members on foreign assignment is having a solid, realistic plan for repatriating them. This is typically one of the toughest challenges facing most international companies with an Acceleration Pool system. The inability to effectively handle the repatriation process, both in terms of the appropriate next assignment and the emotional readjustment that people often have to make, can lead to significant retention problems. Without strong, proactive management of the repatriation process, companies risk losing their very best people and the considerable investment made in them during the course of the international assignment.

Chapter 11

Growth Through
Short-Term Experiences

*"A single conversation across the table with a wise man
is worth a month's study of books."*

—Chinese Proverb

While job assignments are key to an Acceleration Pool member's development, there is another significant development tool that is often overlooked: short-term learning experiences. These include organizational and extra-organizational events such as department presentations, long-range planning discussions, and professional meetings.

As the name implies, short-term experiences are relatively brief, compared to job assignments. In addition, they sometimes offer an opportunity for listening or observing skills rather than mastering them.

Short-term learning experiences usually can be found within the organization, but there might also be outside opportunities with a customer, a vendor, or a community or professional organization. The use of short-term experiences as a development strategy is increasing as organizations find that they need faster development in a broader array of job challenges and organizational knowledge. Following are some examples of various short-term learning experiences.

---

denotes that information on this topic is available at the *Grow Your Own Leaders* web site (www.ddiworld.com/growyourownleaders).

Experiences Within the Organization

- Coordinate a politically or culturally sensitive event, such as a visit from an overseas delegation.

- Represent the organization at a government conference.

- Attend or present at a professional meeting or industry convention.

- Conduct a study of the organization's diversity.

- Attend the company's or unit's long-range planning presentation.

- Participate on the team that briefs the chairman on questions that might arise at stockholder meetings.

- Manage a project team or task force.

- Manage or be a part of a virtual team.

- Facilitate a leadership training program.

- Develop a training program that targets a specific group or skill set (e.g., career planning).

- Mentor a coworker.

- Develop a new process or system.

- Take responsibility for a process (e.g., distribution, payroll).

- Critique practice presentations given by senior officers (e.g., ones intended for the board of directors or another prestigious group).

- Interact with people from different disciplines, cultures, or countries who have different perspectives.

- Participate in a manufacturing, finance, or accounting council that spans the organization.

- Volunteer for a brief international assignment.

- Take responsibility for company guests visiting from another location in the organization or from another company.

- Be part of a team that manages a large-scale project, such as moving an operation.

- Get involved in outsourcing decisions.

- Write a report on a sales project or an analysis of the competition.

- Interview key executives for a company survey (e.g., determine the need for a new program).
- Write a project report.
- Debate others over a project or issue.
- Conduct a portion of an orientation program for new employees or tell a new employee about the organization.
- Manage a global team.
- Train someone in a technical area.
- Manage a continuous quality-improvement team.
- Write a proposal for a new project.
- Teach a course as part of an executive development program.

Teaching Organizations

Several management thinkers are promoting the short-term experience of having an Acceleration Pool member teach his or her direct reports and other employees. GE, Allied Signal, and other organizations are moving toward becoming *teaching organizations* in which leaders actively pass along their knowledge and skill to others in the company. Teaching organizations insist that their managers learn how to teach and then use those skills to develop their people, keep them informed, and measure their success (Ellinger, Watkins, & Bostrom, 1999; Tichy & Cohen, 1998). Acceleration Pool members who become teachers learn as they prepare for the class and deliver their material. They gain commitment to the material they are presenting through the act of communicating and defending the concepts.

Experiences with a Customer, Vendor, or Outside Organization

- Visit a customer's site or a supplier's facility.
- Work on a customer's new product development committee.
- Troubleshoot a problem for a customer or supplier.
- Attend a customer's or vendor's convention.
- Take a temporary assignment in a customer or supplier organization.
- Negotiate with a customer or vendor.

- Speak at a vendor's meeting (e.g., sales conference).

- Teach a customer how to use a new product.

- Benchmark how exemplary companies handle a business issue or process (individually or as part of a team).

Experiences Within the Community/Profession

- Lead a United Way fund drive.

- Lead a strategic-planning committee for a charitable organization.

- Help a charitable organization develop a vision or mission statement.

- Work with hospital administrators to help them apply a quality improvement methodology or other program.

- Work with the local school system to ensure that graduates have the skills they will need for the job market.

- Evaluate community perceptions of the company.

- Lead a Junior Achievement group that focuses on creative business ideas.

- Serve on a professional committee that is developing guidelines, policies, or procedures.

- Coordinate a convention for a professional group.

- Critique articles submitted for a professional publication.

- Attend a professional conference in another country.

- Serve as a member of a board.

Board Membership

Many organizations demonstrate citizenship through representation on local or national boards of directors for nonprofit agencies, organizations, or special interest groups.

Encouraging or appointing pool members to assume board roles can be a very powerful development assignment. Such assignments offer creative opportunities to focus on development priorities and networking opportunities with capable leaders, both in an environment outside the individual's comfort zone. Sample development goals that might be met by this practice include:

- **Exposure to alternative business operating models.** For example, observing the fiscal conservativeness associated with nonprofit organizations might add a perspective of fiduciary discipline to pool members.

- **Strategic focus.** Boards are responsible for shaping the strategic direction of the organization. Board members are typically not expected to get involved in daily operational activities. Therefore, pool members who struggle with an inordinate operational focus might benefit from a role on a well-developed board.

- **Marketing or fund-raising experience.** Most boards expect members to assume responsibility for some aspect of promoting the organization, ranging from general advocacy to active involvement in marketing and fund-raising.

- **Networking.** Many boards comprise highly influential, accomplished individuals. Fellow board members offer models and informal mentoring opportunities to pool members. Boards are commonly developed to include members who offer a mosaic of complementary skills and backgrounds; thus, they are likely to present a different view of the world than is typically encountered by pool members immersed within their own organization.

- **Media/Community relations.** Board roles often provide opportunities for practicing organizational diplomacy to community partners, funding agencies, and the media.

- **Start-up.** Some board assignments offer opportunities to experience the inception of a program, community consortium, or even a small business subsidiary. A board-related development experience allows a pool member to experience the challenges of "birthing" a concept outside of his or her own role. If properly framed, it can offer great insight into defining a vision, mobilizing resources, establishing infrastructure, etc.

- **Source of pride.** Lastly, board assignments give pool members an opportunity to serve as stewards of their organization's reputation and image in the community. Retention objectives can be met as pool members increase their organizational identification and develop pride in serving as their organization's representative to an important cause.

Competency Development

Short-term experiences can be effective in helping to build certain competencies, as Table 11-1 shows.

Table 11-1: Building Competencies Through Short-Term Experiences	
Competency to Be Developed	**Short-Term Development Experiences**
Interpersonal Skills	
Building Strategic Relationships	• Serve on a committee led by someone who models excellent partnership behavior. • Lead a committee that requires strong partnerships across various functions of the organization or with a key customer. • Conduct a survey that collects information on the success of organizational relationships.
Building Trust	• Work as an advisor to a group that was recently restructured or downsized. • Conduct a training program on building trust.
Communicating with Impact	• Work as a public liaison for a local charity or a fine arts group (e.g., the city's ballet company). • Volunteer to write and distribute a team's progress reports.
Cultural Interpersonal Effectiveness	• Serve on a committee charged with recognizing the contributions of the organization's minority employees. • Work on a team that finds corporate internships for gifted minority youths.
Persuasiveness/Sales Ability	• Offer technical support to a sales team preparing for a major presentation to a prospective client; observe and give insights. • Solicit money for a good cause.

Table 11-1: Building Competencies Through Short-Term Experiences (cont'd)

Leadership Skills

Change Leadership	• Coach a team through a change process. • Implement a change in a unit. • Teach a course in change management that contrasts change initiatives that worked and those that didn't.
Coaching/Teaching	• Shadow a leader who is an excellent coach. • Act as a coach or mentor to someone within or outside the organization.
Delegation	• Plan a corporate anniversary event, assigning responsibility and authority to various committees. • Lead a committee and delegate key tasks to its members.
Developing Organizational Talent	• Conduct a retention survey—find why people leave. • Mentor/Coach a new employee and ask for feedback on success.
Empowerment	• Lead a committee and delegate key tasks to its members.
Selling the Vision	• Make speeches in a political or community campaign. • Join a team charged with implementing a new strategy.
Team Development/ Team Leadership	• Join a short-term task force. • Lead a company or vendor committee that is troubleshooting a quality problem. • Actively participate in the start-up and ongoing functions of a team, including chartering the team, creating a mission statement, and seeking feedback from internal partners.

Table 11-1: Building Competencies Through Short-Term Experiences (cont'd)

Leadership Skills (cont'd)

	• Survey team members' satisfaction with their progress as a group.

Business or Management Skills

Drive for Results	• Write a case study of the best-performing unit in the organization.
	• Serve on a committee led by a person known for getting results.
Economic Orientation	• Attend meetings featuring outside speakers on economics and politics.
	• Assume responsibility for financial analysis of a project (e.g., an alliance or small acquisition).
Establishing Strategic Direction	• Join a strategy-development team inside the organization or with a charity or arts organization.
	• Teach a course on strategy that requires a review of the methods proposed by strategy experts.
Global Acumen	• Lead an international committee to develop a performance appraisal or selection system.
	• Meet with international representatives to find a solution to a common problem, such as how best to share electronic files worldwide.
Managing the Job	• Organize the company's United Way campaign.
	• Lead a committee that is planning the organization's annual holiday event.
Marketing and Entrepreneurial Insight	• Attend customer meetings to define their needs.
	• Find out which vendors provide the best customer service and visit their organizations.

Table 11-1: Building Competencies Through Short-Term Experiences (cont'd)	
Business or Management Skills (cont'd)	
	• Join the marketing committee of an arts group.
Mobilizing Resources	• Join a committee charged with implementing a strategy or making a major organizational change.
	• Help plan a major community event (e.g., a parade, picnic, holiday celebration).
Operational Decision Making	• Lead a community organization that is facing difficult decisions or challenges (e.g., relocating a school for the blind).
	• Join a committee led by a person with excellent decision-making skills.
Personal Attributes	
Adaptability, Energy, Executive Disposition, Learning Orientation, Positive Disposition, and Reading the Environment	• Observe people who model certain key attributes.
	• Write an article that defines the specific behaviors associated with success in an attribute.
Technical/Professional Knowledge and Skills	• Attend professional meetings.
	• Help select articles for a professional journal.

Short-Term Experiences in Action

In our work we've seen many examples of spectacular payoffs from short-term learning events. In one organization, for example, an up-and-coming young executive was sometimes making poor interdepartmental presentations; on other occasions, however, she did an excellent job. The problem was not a lack of skill but rather a lack of preparation. Although the executive had been given feedback telling her that she needed to devote more time to preparing for her presentations, she was adamant that the immediate task of running her department was more important than diverting time to prepare. Finally, she was asked on two occasions to watch the CEO rehearse a presentation and then give him feedback. By seeing how much time and effort the CEO put into his presentations, she came to appreciate the importance of preparing. Subsequently, she devoted an appropriate amount of time and energy to getting ready for her own presentations.

In another organization management was thinking about assigning a fast-track manager to the company's Paris office, where he would interact with high-ranking French government officials. The manager was a bit unpolished in social situations. He didn't have a passport and had never been out of the United States. In fact, he hadn't spent much time outside his rural hometown. The consensus of everyone who knew about the potential assignment was that, although he had excellent technical skills and had proven himself in other parts of the organization, the manager would likely feel and look ill at ease.

Rather than throw the manager into a situation in which he would have to learn from making embarrassing mistakes, the organization sent him along with senior executives on trips to France. Management also made sure that he was involved when the organization entertained associates from the French office and French clients who were visiting. He was sent to an industry convention in France and was even given lessons in basic conversational French. The manager was very bright and a quick learner, so he soon had the skills he needed to be successful.

Building Social Skills

That manager's story is not unusual these days. Indeed, our experience suggests that an alarming—and increasing—number of technically gifted people who are poised to enter senior management ranks do not have the necessary social skills for executive positions. High-tech geniuses accustomed to wearing jeans, eating fast food, and working alone are now often finding themselves in unfamiliar—and uncomfortable—social situations. Their new responsibilities might require them to deal with buttoned-down bankers or representatives of investment houses or to make informal presentations over formal dinners. These fast-trackers need experience in such situations before they become the center of unwanted attention and wind up embarrassing themselves and the company. That is, they need to be put into learning situations in which they can observe the kind of behavior that is expected of them. For example, a company might assign an Acceleration Pool member to accompany its investment banker to presentations given by financial officers of other firms.

This problem is not limited to high-tech entrepreneurs. Many newly appointed senior managers are unfamiliar with how executives should behave on field visits or when entertaining clients—largely because they have not had the chance to see more-experienced executives in action. Before the downsizing of the 1980s and early 1990s, many management trainees learned appropriate executive behavior by working as an assistant to a senior company officer. The trainee would do whatever was required, including drive the executive from one meeting to another, carry bags, run errands, and so on. The important learning point was not so much what the trainee did—it was that he or she observed firsthand what the executive did and how the executive did it. The job wasn't very exciting or challenging, and it certainly wasn't crucial to the organization's success; in fact, that's why the jobs were eliminated in waves of downsizing. But the position did orient the trainees to some of the more subtle skills executives must have, such as:

- Recognizing the importance of seating arrangements around a conference or dinner table (particularly if Asians are involved).

- Knowing to send thank-you notes and notes of encouragement.

- Being able to handle impromptu situations in which an executive is suddenly asked to "say a few words about the future of the organization."

- Recognizing when to leave a party. (Because many people will wait until the senior person leaves, a visiting executive shouldn't stay too late.)

- Knowing when spouses and significant others should be invited to a function and when they shouldn't.

These kinds of social skills must be learned, and short-term learning events are an excellent way to teach them.

Plan Ahead—But Be Flexible

Acceleration Pool members should get involved in as many different short-term learning experiences as possible. Learning opportunities should be discussed and identified during development planning meetings with the member's manager and mentor.

That said, it's also important to realize that many short-term development events can't be planned. Business is full of surprises. For example, there always will be the delegation from South Africa that decides to visit the corporate office with little or no notice, or the unexpected news that the company has been chosen as the corporate flagship for a high-profile community charity campaign. So, managers and mentors need to be constantly on the lookout for new learning opportunities and be prepared to move swiftly to assign Acceleration Pool members when those opportunities arise.

Chapter 12

Growth Through Training/Executive Education

"Leadership and learning are indispensable to each other."

—John Fitzgerald Kennedy,
U.S. President & Author of *Profiles in Courage*

In an Acceleration Pool system, training plays an important role in helping pool members develop competencies and, to a lesser extent, in building organizational knowledge. Training also can strengthen an individual's motivation and reinforce the organization's vision and values.

In this chapter we will cover issues important to training people at all levels of an organization because all levels, including supervisors and individual contributors, can be represented in an Acceleration Pool. We recognize that the appropriateness of formal training declines as individuals rise in the organization (see Figure 9-1 in Chapter 9). Often, middle and senior managers do need training—even if the word *training* evokes images of boring classroom experiences, or worse. Throughout this chapter we will note training methodologies uniquely appropriate for individuals at high organizational levels. The challenge to training experts is to deliver training to middle and senior managers in a way that is fun, short, and full of "take-home value."

There are three basic types of training typically used by Acceleration Pool members: *transition training, prescriptive training,* and *special training.* Training comes in many forms, ranging from traditional classroom courses

☞ denotes that information on this topic is available at the *Grow Your Own Leaders* web site (www.ddiworld.com/growyourownleaders).

to online self-directed learning to individualized, one-on-one training for senior managers. This chapter examines how the three types can be used to develop Acceleration Pool members and discusses how to determine the most appropriate delivery methods.

Transition Training

Most organizations offer some form of classroom-based transition training to help rising leaders adjust as they move up through the organization. Typically, transition training is offered when individuals move into supervision, middle management, or strategic management—times when they are facing major changes in job skills, knowledge, and responsibility requirements.

Transition training has three components:

- **Roles (what)**—The responsibilities of individuals at the target level. For example, the roles of a supervisor might include being a coach, team builder, and talent developer. Roles are driven by the job content and the values of the organization (e.g., the organization's stand on diversity, customer service, empowerment).

- **Competencies (how)**—The behavior (skills) required to accomplish the roles. For example, making presentations and leading teams might be skills required of someone who is moving to the next level.

- **Systems (with)**—The organizational systems and procedures needed to accomplish the roles. For example, a new supervisor would need to know the organization's performance management and budgeting systems.

Because they bring together people from various parts of the organization, transition training programs also help participants develop important contacts with colleagues throughout the company. Acceleration Pool members reaching a certain organizational level usually receive the same transition training as everyone else who has reached that level.

Transition into Supervision

Delivery methods and content for transition training vary greatly by level. At the supervisory level some portion of the learning might occur via web-based training (WBT). When classroom training is used, it often is delivered in-house during several sessions, possibly days or weeks apart. Roles, competencies, and systems are commonly taught at the same time using behavior modeling technology. First, trainees learn the importance of a role (e.g., performance coach) to their job success. Then, they learn the organization's systems relative to that role (e.g., performance management systems). And finally, they learn, practice, and receive feedback on the behavioral skills needed to help a direct report set goals and review progress toward them (Byham & Pescuric, 1996). A meta-analysis of 97 studies of behavior modeling shows that it is uniquely and consistently effective in developing interaction skills (Taylor, 1994). Figure 12-1 outlines the learning process for a behavior modeling training module.

Figure 12-1: Learning Process for a Behavior Modeling Training Module

One-on-one and team interaction skills, such as reaching group agreement or introducing change, are best developed using behavior modeling, which Involves:

1. Discussing how the behavior (skill) being taught can have a positive impact on a key role or responsibility (e.g., being a coach).

2. Determining the underlying steps or process in the behavior (e.g., steps in effective coaching).

3. Seeing a positive model video of someone effectively using the appropriate steps or processes (e.g., an effective coaching interaction).

4. Practicing using the interaction steps/processes in an interaction, followed by feedback. (Everyone practices and receives feedback in every module.)

5. Determining how the steps/processes might be applied in a variety of challenging, yet realistic, situations.

6. Planning an on-the-job application.

The organization's systems and forms are used in the practice sessions.

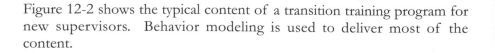
Figure 12-2 shows the typical content of a transition training program for new supervisors. Behavior modeling is used to deliver most of the content.

Figure 12-2: Sample Curriculum of a Transition Training Program for New First-Level Supervisors

- Preparing Others to Succeed
- Facilitating Improved Performance
- Following Up to Support Improvement
- Helping Others Adapt to Change
- Guiding Conflict Resolution
- Performance Planning: Setting Expectations
- Delegating for Productivity and Growth
- Targeted Selection Interviewing Skills

Transition into Middle Management

For the new middle manager, transition training programs rely more on discovery learning and experience sharing. Feedback from direct reports and peers often is integrated. Sessions are compacted into two or three days, and programs are usually delivered at a local hotel or the company training facility. As with transition training for new supervisors, all three of the components (what, how, and with) are usually addressed in the same program—some through behavior modeling training, and some through discussions and other means. Figure 12-3 shows the content of a typical middle-management program.

Transition into General Management

When people reach a level at which they have to be involved in strategy and long-range planning, and they must take an organizationwide view of what's happening, they have reached general management. At this level transition training focuses more on roles. It is assumed that individuals reaching general management have developed sufficient behavioral competencies, such as planning or leading, and if not, that deficiency will be dealt with on a case-by-case, prescriptive basis (see the next section). It is also assumed that the individual has acquired knowledge of the organization's systems or will acquire it as needed. The only thing that's left

---

Figure 12-3: Sample Curriculum of a Transition Training Program
              for New Middle Managers

- Motivating Through Empowerment/High Involvement
- Coaching/Teaching
- Delegating and Monitoring
- Operational Decision Making
- Leading Through Vision and Values
- Helping Others Adapt to Change
- Planning and Critical Path Analysis
- Generating and Recognizing New Ideas and Solutions
- Developing Others
- Trust: Strengthening the Foundation
- Company Budgeting and Planning Systems

---

is knowledge of the roles. Surprisingly, an increasing number of managers are reaching strategic leadership positions without a clear understanding of what they are responsible for—the roles they must play to assure organizational success—and if they know the roles, they aren't very good at them. We believe that these knowledge and skill gaps have been caused by the elimination of organizational layers, such as "assistant to" and "deputy" positions, that provided excellent orientation opportunities in the past.

Shared participant feedback is an important learning element in higher-level programs. Broadening organizational knowledge and making contacts throughout the organization are major "bonus" outcomes. Until recently, internal strategic-level programs were rare, but now more and more organizations seem to be recognizing that many individuals entering senior management need an orientation to the roles they must play. Organizations are conducting programs to meet these needs.

A good example of an executive-level transition program that focuses on roles is DDI's Strategic Leadership Experience[SM] (SLE), which teaches the nine strategic leadership roles shown in Figure 12-4. The SLE uses a highly involving, computerized management game that allows participants to try the roles while running a simulated organization for "three years." Participants realize the importance of the roles and gain insight into the effective behavior associated with each. They can compare their success at the game to that of their peers, which keeps them highly motivated. At the end of each business cycle (i.e., "year") as well as at the end of the game, participants share insights and strategies.

Figure 12-4: Sample Curriculum of Strategic Leadership Experience^{SM},

Figure 12-4: Sample Curriculum of Strategic Leadership Experience[SM], a Transition Training Program for Aspiring or New General Managers

The SLE program is built upon nine leadership roles played by strategic managers. The nine roles are:

1. **Navigator**—Clearly and quickly works through the complexity of key issues, problems, and opportunities to affect actions (e.g., leverage opportunities and resolve issues).

2. **Strategist**—Develops a long-range course of action or set of goals to achieve the organization's vision.

3. **Entrepreneur**—Identifies and exploits opportunities for new products, services, and markets.

4. **Mobilizer**—Proactively builds and aligns stakeholders, capabilities, and resources for getting things done quickly and achieving complex objectives.

5. **Talent Advocate**—Attracts, develops, and retains talent to ensure that people with the right skills and motivations to meet business needs are in the right place at the right time.

6. **Captivator**—Builds passion and commitment toward a common goal.

7. **Global Thinker**—Integrates information from all sources to develop a well-informed, diverse perspective that can be used to optimize organizational performance.

8. **Change Driver**—Creates an environment that embraces change; makes change happen, even if the change is radical, and helps others to accept new ideas.

9. **Enterprise Guardian**—Ensures shareholder value through courageous decision making that supports enterprise- or unit-wide interests.

In addition the program familiarizes participants with the common executive derailers and facilitates their self-insights about potential problems.

Prescriptive Training

Acceleration Pool members often participate in training activities built around their specific needs, as delineated on their Development Priority Lists. Figure 12-5 provides some examples of topics covered in prescriptive training.

Figure 12-5: Examples of Topics Covered in Prescriptive Training Programs

- Seeing self as others do and seeing your actions as others will.
- Communicating (public speaking, news conferences, television interviews).
- Crafting partnerships.
- Financial issues in global competition.
- Building global marketing competitiveness.
- Strategic decision making and creating strategy.
- Strategic alliances.
- Executing business strategy.
- Planning in a changing world.
- Global effectiveness.
- Managing change/Innovation.

For pool members at the middle-manager level and below, training can be delivered to groups with common needs. It can also be delivered through internal or external open-enrollment or electronically delivered programs (e.g., web-based training). (See Table 9-2 in Chapter 9 for information on competencies that can be developed through training efforts.) Prescriptive needs of middle and senior managers can be met by attending short programs run by universities or training companies and by participating in one-on-one training—often combined with coaching. A popular prescriptive program at this level is DDI's Executing Business Strategy[SM], which prepares managers to implement an organizational strategy that they developed or that was handed down to them. An outline of this program is provided in Figure 12-6.

> ## Figure 12-6: Examples of Content in Executing Business Strategy[SM]
>
> - Identifying focus areas for the next three to five years.
> - Developing a clear accountability system to drive focus areas.
> - Matching organizational talent with key positions/roles.
> - Aligning organizational systems with focus areas.
> - Developing measurement systems to track progress.

Conventional University Courses

Colleges and universities offer a cornucopia of learning opportunities to fit specific developmental needs. The challenge is finding the right course or series of courses that meets quality standards and pool members' time constraints. When choosing university courses, remember that:

- The goal of most academic management courses is knowledge development, not skill development.

- Course outcomes depend very much on the instructor.

- Course highlights and descriptions often have very little to do with the actual content.

- The age and experience makeup of the class will greatly affect the learning experience.

- Certain "soft" programs offer advanced degrees but not advanced insights.

- It is very difficult for most managers to fit their learning into an academic schedule—even night school. Thus, many well-meaning managers either fail to finish academic courses or miss so many classes that a self-directed learning curriculum would have been more appropriate.

- Evening academic courses often conflict with family life.

Despite the ubiquity and high quality of some academic courses, we have not seen much use for them in filling the specific development needs of Acceleration Pool members. These courses just aren't flexible enough nor have enough bottom-line impact. An organization might be better to consider self-directed learning options, such as courses on "accounting for non-accountants" instead of conventional academic accounting courses.

Short, Open-Enrollment University Executive Programs

Thousands of training programs specifically designed for managers and executives are available from colleges and universities throughout the world. These range from one- or two-day events to programs lasting eight weeks or more. The programs are offered on campus, at executive conference centers, or via the Internet. Because the choice of offerings is so varied, making smart buying decisions is difficult. A few words of advice:

- Compare course offerings against the competencies or knowledge a pool member is trying to develop. The training must have a measurable, meaningful goal.

- Remember that most university executive programs are not designed to build skills. Their purpose is to transfer knowledge or provide information on new developments.

- Consider the other participants' backgrounds. What will be the impact on other participants' learning if 25 percent of the class is from a single country or region? Seventy-five percent? Broad diversity is usually best.

- Don't underestimate the importance of contacts made at residential training programs. Participant surveys often show that trainees perceive this to be the most valuable part of the experience. These contacts allow participants to benchmark their organizational practices against other companies and their personal styles against those of other successful executives.

- Don't be overly impressed by the school's football record, the size or location of its executive training center, or, for that matter, where your organization's CEO got his or her degree. The quality of instruction is most important.

- Realize that good university classroom lecturers often make poor executive educators. They lack involvement and do not have a vested interest in behavioral change. Check out the instructors' ratings and ask for references.

- Decide whether the course or program is a prescription for a diagnosed training need or transition training that should be experienced by everyone in the Acceleration Pool or at an organizational level. Both can be effective strategies when used appropriately. However, a prescriptive program can easily become a rite-of-passage transition program, and thus, many people will attend who don't really need to and who would benefit more from another experience instead. We know of several companies that have named their high-potential talent program after the university training program that all of their high-potential pool members attended.

• Recognize that the quality of university programs changes over time. Instructors as well as their research interests change and, thus, so does what they emphasize in class. Check the current ratings of programs. Many university programs are resting on their laurels when they should be keeping up to date on what is new in management and leadership.

In general longer executive education programs (8 to 15 weeks) are being discarded for shorter, more targeted programs. Companies want programs with "take-home value"—that is, programs that are topical and based on organizational issues. Shorter, open-enrollment courses sponsored by universities remain popular around the world, but there's been little growth in their use except in Asian and developing countries. Instead, universities have noted much more interest in courses developed especially for organizations (Bassi, Cheney, & Lewis, 1998).

How to Check Out University-Based Programs

Almost all universities offering executive programs provide descriptions of them on their web site. In addition, try these sources:

• *International Executive Development Programmes,* published by Kogan Page Limited. It includes program overviews and contact information (www.venda.com/vendanet/iedp/).

• *Bricker's International Directory.* It is an informative guide to more than 700 management education programs offered by universities and nonprofit organizations worldwide. There is a cost involved (www.petersons.com/brickers/bsector.html).

One-on-One Training for Executives

Organizations are beginning to recognize that getting executives into formal training programs is extremely difficult, and getting them to do web-based training, no matter how web savvy they are, is virtually impossible. An alternative is one-on-one training, in which an instructor delivers the same material covered in classroom training, but in a greatly abbreviated version that meets the executive's specific business and personal needs.

One-on-one training is not the same as executive coaching, which usually involves helping the executive discover solutions to his or her problem situations—although there can be some elements of training in a coaching situation. A common application of one-on-one training occurs when an organization adopts a new companywide selection interviewing system. All supervisors and managers go through a two-day interviewer training program that provides them with opportunities to practice interviewing real-life job applicants and then receive feedback. Recognizing that the new system's success hinges on modeling, support, and reinforcement by senior management, while also realizing the difficulty of getting senior managers into training, the organization arranges for each executive to receive a two-hour, condensed version of the training. This is followed by feedback on the executive's use of the skills when the instructor observes the interviews with the people whom the executives would have had to interview anyway. The same instructor conducts both the two-day and the two-hour versions of the program. There usually is no follow-up for executives.

The best approach we have seen for building executives' performance management skills (i.e., developing their own performance plans, critiquing and aligning the plans of others, discussing with their boss and their direct reports their achievement or failure to achieve goals) was built totally around one-on-one training. After one hour of teaching the basic principles, the instructor helped each executive complete a performance plan and also review the plans submitted by direct reports (tasks that the executives would have had to do anyway). Then the instructor and executive discussed how the executive should work with direct reports to improve the quality of their performance plans.

When it was time for them to review their direct reports' success relative to the goals, the executives received another hour of one-on-one training, followed by a planning session on how they would handle each direct report's performance discussion. If a problem was anticipated, the trainer and the executive role-played the discussion. The executive and the instructor sometimes met to debrief particularly difficult performance discussions. The instructor returned each year to provide help and insight. After three years all members of the senior management team were successfully using the performance management system—to the best of our knowledge, a first in North American industry. Implementing the system was expensive, but the results were well worth the investment. All executives felt that the increased clarity of purpose, from the specific strategy-related goals that were developed, paid for the cost of the instructor many times over.

As in the previous example, one-on-one executive training works very well when developing behavioral skills, such as interviewing, conducting performance management (appraisal) discussions, holding 360° or other feedback discussions, negotiating, coaching, and developing leadership talent. Both the cognitive material and the behavioral models can be presented, and the executive can role-play situations with the instructor. The instruction is timed so that it immediately precedes an opportunity for the executive to use the skills on the job. Then, in the ideal situation the instructor observes the real-life application and provides feedback.

One-on-one instruction does not work as well in the development of cognitive and management skills, such as analysis, judgment, and visionary leadership. The value of the classroom discussion is difficult to replicate in a one-on-one situation. Executive coaching is a better alternative (see Chapter 13).

Special Training Experiences for Acceleration Pool Members

In addition to participating in the transitional and prescriptive leadership-training programs that are provided to all rising employees, Acceleration Pool members attend training events that are designed specifically for them.

Acceleration Pool Orientation

When there are enough eligible participants, some organizations sponsor a half-day orientation program for the people entering the Acceleration Pool. This is not meant to build skills but to acquaint members with their responsibilities in the pool, the roles of the mentor and the coach, and the advantages of being in the pool. These orientations also provide information about the process for diagnosing development needs, preparing Development Action Plans, and building a Career Development Portfolio to document development. Representatives of the organization's Human Resource department typically conduct these orientation sessions.

Major Training Events

Organizations that have Acceleration Pools typically provide at least one development program specifically designed for pool members. These programs:

• Symbolically show that pool members are unique and important to the organization.

- Bring pool members together so they can network and build relationships.

- Introduce pool members to the organization's top executives, opening the door for future contact.

- Provide unique content that is important to members' success at the executive level or that relates to specific organizational initiatives.

- Give pool members a feel for high-level decision making.

- Facilitate team projects, such as action-learning projects.

- Help pool members see how they stack up against their peers in the organization. Individuals who consider themselves to be stars in their own departments can gain valuable insights by meeting high fliers from other work groups.

The content and timing of such events vary greatly. Programs can be held on- or off-site and typically last one to two weeks. Often the CEO attends portions of the program and sometimes leads sessions that stress major issues facing the organization. General Electric CEO Jack Welch, for example, is a strong proponent of involving top executives in management training. "I would never want to run this company without Crotonville (GE's management training center in New York)," Welch told *The Wall Street Journal*. "About 5,000 people go through there each year. I will see 1,000 myself for four hours" (Hymowitz & Murray, 1999, pp. B1, B4).

Often such programs emphasize the unique strategic challenges facing top management. Organization-specific management games and case studies can be used to start discussions and spark insights. Outside speakers, such as investment analysts or management gurus, might be brought in to contribute as well.

Although the specifics of such programs vary, some general rules of thumb should be considered in determining activities. Typically, effective programs designed for Acceleration Pool members:

- Are held off-site.

- Recognize that participants will value the opportunity to get acquainted with top management and hear their ideas on the organization's direction. As a result, executives should allocate adequate formal and informal time to the program—rather than just fly in, make a speech, and leave. It's also important to make sure that participants don't have other assignments that prevent them from interacting with the senior executives.

- Have an explicit goal of helping participants get to know one another and network. A good way to foster peer relationships is to employ many small-team activities and intentionally shuffle people from team to team.

- Provide short training nuggets—just in time, just enough. For example, providing participants with training on team chartering or team decision making just before project teams are formed can be very effective. The new knowledge and skills can be applied immediately and save teams a great deal of time as they pursue their goals.

- Push participants. Pool members typically want to get the most out of the experience and expect to work day and night. However, it's also important to provide exercise or break time and some time during work hours to check on "back home" responsibilities. Remember that "back home" might be several time zones away.

- Use a variety of training methods (e.g., company-specific management games or case studies, in addition to group discussions and lectures).

- Assign teams to develop a unique solution to a challenging business issue. Teams might compete to find the best solution or each take on separate parts of a problem. The teams ultimately report their recommendations to representatives of senior management. (These projects do not require the same amount of research or time demanded by an action learning project.)

- Make people feel as if they are special and that the organization cares about them. One way to do this is to bring in prestigious people from outside the organization to make presentations and lead discussions.

- Develop international acumen. Make a point to have a mix of international representatives on teams and consider international topics in cases and research assignments. Hold portions of the training or data-gathering sessions in different countries.

- Help participants develop their interpersonal competencies. Participants should set personal learning goals for the training program—based on their Development Priority List—and work with their team to accomplish the goals. For example, an individual might want to build her collaboration skills while participating in a training program focusing on strategy. Some organizations make outside coaches available to provide feedback for skill development during these programs.

Beware of Internal Poachers

Sometimes, senior managers speaking at an Acceleration Pool training event use it as an opportunity to "poach" talent from other parts of the organization. Working like talent scouts, they sometimes roam a meeting and look for potential superstars, whom they later corner, compliment, and court to fill roles in their business units. This sort of internal recruiting can be problematic for a variety of reasons:

- Individually driven talent identification and promotion can fly in the face of organizational efforts to grow and share talent in ways that best support the total organization.

- Poachers might use poor criteria in evaluating participants. Ask several of these executives what they're looking for, and you're likely to get many different answers. Such inconsistencies can undermine the organization's efforts to communicate a consistent leadership model.

- Some of these events involve a mechanism for assessing participants as well as training them (e.g., on-site coaches who provide structured evaluations of individuals during and after the event). Executives who "work around" these objective assessments are not only highly prone to making promotion mistakes, they can also discredit the assessment process by conveying their preference for their own judgment methods.

Action Learning—Team Projects

Many training experiences designed specifically for Acceleration Pool members use a variation of *action learning,* whereby teams of 6 to 16 people tackle real-life business problems or challenges outside their usual areas of expertise. The purpose of such assignments is to prepare participants to deal with strategic issues and develop decision-making tools and methods. Depending on the program's design, participants also can learn the importance of networking, understand the different styles and methods represented by other members of their action learning team, practice leadership skills, and learn how to solve problems collaboratively in small groups.

For example, action learning assignments might involve tackling issues such as:

- "How can we fundamentally change the rules of competition in our industry?"

- "Is the market for Product X ready for a new player?"
- "Could we actually change the basic market assumptions about our products, and if so, how?"
- "How could we start operations in India? Should we?"
- "How could HR add more value to our business?"
- "How can we develop a new strategy for acquiring new clients?"
- "What back-office operations should we outsource?"

The action learning activity, which usually lasts from one to six months, is almost always preceded and followed by an off-site experience of three to five days. The first off-site experience prepares participants to tackle the action learning assignment by helping them understand its importance and its ramifications, and it gets them started by developing team spirit and formulating a plan for approaching their task. Teams then go off to work on their assignments. In the later classroom event, all the participants present their team's recommendation to the other teams and the CEO or other senior managers. The before-and-after off-site experience, where several teams are in attendance, also provides the opportunity for other development activities, such as speeches by senior officers of the company. Some organizations also provide training in team leadership and other skills that can immediately be applied.

We have found that the key to effective action learning is ensuring that the task is meaningful to the organization. The best topics cut across organizational unit functions and deal with issues that are popularly accepted as in need of repair or that obviously fit with the organization's strategic objectives. Having meaningful assignments instills in participants the sense that they are being trusted with an important issue. Most action learning teams are assigned a single topic, but some organizations provide a short list of topics from which teams can choose. Entire action learning teams are usually not involved in implementing their recommendations, but one or two team members might be. Because of the intense interest and "ownership" generated by team members' participation, we advise that organizations keep the teams informed about what is happening with their recommendations. Even if their ideas are not implemented, understanding the reasons why will help their development.

Action learning teams should be diverse and include people from throughout the organization and around the world, with appropriate race and gender representation. Teams often are virtual, but some have periodic face-to-face meetings. Also, an action learning experience might involve considerable travel while the team collects basic data.

Some organizations take members of an action learning team away from their jobs for the duration of their project. Most, however, make participation an extra assignment, thereby adding to the stress of already-busy executive candidates. The managers of Acceleration Pool members who are on action learning teams should understand that their charges' participation will consume a significant amount of time.

Many organizations assign executives to advise (or sponsor) each project team. These advisors are well versed in the issues being researched and can provide background information and answer questions as they crop up. An advisor's most important duty is to ensure the team doesn't get too far off track. In most settings advisors should be careful not to make recommendations to the team—their job is to provide support and open doors. The idea behind action learning is to get a fresh perspective from the team, and thus, the advisor should not become an expert who dominates the process.

In addition, organizations often provide coaches who are experts in group dynamics and personal development. These professional coaches are typically involved as the team is forming, especially if there is some kind of team-building activity designed to get the team off to a good start. Also, coaches help each team member set specific learning objectives for the action learning experience. This is important because pool members will benefit most from a program if they have targeted personal development needs beforehand. The professional coaches periodically check in with the team during the action learning experience and provide feedback based on their observations and the results of team member surveys.

It is extremely important for action learning team members to recognize that there are two purposes for their participation: to come up with a good plan or recommendation and to develop decision-making and interpersonal skills. This is where the professional coaches can really add value. Some teams begin each meeting with a discussion of what they have learned individually since the last meeting; others use some sort of journal to document what they've learned as individuals and as a team. It's crucial that in the final team meeting after presenting their recommendations, team members have a chance to focus on the quality of their recommendations, their individual learning, and how the learning can be applied to their jobs. Again, coaches are very helpful in this process.

Action learning programs are effective because they get people heavily involved in the activity. If a program is designed correctly, team members are totally committed and enthusiastic and are truly at a teachable moment—a time when they are open to trying and learning new things. In our experience it is amazing to see how quickly people become experts in areas totally outside of their normal work. They are highly motivated because the projects are typically more strategic and more challenging than any initiatives they have ever had to deal with before.

Action Learning—Individual Projects

While traditional action learning teams are built around group projects, it is becoming more common to have each team member take on an individual project. Team members then coach their teammates and support one another's efforts. Often, the project involves applying a concept learned during a previous skills-training segment. For example, each team member might decide to introduce empowerment into their work units and document the results.

We know of a midsize, high-tech organization that decided its teams would tackle "change." The organization had become less nimble than it once was, and the management team thought the organization was becoming bureaucratic and not as willing to accept new initiatives. To tackle these issues, the management team divided their 12 Acceleration Pool members into two teams of 6. Each mid-management participant on each team chose an area in which he or she would make some significant changes. Team members discussed their goals and their plans for implementing each change. Then they began the implementation, checking their progress with one another every other week. At the end of the allotted time (six months), they met again to compare notes and make a presentation to the senior management team that summarized their individual accomplishments and discussed their combined learning.

Action Learning—Individual Projects with Team Members from Different Organizations

A few companies, mostly in the United Kingdom, are experimenting with individual action learning projects in which the participants are from different companies. They report considerable success, especially at higher organizational levels where it is difficult for one company to come up with a sufficient number of high-level people to form a team.

Making Better Decisions About Training

Training is a major Acceleration Pool expense and one area in which many cost savings and improvements in efficiency can be realized. To help you make sure your organization's training accomplishes its objectives, we have provided considerable guidance on the Grow Your Own Leaders web site. The topics covered on the web site are summarized in the remainder of this chapter.

Essential Components of Effective Pool Member Training

A good place to start is by comparing your organization's training efforts against a list of essential components of effective training programs, making sure you are using the most effective strategies and training delivery options. Each of your organization's training opportunities should be weighed against these 11 components of effective training:

- Focus training efforts on maximum ROI.
- Know what you want to achieve.
- Choose the appropriate training mode.
- Customize training—but don't overdo it.
- Spread training over time.
- Provide opportunities for practice and test skill acquisition.
- Build confidence to apply the learning.
- Use quality instructors.
- Select the right venue.
- Prepare learners to learn.
- Have as many executives involved as possible.

Training Delivery Options

Are you using the most cost-effective and efficient mode of training delivery, including self-directed learning via CD-ROM, the Internet, company intranets, and distance learning via videoconferencing?

Training Sources Outside the Organization

We discuss the strengths and weaknesses of various categories of training that are popular in executive development, including:

- Classroom, Internet-based, and weekend university degree-granting MBA programs.

- Short, open-enrollment university executive programs.

- Short courses developed specifically for an organization.

- Transition and prescriptive programs conducted by training resource organizations.

- Public seminars and workshops.

- Experiential/Inspirational programs.

Common Pool Member Training Needs and Effective Strategies for Meeting Them

Some development needs covered are business strategy, ethics, judgment, planning and organization, negotiation, interaction skills, attitudes, knowledge, values, and technical skills.

How Can Training Be Made Efficient and Thus Provide a Better ROI?

- Evaluating training options.

- Computer-based support.

- Learning support.

- Supporting training on the job (performance support).

Determining If Training Works Before You Invest

It's easy to get fooled when purchasing training. Vendors often make claims with no documented evidence. Purchases often are based on the prestige of the organization or one of its speakers. In this section on the web site, we discuss training program evaluation and answer questions such as, "How is training effectiveness evaluated?" and "When should a research study be required?"

By providing this information on training, we are not attempting to make the executive reader a training expert. Rather, we are trying to make the executive a more educated consumer of training. A lot of money is wasted by putting the wrong person in the wrong training program that's delivered in the wrong way and at the wrong time in the person's career.

Summary

Sending an individual through a training program is seldom enough to close an important management development gap, but training can contribute significantly to closing that gap. Training must be combined with opportunities for on-the-job applications of the knowledge, skills, or behavior taught in the training, and it must be reinforced by coaching and appropriate feedback before, during, and after the application. Properly chosen training—delivered in a classroom, over the Web, or one-to-one— can materially speed learning in many situations. Why have managers waste their time trying to figure out how to do something correctly? Helping them learn the required knowledge or behavior and letting them spend their valuable time practicing and having success is much more effective. Unfortunately, most training offered to managers and executives is a waste of their time and the company's money. It doesn't build the knowledge, skills, and behavior required or spends an inordinate amount of time doing it. The challenge is for organizations to be educated consumers of training.

Chapter 13

Growth Through Professional Coaching

**PepsiCo, Nortel, Steelcase, AT&T, Quest Diagnostics,
U.S. Postal Service, General Motors, Whirlpool, Mercedes-Benz,
Wal-Mart, BP Amoco, H.J. Heinz, Kellogg's, Staples, Alaskan Airlines
Group, Schering-Plough, Boeing, American Family Insurance, Michelin,
Technical Data, Bank of America, Motorola, Cisco Systems,
Deloitte & Touche, Ernst & Young, ComEd, H&R Block,
American Express, Coca-Cola, Colgate-Palmolive, Vistana,
Pharmacia & Upjohn, and many more!*

* Partial list of organizations that have used executive coaches.

New executives quickly learn that the support systems that once helped them deal with complex and difficult challenges are no longer there to protect them. As they step up to broader, more ambiguous roles, they find that there are simply fewer peers, or even higher-level executives, who have the perspective, skill sets, or time to advise them and act as a sounding board for their ideas.

Often Acceleration Pool members have spent time in competitive situations and know how coaches have helped them, whether it be on the sports field or in other goal-oriented endeavors (e.g., mountain climbing, debate club).

For many pool members, the expression "It's lonely at the top" rings true. They are hungry for a neutral advisor dedicated to understanding their

denotes that information on this topic is available at the *Grow Your Own Leaders* web site (www.ddiworld.com/growyourownleaders).

special challenges—someone who can offer wise advice that enables them to optimize both their performance and career growth.

From this set of dynamics, the concept of the executive coach has been born. As coaches can help athletes reach peak performance—refine their golf swing, improve their time, enhance their conditioning and technique, etc.—it certainly seems sensible that expert coaches should be able to do the same for executive performance. This chapter demystifies the use of coaches, both in the Acceleration Pool arena as well as in other key applications.

What Is an Executive Coach?

The term *executive coach* often is thrown about loosely these days. Executive coaches have been compared not only to athletic coaches, but also to teachers, trainers, mentors, personal psychologists, sounding boards, friends, shadow consultants, trusted confidants, mirrors, consciences, healers, masters, village elders, and even fashion advisors.

In our view a coach is a *catalyst* or *facilitator* of individual development and performance. Effective executive coaches are seen as strategic business partners whose business experience, diagnostic insight, and proactive guidance offer tangible value to leaders. Perceived "value added" and "good chemistry" are keys to successful coaching relationships.

Strong coaches establish credibility and trust in a manner that invites executives to shed their egos long enough to benefit from diagnostic insights, ongoing (accurate) feedback, performance suggestions, and career advice. Sustaining a busy executive's interest and participation in a process that requires ongoing time and emotional energy is no small achievement.

But exactly what do professional executive coaches do?

Executive coaches offer a complex array of services. The diverse range of an executive's need for coaching (e.g., accelerated development or remedial) and his or her career stage (i.e., aspiring, transitional, mid-career, or mature) certainly suggest different coaching approaches. The conceptual model in Figure 13-1 shows the support offered by executive coaches.

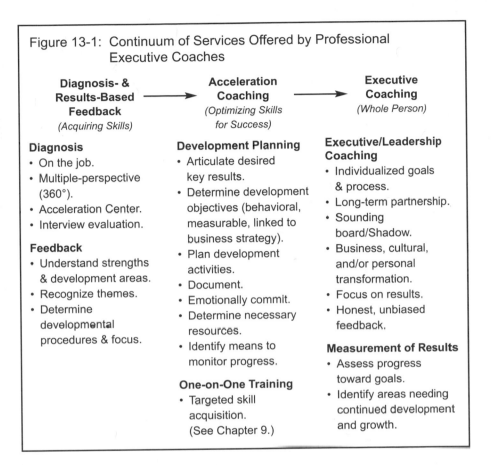

Figure 13-1: Continuum of Services Offered by Professional Executive Coaches

Diagnosis- & Results-Based Feedback *(Acquiring Skills)* →	Acceleration Coaching *(Optimizing Skills for Success)* →	Executive Coaching *(Whole Person)*
Diagnosis • On the job. • Multiple-perspective (360°). • Acceleration Center. • Interview evaluation. **Feedback** • Understand strengths & development areas. • Recognize themes. • Determine developmental procedures & focus.	**Development Planning** • Articulate desired key results. • Determine development objectives (behavioral, measurable, linked to business strategy). • Plan development activities. • Document. • Emotionally commit. • Determine necessary resources. • Identify means to monitor progress. **One-on-One Training** • Targeted skill acquisition. (See Chapter 9.)	**Executive/Leadership Coaching** • Individualized goals & process. • Long-term partnership. • Sounding board/Shadow. • Business, cultural, and/or personal transformation. • Focus on results. • Honest, unbiased feedback. **Measurement of Results** • Assess progress toward goals. • Identify areas needing continued development and growth.

Focused Acceleration Coaching

Generally, when professional executive coaches are used as part of an Acceleration Pool strategy, the nature of support falls to the left and center on the continuum. The coach often plays a role in collecting diagnostic data that complement nomination and/or Acceleration Center data, and then in interpreting and communicating trends or themes in a *feedback* session. Coaches are particularly valuable in helping pool members better understand the unique derailers that might impede their performance and career progress. Coaches help pool members anticipate situations in which they are likely to fall prey to derailing behaviors; they also work with their clients in developing strategies to compensate for these behaviors.

In organizations where Acceleration Pool systems (i.e., assessment, feedback, and development planning) are not working well, professional executive coaches fill the void, particularly in development coaching after assessment feedback. The coach focuses on helping pool members construct concrete development plans and a means to measure and monitor progress. The number of acceleration coaching contacts varies but typically ranges from one to three focused interactions. Ideally, the coaching involves some degree of ongoing contact intended to help pool members stay on track with their development. In cases where organizations have well-run Acceleration Pools that incorporate accurate diagnosis and feedback and have (at least some) internal managers and mentors who are effectively doing their jobs, the most common form of coaching offered to Acceleration Pool members is accelerated coaching around one or more competencies or derailers. The coach might be solicited if the pool member or the Executive Resource Board feels a catalyst or a facilitator is needed to speed along development. The number of coaching sessions depends on the number and complexity of development targets. Commonly, the coach and pool member meet once a month for the first six months.

Broader Executive Coaching

Beyond the straightforward context of speeding pool member development, executive coaches also can be deployed to address more complex or deeply entrenched executive performance challenges. We would classify these more broadly focused relationships (described at the right end of the continuum) as classic executive coaching. These relationships often are more enduring and allow support of a "whole-life" development game plan. Support is tailored to clients' unique needs and motivations. As a result, coaching might target a wide spectrum of challenges, including professional and personal stress, strategic thinking, personal wellness, financial management, or avoiding political land mines within the organization. Executive coaches who are engaged in these types of long-term relationships make themselves accessible both on an as-needed and regularly scheduled basis (e.g., monthly, quarterly).

Executive coaches might also be employed for intense, short-term interventions over two or three sessions. For example, a coach might be brought in to help an executive prepare for and adapt to an upcoming international assignment or to overcome a relationship barrier with a key partner. As the nature of support becomes increasingly tailored at the right end of the continuum, interventions often require significantly more sophistication and skill from coaches.

Is Coaching Just a Passing Fad?

Unquestionably, executive coaching is very trendy right now. The benefit of such coaching has been heralded in the *Wall Street Journal, New York Times, Washington Post, Business Week, Fortune, Inc., Harvard Business Review,* and popular HR journals such as *Training*. A plethora of consulting firms and independent consultants are marketing executive coaching services.

Growth of this executive coaching "industry" has led to hard questions about many aspects of coaching practices, including training and ethical standards, effectiveness research, and best practices. Many concerns about the impact of coaching remain unanswered, as popularity of executive coaching has grown largely through anecdotal legend, word of mouth, and the trumpeting of success stories in the business media. Although the jury is still out, it is hard to refute executives who report transformational experiences because of the support of wise, objective coaches whose judgment they trust.

Besides the direct benefits to the individuals involved, there are other reasons for using coaches. In some organizations receiving a coach connotes status and a visible statement of the company's willingness to assume an individualized stake in an executive's future success. In other companies executive coaches have become a new rite of passage and, like high-profile university or in-house programs, an envied message about perceived value. As a result, some organizations view investment in coaching as a key facet of a retention strategy for highly valued executives.

Why Choose Executive Coaching?

Although we believe that the coaching trend is more than a fad, we also know that paybacks are not assured. If, in fact, coaching was a panacea for all executive development challenges, there would be a run on coaching, and other options, such as learning events, networking, and developmental assessments and feedback, would have less appeal. The increasing popularity of all these options reflects the view of most organizations— that coaching is only one development alternative, but one that must be applied for the right reasons. Coaching is an expensive, time- and labor-intensive process—it is judicious to employ coaches when they offer an optimal acceleration alternative for a specific individual.

A few organizations make a blanket decision to offer all Acceleration Pool members an executive coach. Most organizations use coaches on a selective basis, when they feel the return on investment from a coach will make most sense. There are three key situations in which a coach will add significant value:

- Coaching for career or role transitions.

- Coaching to address a specific challenge or problem.

- Coaching to avoid problem areas.

Coaching for Career or Role Transitions

- **Key career transitions.** In our view supporting executives through their career crossroads is an area in which coaches have significant value. Key transition targets, such as the executive making an important mid-career move or the seasoned executive wanting to leave a legacy of knowledge, are fertile areas for coaching. The major benefit a coach offers during these transitional phases is in helping executives pause, take stock of the bridge they are attempting to cross, and figure out how to proceed, given their skills, interests, and available time.

  A professional coach also can pull the mid-career executive out of "autopilot" by helping the person revisit professional goals, regain focus, shed bad habits, and rededicate efforts. Such "back-on-track," remedial coaching can rejuvenate floundering executives who need to regain perspective and establish priorities.

- **On-boarding.** Assimilating executives into new assignments (internal promotions or external hires) is one of the most powerful applications of coaching. Individuals at different points on their executive career paths face very different issues—they also present unique coaching challenges. For example, coaches will offer special value to, and perhaps even "save" the credibility of, novice executives immersed in environments that require quick assimilation or perceived sure-footedness. Newcomers might well learn the ropes in their own good time; however, without the help of a coach, they might be too late to gain the respect of an organization that is closely watching their early performance. This is particularly true if the executive's predecessor was highly respected. Coaches can also play a significant role in addressing culture assimilation for more-seasoned executives.

  Coaches reduce a person's ramp-up time. Support might include collecting data about the new environment (including key business and relationship dynamics) through interviews, team observations, and targeted diagnosis of the individual relative to the new team's needs and expectations.

Figure 13-2 outlines examples of common career transitions and development challenges experienced by executives at each juncture.

Figure 13-2: Common Career Transitions and Development Challenges Facing Executives

	Aspiring/Novice (1–2 yrs.)	Transitional (3–4 yrs.)	Tenured (5+ yrs.)
Key Transitions	• Unfamiliar responsibilities. • Proving self.	• Developing new directions. • Handling external pressures. • Focus.	• High stakes. • Leaving legacy. • Optimizing potential. • Avoiding intolerance.
Challenges/ Opportunities	• Tolerance for ambiguity. • Dealing with wider range of people. • Team challenges. • Seeing things from a broader point of view. • Anticipating own impact. • Accountability with less control. • Coping with change. • Executing strategy.	• Increased scope. • Increased visibility. • Managing business diversity. • Job overload. • Influencing without authority. • Adverse business conditions. • Facilitating and/or embracing change. • "Whole-life" balance. • Shaping strategy.	• Creating change. • Maintaining enterprise perspective. • Modeling a learning culture. • Adverse business conditions. • Breaking out of a rut, avoiding obsolescence. • Creating long-term strategy & vision.
Common Coaching Focus	• Acceleration. • Skill focused.	• Acceleration. • Transformational (i.e., whole person). • Remedial.	• Transformational. • Remedial. • Legacy.

Coaching to Address a Specific Challenge or Problem

- **Overcoming interpersonal/relationship issues.** This is the classic coaching scenario—reshape an otherwise promising executive who is perceived as abrasive, lacking social polish, or politically incorrect. Professional coaches often must wield a "velvet hammer" to get through to executives who will dramatically enhance their likelihood of success if they can improve specific relationship skills. Coaches often do this by observing or shadowing executives to identify problems and then offering alternative behavioral strategies. This task is especially challenging with executives who are poor listeners, argumentative, or socially obtuse (i.e., they don't recognize how their actions affect others).

• **Building a specific skill or competency.** Many coaching interventions have one objective: facilitate the development of a targeted skill or competency. This is a very common application of coaching for Acceleration Pool members, particularly when there is a dearth of internal models. For example, for a pool member who has a development need in strategic thinking and financial acumen, a coach might bolster the person through his or her first business-planning cycle. A coach might also be employed to address professional impact or presentation skills with individuals who need more polish and presence.

• **Diversity issues.** In organizations having significant obstacles to the progress of target populations (i.e., women, minorities), coaches can serve as advisors or even role models for members of these groups who might feel isolated in a homogeneous executive culture (i.e., white male). Coaches provide a haven for open expression and offer a balanced perspective on real versus perceived obstacles. Consider this case study:

> "Jennifer" always questioned why she hadn't yet been asked to sit on F&M's global HR council. Was the general feedback about her need to build stronger business acumen and executive demeanor fair, or had she simply hit the classic female "glass ceiling"? No one had offered specific ideas for her to make progress in her so-called deficit areas. Looking just at the predominantly male HR council, Jennifer began to believe her gender was a significant obstacle to advancement. In fact, her frustration was building to the point where she considered leaving the organization.
>
> F&M's operating committee knew that their organization was not an easy place for women and minorities to work, and they were committed to change. Jennifer, along with other targeted players, was assigned an executive coach. As Jennifer shared her perceptions, her coach acknowledged the real challenge that

women faced in establishing credibility at F&M and cited several specific anecdotes as examples of unfair treatment. Nevertheless, the coach also encouraged Jennifer to get specific feedback from her colleagues. With her coach's help Jennifer fashioned a set of interview questions. She then asked her coach to interview several colleagues about targeted areas of concern.

The interviews confirmed previous feedback and also offered Jennifer specific behavioral examples of her development needs. Her coach helped Jennifer accept the feedback as relevant and made some simple suggestions as to how she might be seen as more credible in key strategic discussions. For example, feedback suggested that Jennifer's expression of concerns would offer more value if she coupled her "issues" with recommended alternative courses of action. Jennifer worked hard to act on her feedback and the more balanced perspective she gained on her development areas. As a result, she was pleased, although not surprised, when she was finally invited to join the global council.

- **Executives facing team issues.** Targeted interventions might partner a coach with an executive to address challenges that are significantly diminishing his or her team's effectiveness. A coach can help the executive to recognize the root cause of rifts or conflicts, respond appropriately to a crisis in leadership confidence, or better empower the team to address its own challenges.

- **Reluctance to accept feedback.** Coaches offer neutrality and the opportunity for candid, direct feedback to executives who otherwise might not want to hear the message. For example, a coach respected at senior levels might offer "outsider" insights that would carry more perceived credibility than the same message delivered by an insider. This is particularly true when there is a lack of trust within the management ranks, when there are no dependable observers who can provide specific behavior examples, or when an individual's history of personal resistance has limited meaningful feedback.

Helping a COO Cope with Pressure

DDI contracted with a major agricultural organization to provide services in support of a board-mandated succession management initiative. More than 70 senior executives and the COO participated in an Acceleration Center and executive coaching process. Each participant worked with a DDI executive coach to identify developmental priorities and plan developmental actions. In the process of working with the group, we uncovered numerous organizational trends. For example, many executives—including the COO who, for all intents and purposes, served as the CEO—showed development needs in the competency *Building Trust.* During feedback sessions many participants complained that a culture of fear and backbiting had permeated senior management. While they acknowledged that their development needs were valid, they reported that change was especially difficult in the current environment. The COO was repeatedly identified as perhaps the primary offender in this area, having a reputation for embarrassing executives during meetings and ranting publicly about leadership failures. The COO's frequent outbursts and impatient, aggressive style had begun to cause many other executives to mimic many of the same tactics.

In coaching sessions with the COO, these issues were addressed candidly. The DDI coach linked behavioral examples from the Acceleration Center to trends occurring in the work environment (e.g., low trust) and confronted the COO with the possibility that he might be damaging the culture. Through several honest and, at times, heated conversations, the COO began to acknowledge his vulnerabilities and disclose his motivations. It became clear that the COO was desperately concerned about the near-term health of the organization and felt that motivation through anger and urgency was his only recourse. The coach and the COO explored the impact of these actions and contrasted the likely outcomes of alternative approaches.

The COO soon began to realize the negative effect his actions were having on the company and reflected deeply on the issues. He even cancelled a day's meetings after one especially productive coaching session so he could take time to think about what had been discussed. Since then, the COO has begun to work on his style, and reports from other company executives have confirmed that change is taking place. As of the writing of this book, at least six executives have reported to DDI that their participation in the assessment and coaching process, along with the COO's evidence of change, have led them to reverse their intentions to leave the organization.

Coaching to Avoid Problem Areas

• **Avoiding derailment.** Using a coach to chaperone executives around interpersonal blind spots (as we just described) can help Acceleration Pool members steer clear of derailers that might otherwise interrupt a successful executive career. Navigational assistance is often needed because, as previously mentioned, most executive derailers represent too much of a good thing: Confidence turns to arrogance, conscientiousness and dependability evolve into rigidity/risk aversion, and assertiveness manifests itself as defensiveness or being argumentative (see Chapter 6). Thus, executives often are derailed by the same behaviors that drove them to success in lower leadership roles (e.g., operational excellence turns into operational focus when it should be strategic focus).

Coaching to avoid problem areas also includes helping executives to get "unstuck" or to break seemingly incorrigible bad habits. Coaches often are brought in to offer a mirror to talented executives to help them recognize when their overreliance on familiar behavior patterns is affecting performance and perceived organizational credibility. For example:

> "Scott," a popular plant manager, was known for running a very tight ship on the manufacturing floor. His personal warmth softened the results-oriented, command-and-control style he had learned in the Navy. Somehow, this mix resulted in a style that was highly effective with plant associates. However, Scott's directive, albeit friendly, approach became a liability after he was promoted to director of quality assurance. Success in his new job depended on the power of persuasion and influence rather than formal authority, and Scott didn't recognize the changes he needed to make in his managerial style. His executive coach offered Scott candid feedback on internal stakeholders' perceptions that he operated with too much "tell" and not enough listening. The coach also laid out specific examples of alternative approaches that he could use to sell his ideas. After reflecting on the coach's feedback, Scott recognized himself in the coach's observations. With continued coaching and ongoing feedback, Scott made behavioral changes that dramatically improved his effectiveness.

- **Highly political, competitive, or high-pressure cultures.** The more intricate the organizational culture, the more likely individuals will yearn for help to navigate it. Seasoned coaches offer their charges objective suggestions for dealing with competing agendas and bolster the confidence of executives who must overcome tendencies toward learned helplessness. Professional coaches also can provide a "mirror" to help executives understand how their actions are being perceived, thereby helping them avoid potentially fatal career mistakes.

Factors That Increase the Likelihood That Coaching Will Work

Desire to Change (Be Coached)

We have seen executive coaches assigned to individuals who have no interest or intention of developing themselves. Individuals who do not feel the need or see the value of personal development will obviously be far less likely to show improvement. However, personal resistance to coaching should not be considered the "kiss of death" because this resistance can be overcome in many cases (see Sponsorship, Accurate Diagnosis of Development Needs and Business [Strategic] Linkages in this section).

This issue also speaks to a common question: Should coaches be *assigned to* or *chosen by* the Acceleration Pool member? To answer this question, we must consider the purpose of the coaching engagement. Pool members who need to build specific skills (e.g., presentation skills) might be more willing to accept an assigned coach who has a proven track record in other parts of the organization; however, broader objectives, such as managing a major job transition or restoring a reputation after a failure, might require a closer look at the personality match between coach and pool member. In these cases the pool member's involvement in choosing the coach increases the likelihood of long-term success.

Sponsorship

The desire to develop a pool member might become irrelevant if there is no sponsorship of the changes to be made. We have seen many coaching engagements fail because they were conducted "in a vacuum." Executive coaches are sometimes deployed as surrogate managers who are expected to turn around performance problems that managers themselves have been unable to correct. These approaches rarely work because most development strategies require the involvement and input from the individual's manager. A triumvirate, consisting of the individual, coach, and manager all working together to support a development strategy, is required if performance turnarounds are expected.

Accurate Diagnosis of Development Needs

As we outlined in Chapter 7, Diagnosing Strengths and Development Needs, knowing *what to develop* is essential before trying to develop it. A solid coaching relationship begins with reliable data about the individual's development needs. It also bears mentioning that the individual's acceptance of that diagnosis is critical to success. Coaching relationships often begin with both parties reaching agreement on development priorities. Once these priorities are established and agreed upon, execution of the development strategy can begin. The usual high rate of acceptance of feedback based on Acceleration Center findings is one of the main arguments for coupling Acceleration Centers and professional coaching.

Clear Plan with Clear Objectives

Chapter 8 outlined a developmental strategy based on the importance of crafting a specific development plan with clear measures of progress and success. No coaching engagement should be launched without a clear notion of the expected outcomes.

Business (Strategic) Linkages

Helping individuals appreciate the business impact of their personal development often requires an experienced coach and the input of key internal stakeholders (e.g., the individual's manager). Linking personal development to business strategies also can help persuade "standpat" executives to rethink the value of development. Again, collaboration between the executive coach and the individual's manager is essential to achieve maximum impact.

What Is the Profile of an Effective Executive Coach?

In our experience there is no single ideal profile for an effective *executive coach*. Instead, it depends on the desired outcome of the coaching assignment and the personal characteristics of the person being coached. Chemistry with target executives will be driven by the coach's total package, namely the skills, business experience, and personality mix he or she has to offer.

More seasoned executives and executives with complex needs, such as imminent derailment, have a greater need for perceived compatibility with coaches whose experience, sophistication of skills, and style are seen as credible. Acceleration Pool members tend to be more open-minded about who the coach is, as long as he or she helps to jump-start development through value-added support in feedback and development planning.

From a practical standpoint someone in the organization needs to play the role of "matchmaker" as well as financial sponsor for executive coaching relationships. Generally, the Human Resource department will assume responsibility for researching and recommending various coaching options to internal clients. However, depending on the reason for using the executive coach, the pool member's manager or mentor might be involved in defining the "specifications" for the coach, if not actually selecting the person. Because interpersonal chemistry often is difficult to predict, corporate matchmakers need to make the best possible recommendation, given what they know about the pool member's development needs, experience, and personal style.

What to Look For

Some consulting organizations strongly believe that all coaches should be licensed psychologists. Our experience is just the opposite; we believe that—as with too much of many good things—using too many psychologists can have a downside. (Note that all three authors of this book are psychologists!) We have found that diversity in background across coaches brings richer matches to client engagements. DDI has had coaches who arrived at their calling with an amazing array of backgrounds: former CEOs and other senior executives (banking industry, high tech), psychologists (industrial/organizational, clinical, and social), social workers, former university professors, elementary school teachers, grant development officers, former plant managers, retired naval officers, and ex-police chiefs.

There is also debate over whether coaches should come from within or outside the organization. This should really be a secondary consideration— the quality of the relationship and the coach's skills need to be the primary concerns. Organizations often choose external coaches because of perceived confidentiality or trust issues, time constraints, limitations on internal coach's skills, or questions regarding the executives' need to receive an external perspective. In some organizations external advisors might enjoy more credibility than their internal counterparts, simply by virtue of being outsiders. This is a source of frustration to many capable, internal HR professionals, but it is a reality. Fairly or unfairly, external coaches might be viewed as untainted by bias and armed with a broader real-world perspective than insiders. As with any assumption, this view needs to be tested. Notions of superior perspective are dependent on the external coach's skills, depth of insight, and experience.

There are upsides to using internal coaches. Some organizations view internal coaches as a more cost-effective model, as fees charged by external coaches often range between $1,500 to $5,000 per day. Obviously, internal coaches are not free, but neither are they an out-of-pocket expense. Internal coaches also know more about the organization, industry, and the people with whom the executive will be interacting.

As you can see, deciding on whether to use internal or external executive coaches often requires a series of trade-off decisions. It is not necessary for an organization to use either all of one or the other—a mixed model is very workable.

On one point there is consensus—an effective executive coach is seen as a "strategic value creator." In other words, the coach instills in clients a feeling that they have improved because of their relationship with the coach.

Following are additional observations on characteristics of executive coaches who make an impact. Obviously, a coach who has the full repertoire listed below would be suited for the most sophisticated of coaching engagements; many coaches can be effective with a relevant subset of these characteristics.

- **Credibility.** Credibility is earned through demonstration of extensive business or life experience. The coach projects credibility and can be seen as offering a strategic, high-level perspective as well as being able to directly and personally (i.e., not theoretically) relate to the client's world. Being able to "walk in the shoes" of the client is key. Confidence builds as the coach shows the ability to go "toe to toe" with clients, sharing personal stories and anecdotes.

- **Business acumen.** Coaches who clearly understand the business challenges, priorities, and market drivers that affect their clients make good strategic partners. They also must recognize their limitations in this area.

- **Political savvy.** Shrewd coaches offer a degree of protective "radar" to busy executives, offering observations, insight, and guidance on navigating political terrain. Their impact in this domain is directly related to their own natural acumen for recognizing political land mines and their skillful ability to offer survival advice.

- **Contemporary point of view.** Seasoned executives fear becoming obsolete—yesterday's style leader. To avoid their own obsolescence, coaches who stay ahead of current leadership paradigms—almost offering a futurist perspective on tomorrow's challenges—are highly valued. Reliance on a tried-and-true bag of tricks can quickly render coaches obsolete.

- **Emotional intelligence.** Strong coaches tend to be personally introspective, which enables them to accurately read individual motivation and organizational dynamics, even from a distance. They also model their interpersonal perception through thinking out loud. Their approach helps clients build better "lenses" for interpreting behavior around them.

- **Tough love.** Coaches often are asked to deliver tough messages and to ensure ongoing focus on addressing remedial issues. This role requires a delicate balance of extreme candor with an understanding of how to work with different individuals and their tender egos. Remember that most executives are accustomed to hearing primarily positive feedback about their achievements. Effective coaches understand the best way to get their developmental feedback across without the client shutting down.

- **Chemistry and challenge.** Executives will return to coaches with whom they feel a personal connection on an emotional, intellectual, or social level. Obviously, few formulas adequately predict chemistry; coaches build bonds in many different ways. Executives tend to sustain attention to coaches they find personally stimulating, challenging, or otherwise attractive. These are likely to be individuals with a broad range of interests (or at least similar interests to their own) and a clear abundance of rich life experience. Other traits that might lead to long-term matches include respected intellect, complementary skills (i.e., the coach fills the executive's "gaps"), or technical prowess.

- **Creativity.** Executives rarely apply the same creativity to fulfilling personal development needs as they do with their business. Creative coaches can spark thinking outside typical executive self-development paradigms. Such coaches might offer a different "angle" on professional or personal growth, particularly relative to integrating self-development directly into meeting business objectives, work-life balance strategies, and future career directions.

Coaching Strategies and Techniques

Executive coaches use a range of process models to support interventions. At the simplest level of analysis, most coaches employ some form of diagnosis-prescription model. Also popular are coach-driven "tryout assignments" around events that naturally occur in the executive's work life. These assignments give executives a chance to "try on" new behaviors.

Coaches might work closely with their clients' managers, both to maintain an ongoing dialog about progress and to collaboratively identify development opportunities and internal support resources. Obviously, coach and client need to establish a mutual understanding about what can be shared and what needs to remain confidential.

Some coaching practices include:

- **Journalizing/Diaries.** Used for both self-insights and coach's insights regarding behavioral patterns and trends.

- **Shadowing.** Coaches might spend time at various points observing executives in their own environment, across a variety of situations and challenges.

- **Brokering other development options.** Coaches might research best-fit educational programs or seminars or facilitate networking opportunities and other strategies tailored to their clients' needs.

- **Regularly scheduled (e.g., quarterly, monthly) progress checks.** Coaches help executives stay focused on their goals through mutually agreed-upon follow-up calls and discussions. Coaches also are typically on call for real-time coaching, as the need arises.

- **Progress measurement.** Follow-up assessments (e.g., multiple-perspective [360°] surveys), objective results, and interviews with peers, superiors, or partners are common milestone measurement strategies.

A Word About the Distinction Between Therapy and Coaching . . .

Most professionals engaged in coaching are careful to differentiate the consulting support they offer from clinically focused "therapy." Executive coaches generally focus their support toward reasonably well adjusted individuals facing key leadership challenges in a business setting. Conversely, clinical interventions often address deeper underlying issues that result in emotional or behavioral dysfunction across many aspects of life.

Although this distinction is well endorsed, navigating the difference between potentially derailing interpersonal dysfunction and more deep-rooted pathologies can be tricky. Coaches must be diligent in recognizing when an executive's coping or relationship issues are severe enough to indicate therapeutic referral. Two emergent trends point to a need for diligence in this area. First, there is an increasing attraction for executives who are juggling work-life balance issues to coaches and/or "epiphany experiences" that offer "whole-life" development. Executives who have vague boundaries between their personal and work lives want, and deserve, experiences that add holistic value to their roles across professional, family, and friendship realms. Even so, it is important that the Executive Resource Board's interventions remain focused on "functional" behavior versus any issues associated with deeply rooted psychopathology.

Second, some executive coaches use a more clinical style than we might recommend. This means that coaches spend an inordinate amount of time discussing feelings, motivation, personality, or values. While these discussions can spark "ah-ha" reactions in their clients, they add little enduring value until clear linkages are articulated to behavior and business strategy. Some coaches are outstanding at such behavioral integration; they have powerful impact because their observations are seen as uncanny and their behavioral suggestions highly relevant. Other coaches are not as sophisticated; they might suffer from poor business acumen or poor agility in interpreting data. As a result, they miss opportunities to integrate insights with strategic business contexts.

The slide toward therapy and away from coaching has been amplified by the impact of managed health care, which has led some mental health providers (including clinical psychologists and social workers) to reinvent themselves as *executive coaches.* As educated consumers, organizations should be wary of coaches who might be tempted to take an overly therapeutic approach. Before starting their executive coaching relationship, Acceleration Pool members should be oriented (likely by the HR group). Orientation should reinforce the important distinctions between coaching and therapy and remind pool members that the most successful, business-relevant strategy is to focus on their behavior.

The Receiver's Role: How to Get the Most out of a Coach

Finding the right coach is only half of the equation. Obviously, the caliber of the coaching relationship will be directly proportional to the effort that recipients put into it. Early in the relationship, most coaches will facilitate development of a coaching "contract" that clarifies mutual expectations, desired outcomes, and accountabilities for each party. Advice to executives entering a coaching relationship is fairly basic but deceptively important. Here are some tips for getting the most out of an executive coach:

- Be willing to maintain openness and vulnerability—trust the coach.

- Tell your coach what you need. Coaches are not mind readers. Are you looking for a catharsis? Candor? Positive feedback? Keep this dialog open—your needs will shift as you grow and change.

- Help your coach understand your motivational hot buttons—how you learn best, when you need a kick-start, your bad habits, and any chronic personal challenges.

- Think about professional goals and challenges in relation to a whole-life approach or patterns that have created issues. Extrapolate your learning to all elements of your life.

- Share ongoing perceptions about how the overall process is going and where adjustments need to be made. Your coach wants performance coaching as well.

Summary

In this section of the book, Strategies for Accelerating Development, we have discussed four sets of tools available to organizations in the development of Acceleration Pool members (assignments, short-term experiences, training, and professional coaching). Reliance on any one set of tools, such as assignments, or one tool, such as an action learning program, will not in itself bring about the accelerated development needed.

The major challenge facing pool members and their organization is how to use these tools creatively. We have seen thousands of development plans created by individuals for themselves or by senior management for them. Overall, these plans have been extremely uncreative. In our experience this lack of creativity is the reason that most development plans are never implemented and, if they are, that few lead to the expected level of development. In Chapter 8 we discussed how pool members can construct creative development plans using the Development Action Form. In the next two chapters, we'll cover the roles and responsibilities of the pool members' manager and mentor and the Executive Resource Board, which has control of some key development tools, such as attendance at special training/development events, professional coaches, and most assignments.

SECTION V

ENSURING ACCELERATION POOL SUCCESS
KEY PROCESSES, ROLES/ACCOUNTABILITIES, MEETINGS, AND OTHER MECHANICS

Our last section focuses on the processes and logistics associated with successful and enduring implementation of Acceleration Pools. The important development-facilitator roles of supervisors and mentors are described in Chapter 14. Chapter 15 discusses tactics to maximize the effectiveness of talent review discussions (where placement and development decisions are made), and Chapter 16 explores in detail the important role of the CEO. Finally, succession management, HR, and consulting practitioners will appreciate Chapter 17's discussion, Getting Started.

Chapter 14

Key Partners: Supporting Growth

"What I have come to learn is that young people are far more capable than we think they are. If you just give them the ball and help them as they run with it, you'll be surprised almost every time."

—Roger Mowen, Sr. Vice President of Marketing, Eastman Chemical

Throughout our book we have referred to three individuals who play the key roles in the day-to-day growth of Acceleration Pool members: the pool member, the manager to whom the pool member reports, and the pool member's mentor. In this chapter we explore their roles and responsibilities further and suggest orientation, training, and reinforcement techniques necessary to make the partnership work.

Acceleration Pool Members Manage Their Own Destiny

We strongly believe that Acceleration Pool members must understand that they carry the greatest responsibility for their development. They must make things happen. They must make sure to complete Development Action Forms for each assignment and to execute their development plans. If they are not getting the coaching and job support they need, they must seek it out. If a relationship with a mentor isn't working, the pool member must try to remedy the situation or get another mentor. It is very difficult

 denotes that information on this topic is available at the *Grow Your Own Leaders* web site (www.ddiworld.com/growyourownleaders).

to develop the required job challenges, organizational knowledge, derailers, or competencies without help from others. Recognizing the pressures on the people who will be supporting them, pool members must use their initiative and creativity to find ways to get the support they need.

It is easy to see how pool members might be confused by the roles of the people who will be helping in their development. That's why it is important to establish role clarity from the beginning—either as part of an orientation session for new pool members or at the first meeting with their manager and mentor to discuss development planning.

Immediate Managers Provide Guidance, Resources, and Encouragement

The Acceleration Pool member's immediate manager (i.e., supervisor) offers task-oriented advice about how to achieve job success and development goals at the same time and offers tangible support when necessary. Some of the tasks the immediate manager must accomplish are described below. The responsibilities are best-practice recommendations, not absolutes. In some organizations an assigned mentor or second-level manager might assume some of the tasks, particularly if the manager has significant skill gaps, is a poor coach, or is not motivated to support the pool member.

- **Help pool members to set clear, realistic, and measurable performance objectives for assignments.** Acceleration Pool members must know what they are expected to accomplish in their assignment and how success will be measured. The organization's performance management system should provide the basis for this discussion.

- **Encourage pool members to manage their own development.** Although pool members come to the direct manager with a completed Development Priority List showing areas they need to work on, this is only the first step. The priorities must be adapted to the current job situation, and this is where most people need help. Pool members new to an assignment might not know what opportunities are available. In addition, people new to the Acceleration Pool might need help completing Development Action Forms for each development target. Pool members appreciate suggestions from the manager, but effective leaders don't tell them what they need to do. Instead, they encourage members to set their own development goals and implementation plans. This approach works well because people who psychologically own their development plans are much more likely to follow through on implementing them.

- **Encourage pool members to set up an initial development-planning meeting with the manager and mentor to discuss development goals and plans.** The pool member should lead the meeting, using the completed Development Action Form as a guide for discussing each development objective. The manager should suggest additional development goals that might be targeted.

- **Work with Acceleration Pool members to conduct ongoing measurements of progress as they apply the new skills or knowledge.** This often is a challenge for pool members, and they often need help (e.g., giving them opportunities for ongoing competency assessment using multiple-perspective [360°] instruments or helping them set up a system to measure internal and external customer satisfaction).

- **Offer implementation assistance.** Given the high expectations of everyone involved, it is important that neither internal politics nor scarcity of resources delays pool members' development actions. Often, managers must pave the way for the pool members to carry out their application plans. For example, a manager might need to see to it that the organization's laboratory gives priority to the samples needed by a task force investigating a new product, or ensure that support departments recognize the criticality of a new device that is under development. Clearing the way for implementation does not mean doing the job for pool members—it simply means making sure they get to see the right people (e.g., the president) and have the necessary resources. Each assignment needs to be a test for the pool member—but it needs to be a *fair* test.

- **Coach pool members so they will be successful.** Coaching involves giving advice or guidance. Every manager knows what coaching is, but many aren't very good at it. Too many feel that the best time to coach people is after they've failed—at which point, the manager explains what a person should have done. While this is helpful, the best coaching occurs before an event, enabling the individual to apply the advice and learn from success. This builds confidence and speeds learning.

A good coach asks how the person intends to handle an issue and then asks questions about aspects of the pool member's plan that might be problematic. By asking open-ended questions, the manager helps the person anticipate possible barriers or land mines. An effective coach enables the individual to solve problems independently, letting ownership of the solution remain with the pool member—which is exactly where it needs to be. Coaching is especially important in helping pool members develop interpersonal skills (e.g., to handle someone who is disrupting a team or who is not pulling his or her weight). In such cases it often is appropriate for the manager to suggest role-playing the situation before it occurs. After the role-play exercise, the manager provides feedback.

Coaching does not mean that the manager always assumes he or she is right. In matters of judgment, it often is best to let a person learn from trying out ideas. After all, many times the individual will be right.

Some managers make the mistake of trying to micromanage or provide all the answers under the guise of coaching. This often happens when the pool member is about to take on a stretch assignment and the manager isn't sure the person has enough training or experience. Solving problems for a pool member or reclaiming assigned responsibilities deflates the person and saps the energy that comes from psychologically owning a project. The proper technique is to "offer help without removing responsibility for action"—one of the key principles of empowerment (Byham, 1988/1991). Simply put, the coach *does not* step in and take over for the pool member; instead, the coach *helps* the person consider alternatives and *encourages* him or her to take the appropriate action.

Because pool members move through jobs relatively rapidly, an important factor in their success is their ability to quickly size up a new opportunity and jump into action. They must quickly build relationships, seek information, make decisions, and communicate directions. The ability of pool members to succeed in job transition can be predicted by data generated through an Acceleration Center. Individuals who are relatively more extraverted and open to new experiences and who have a positive disposition will generally find making transitions easier. Knowing in advance that a pool member might have problems quickly feeling at home in a new position can guide a manager's efforts in getting that person off to a good start.

- **Reinforce the efforts of Acceleration Pool members.** No matter how smart, well educated, or old people are, positive reinforcement is still important to them. Many managers assume that because a pool member seems confident—perhaps justifiably so, considering the person's background and previous successes—no reinforcement is needed. Indeed, some managers seem to feel that such a person is too cocky and that reinforcement will only make him or her more insufferable. But the truth is that a pat on the back, a word of encouragement, and recognition of progress are vital to the success of *all* individuals, no matter who they are. Acceleration Pool members set high standards for themselves—and that makes it all the more important that they be recognized when they are progressing toward their goals and encouraged when they are falling behind.

This is especially true when an Acceleration Pool member is running into trouble. Like all of us, pool members tend to focus on their problems (e.g., a troubled relationship with a specific customer) and forget about all the positive things that they have accomplished (e.g., building strong relationships with other customers). Pool members need to be reminded of their successes even while working on correcting a current problem.

- **Help pool members manage time.** The best development projects are in sync with a pool member's job assignment. Doing well in the project helps the pool member to do well in the job. But, some learning opportunities inevitably will require time away from normal job responsibilities. If the activities are important enough to be development targets, managers need to suggest ways for pool members to prioritize tasks. This will underscore the importance of an assignment or learning opportunity. When developmental assignments are simply added on to existing workloads without explanation or discussion, the pool member might find it difficult to gauge their importance relative to other responsibilities. People usually focus on the areas that are most immediately reinforced, and self-managed learning is not one of them. When managers continually pull their people out of training programs or cancel their attendance the day before the program, they not only cost the organization money by wasting a training slot, they also send a negative message about the importance of learning. Of course, canceling a program is sometimes necessary, but for many managers doing so is driven more by convenience than real necessity.

- **Provide or facilitate feedback.** Ongoing feedback concerning job behavior and decisions is critical to competency and derailer growth. Effective feedback is:

  - Provided as soon after the event as possible.

  - Balanced, covering both what the individual did well and areas for improvement.

– Built around specific examples—what the person said or did.

Immediate managers are usually in the best position to provide feedback. However, as job or committee assignments carry pool members further into working with other managers or clients, it will be important for them to receive feedback from these other sources too. The immediate manager must be ready to assist the pool member in obtaining this valuable performance information.

- **Document the pool member's on-the-job achievements.** The organization's performance management system should be used to document job achievement—or the lack of it. Also, the manager has the responsibility to document achievement of development goals—to the extent the goals were included in the pool member's performance management plan.

In addition to the specific points we've just described, a manager must be sure to use effective leadership behaviors. These include:

- Modeling continuous learning. Managers need to share job-related insights gleaned from past experiences, reading, conferences, or task force participation.

- Assigning responsibilities that become progressively more challenging and giving pool members incrementally higher-profile roles in handling them.

- Providing developmental opportunities through learning experiences, such as the opportunity to attend a convention or be on a committee (see Chapter 12).

- Serving as a sounding board. People often need to talk their ideas through before committing. They need someone who will act as a devil's advocate—challenging and probing for flaws—in a manner that does not diminish or challenge their self-esteem. That keeps the psychological ownership of the idea with the person who conceived it.

Appendix 14-1 provides some insights into transition issues facing pool members that provide an opportunity for ongoing coaching and mentoring.

Training Managers to Facilitate Learning

Very few managers are prepared to provide the development support we've just described. They don't know what they need to do and many times don't have the required skills or confidence. An organization needs to train managers to help them fulfill their important role in nurturing Acceleration Pool members. This task is not as daunting as it might seem—a half-day orientation program can be enough to teach the Acceleration Pool process and answer any of their questions. A three-day behavior-modeling program will provide the necessary coaching and development skills. ☞ If the goal for the organization at large is for all managers to have coaching and development skills, then groups of managers—starting with those who supervise the youngest, least experienced Acceleration Pool members—can be trained each year until the entire organization is covered.

Mentors Provide High-Level Guidance and Track Progress

Mentors are managers with a broad range of organizational knowledge and experience who are willing to help with a pool member's development, career advancement, and personal adjustment to the challenges that come with moving up in the organization (see Appendix 14-1). A mentor is usually not in a direct-line relationship with the Acceleration Pool member and often is at a higher organizational level than the person's immediate manager.

There are two kinds of mentoring relationships: short term and long term. Short-term mentors are more likely to be assigned or matched with pool members as part of the Acceleration Pool process. Long-term mentors tend to evolve informally. These relationships usually emerge from opportunities in which pool members and seasoned leaders cross paths and find mutual chemistry, interests, and opportunities to gain personal growth and insights. While there are clear distinctions between the two, there are also many areas in which the support they offer to pool members overlaps.

Short-Term Mentors

Many successful development programs use short-term mentors, who are typically assigned to a pool member for one to three years. Short-term mentors meet with their charges to help plan development activities and help monitor progress against those plans. They suggest other sources of assistance for pool members. Often, the mentor is a role model of a competency that the pool member needs to develop.

The short-term mentor helps the pool member understand the organization's vision, values, and culture and how those factors relate to what is happening in the organization relative to the obstacles and opportunities facing the individual. People in an Acceleration Pool must understand where the organization is going and the opportunities and obstacles it faces. They need this knowledge to guide decisions they will make in their jobs and about their careers.

Understanding the vision, values, and strategies also helps pool members understand why the target competencies, job challenges, and organizational knowledge required for their development are important. It is not unusual for an organization to simply assume that people understand the significance of such factors, but in reality strategy and other concepts often become distorted as they work their way down through an organization. For example, a company could be furloughing people in one area and hiring in another, and likely, people working in each of those areas might have widely differing views of the organization's direction.

The short-term mentor is also charged with monitoring the relationship of the pool member and his or her immediate manager. If the learning assignment is not working, the mentor can step in and try to remedy the situation. If the situation can't be turned around, the mentor might ask the second-level manager to intervene or suggest that the Executive Resource Board change the person's assignment. Similarly, the mentor often is the person who lets the board know when an executive coach is needed.

We often are asked if relationships between short-term mentors and pool members should be stretched into longer periods. In practice there is no single right answer—it depends on the chemistry between them as well as the direction in which the person's career is moving. In general, however, we believe that companies using a short-term mentoring approach should stick to it. Shifts in mentoring assignments can provide new challenges that can invigorate both the mentor and the pool member. Also, the pool member is exposed to a wider range of insights and contacts within the organization. In addition, if a pool member is moving up rapidly through the organization, it usually makes sense to provide the person with higher-level mentors along the way.

Long-Term Mentors

Long-term mentoring relationships generally evolve informally and can last anywhere from 2 to 10 years or beyond. Long-term mentors do everything that short-term mentors do and more. Typically, higher-level executives will take a liking to certain individuals and take them under their wing. Our experience suggests that the intrinsic motivation of informal, long-term mentors makes them **more** likely to provide career advice, help the pool member network, create opportunities, tout the member's achievements to top management, and offer advice regarding the organization's politics. Long-term mentors also are more likely to help their pool members cope with the personal challenges they encounter by providing long-term support and positive reinforcement, making suggestions for handling company or social situations, and, most of all, being a trusted colleague.

Which Type of Mentor Is Preferable?

So, which is better—the short- or long-term mentoring approach? Because most organizations cannot assume spontaneous relationships will occur (this often is likened to waiting for lightning to strike), we recommend that Acceleration Pool systems start with short-term mentors who rotate every two years. That approach provides a greater degree of flexibility in adjusting mentoring assignments. In some organizations mentoring assignments are random, while other companies take great care to match education, background, goals, interests, and even personality types. They try to come as close as possible to achieving the chemistry associated with a spontaneous mentoring relationship.

Also, having an assigned, short-term mentor does not mean that individuals cannot find an additional mentor on their own—and indeed, there is no reason why a pool member can't have two or more mentors at the same time. Such fortunate individuals are in a good position to cross-check recommendations and get additional assistance. In practice we often find that ambitious pool members are constantly seeking mentors to help them be successful.

In establishing a mentoring system, the issue of whether a mentor should be chosen from the pool member's operating or business unit often crops up. Table 14-1 compares the two approaches.

Table 14-1: The Advantages of Pairing Mentor and Acceleration Pool Members from the Same or Different Business Units	
When They Come from the Same Business Unit . . .	**When They Come from Different Business Units . . .**
The mentor knows more people in the pool member's unit and has a better feel for what's happening in it.	• The mentor knows more people outside the pool member's unit and can thus provide a wider perspective. • The pool member gains greater visibility across the organization. • The mentor can provide access to resources outside the pool member's typical circle.
The mentor can more readily observe the pool member's behavior (e.g., during in-unit presentations) and thereby give more meaningful feedback.	The mentor usually cannot directly observe behavior so must seek examples of behavior before meeting with the pool member.
The mentor might have an existing relationship with the pool member's manager, helping them all to work together as a team.	The pool member might see the mentor as more objective if a conflict arises with the member's immediate manager.
The mentor might have talents in a professional or business area in which the pool member needs to develop.	The pool member's manager might benefit from the exposure to, and building a relationship with, a mentor outside of own business unit.
The mentor can nominate the pool member for assignments within the business unit.	The mentor can nominate the pool member for assignments outside the business unit.

The bottom line is that there is no right or wrong approach; it all depends on the circumstances in question.

The ideal short-term mentor is several levels above the pool member in the organization. However, this often is not possible—sometimes there just aren't enough people higher in the organization to serve as mentors. As a result, many organizations find that the multiple-level separation of mentor and pool member is less feasible as pool members go higher in the organization.

How Many Pool Members per Mentor?

How many pool members can a manager mentor effectively? We strongly believe the magic number is one. Because of the pressures that most mentors experience in their regular jobs, it is very difficult for them to mentor more than one Acceleration Pool member and be effective. We have seen cases in which five to seven pool members have been assigned to a single executive—and in every case the desired mentoring never came about. A few managers can mentor two or even three pool members, but they are very rare.

Such overburdening usually occurs when an organization makes an arbitrary rule about who can be a mentor (e.g., all mentors must be members of the operating committee or another high-level group). There simply are not enough of these people to go around. While top-ranking executives might be ideal, an organization is much better served using people lower in the organization, thereby getting a one-to-one ratio of pool members to mentors.

Many of the common problems that arise in mentoring programs stem from misguided expectations—on both sides. Too many pool members sit back and expect the mentor to do everything in their relationship. If they're lucky, that might happen, but most of the time, it doesn't. Usually, pool members must take the lead in setting up meetings and getting what they want from the relationship. Pool members who take the initiative in making the relationship work report excellent results and few problems. Mentors know their responsibility is important and usually don't mind if a pool member takes the first step in scheduling meetings, etc. As discussed in the previous section, a major step in avoiding misconceptions about the relationships is to have both the mentor and the pool member participate in an orientation session to clarify their roles and agree on how they will confront issues.

When organizations don't have formally appointed mentors, the immediate and second-level managers must assume the mentoring responsibilities.

Mentors Can Help Retain Acceleration Pool Members

There are many reasons that pool members might become frustrated with their immediate manager; yet, they often are unwilling to go over the manager's head and vent their displeasure to higher management. If the pool member has no one to turn to in such situations, the problem grows until he or she seeks a job outside the organization. A mentor is a convenient, trusted, organizationally acceptable ally for an Acceleration Pool member who has a problem. A mentor can evaluate the situation, give advice, and intervene if necessary.

What Acceleration Pool Members Want and Get from Their Mentors

A DDI survey of Acceleration Pool members in a large appliance manufacturing organization found that, in these individuals' experiences, mentors encouraged learning, achievement, and trying new approaches. Pool members valued their mentors as good listeners who kept their confidences. Most of all, the Acceleration Pool members felt that their mentors cared about them and wanted them to succeed.

The survey also found that pool members wanted the mentors to help them meet new colleagues and provide specific feedback regarding their performance in their current job. They wanted their mentors to suggest strategies for specific work challenges and to advise them on dealing with issues unrelated to their work. In short, pool members wanted a wide range of tactical help to make them successful (DDI, 2001).

Mentoring on the Web

As with almost everything else, Internet/intranet and e-mail communications are having a powerful impact on mentoring relationships. Increasing numbers of mentors are interacting with pool members via e-mail—and both sides seem to like it. Using e-mail increases the frequency of contacts and allows immediate responses. Many pool members report that they feel more at ease sending a question via e-mail than asking the same question over the phone. Mentors report that pool members often copy them on job-related correspondence, which helps them to get a better understanding of their pool member's job and development progress. Communicating via the Web is particularly effective if a mentor and pool member are in different time zones or have difficulty in face-to-face meetings.

Group Self-Mentoring

Some organizations are experimenting with the concept of group self-mentoring. This involves having 6 to 20 high-potential individuals self-mentor as a team, with a senior manager acting as a facilitator and coach. The participants bring up personal development issues and share suggested answers, while the senior manager facilitates the meeting process and helps the group find the right answers on its own. The manager's role is not to come up with the answers.

Application of Group Mentoring at Bayer

Bayer USA is experimenting with group mentoring in its Consumer Care Division, in Morristown, New Jersey. Groups of 15 to 16 mid-level professionals and managers meet with a vice president who has volunteered to advise and mentor the group. They peer mentor one another by determining 12 topics of interest to work on throughout a 12-month period. They share experiences, issues, and answers. The group members and the mentor receive training before starting the process.

Ensuring That Help Is Provided

For an Acceleration Pool to succeed, the Executive Resource Board and the HR department must work together to meet a major challenge: getting the immediate manager and the mentor to dedicate the time and energy necessary for success.

One approach is to build the responsibility for developing the pool member into the performance plans of the manager and mentor. If they know that their assigned pool members' progress will be discussed during performance reviews with their manager and that part of their salary increase or bonus is tied to each pool member's success, the mentors and managers are more likely to expend the necessary effort. However, as we've often noted, it is much easier to add a development objective to someone's performance review form than it is to get high-level executives to seriously consider it in appraisal discussions. Still, it does no harm to include such objectives, and doing so serves as a symbol that the organization is serious about succession management.

Another way to put pressure on managers to develop pool members is to include the manager's manager (sometimes called "manager once removed") as part of the team responsible for developing the pool member. The second-level manager can check on the pool member's progress, see that Development Action Forms and other documentation are completed, and make sure that the pool member is getting the planned learning opportunities. The second-level manager can be very effective in ensuring that the Acceleration Pool member's immediate manager does not provide too much help during a stretch assignment or, worse yet, assume responsibility for it. When this happens, the second-level manager must intervene. Also, the second-level manager usually has a broader understanding of the organization's needs. This expanded perspective enables the second-level manager to offset any parochial views held by the immediate leader, who might be reluctant to assign much responsibility to a pool member who will soon be moved to another assignment, or to relinquish a person who is starting to make a significant contribution to the work group.

Some organizations periodically remind managers and mentors of their responsibilities and commitment. This is a tactic often used by HR departments, but it works best if the CEO or COO employs it. Other organizations require those directly involved in a pool member's development to submit reports or attend meetings in which the individual's progress is discussed, or both. This can be an effective tactic, especially if the CEO attends the meetings.

Encouraging managers and mentors to work together as a team and, as such, be responsible for the development of pool members is still another way to engage them more fully in their development tasks. For example, the immediate manager, the mentor, a representative of the HR department, and sometimes even the second-level manager might be formed into a team by senior management. They go through orientation and training together. The HR representative arranges team meetings and makes sure that everyone attends. The net result is that before the planned meetings team members follow through with their responsibilities because they don't want to appear to their fellow executives as if they're not holding up their end of the bargain. Once a year, the team reports to the CEO or the Executive Resource Board on the progress of their assigned pool member.

Another tactic for helping managers and their Acceleration Pool members to take appropriate actions is to remind them—at strategic times—about what they are required to do. Organizations, such as BASF North America,

A Team Approach at PPG

PPG has effectively used a variety of creative strategies to mentoring its high-potential executives. One approach has been to leverage several versions of a mentor "team" concept for the last several rounds of their talent pool process.

One such alternative involved assigning *two* senior mentors to each pool member. This mentor team is charged with working in partnership to support development for the targeted high potential. The mentoring relationship commences once the pool member completes an extensive developmental assessment/feedback process. Generally, both mentors are from outside the individual's own unit or function. Considerable care is taken in matching both mentor partners to each other as well as to the pool member. This strategy was designed to ensure that pool members received sufficient breadth and focus of support as well as exposure outside of their own domains. PPG's approach has resulted in several intended and unintended outcomes. The expected synergy and focus offered by a mentor team generally occur, although there are differences in the sustained quality and consistency of support. The major obstacle has been coordinating meeting schedules. One unanticipated outcome is the opportunity for mentors to develop or enhance peer (i.e., co-mentor) relationships.

In PPG's current cycle, previously identified high potentials (process graduates) are now stepping up to mentor roles. These individuals obviously have special motivation and experience that offers value to new pool members. Further, pool members obviously benefit from healthy diversity in perspective and constructive dialog regarding their development plans. Finally, the mentor partners concept offers an extra witness to the caliber of the development effort, resulting in a heightened sense of accountability for all stakeholders to be fully engaged in the development planning process.

send computer-generated memos to learners and their managers to remind them of their responsibilities before, during, and after training programs. For example, about two weeks before an individual is scheduled to attend a training program, his or her manager receives an e-mail encouraging the manager to work with the person in setting learning and application objectives. More reminders are sent during and after the training.

In trying to focus people's energy on the Acceleration Pool, it's important to maintain perspective. Remember: Managers do see the importance of

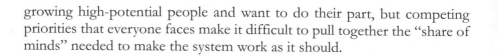

growing high-potential people and want to do their part, but competing priorities that everyone faces make it difficult to pull together the "share of minds" needed to make the system work as it should.

TAP into Acceleration at Bristol-Myers Squibb Company

A relatively expensive but excellent way of encouraging the active participation of the manager and mentor is to involve a professional in the mix. In its Talent Acceleration Program (TAP), Bristol-Myers Squibb assigns each participant an internal Development Guide (an HR professional or psychologist), who serves as an executive coach and as a catalyst for involving the manager and other executives.

These Development Guides are responsible for integrating and delivering feedback on the assessment data, working with participants to create development plans, meeting with them for monthly coaching meetings, and reviewing participants' progress with a senior executive Steering Committee. The coaching has a decidedly strategic focus. More than 25 percent of the time is spent on typical, tactical coaching (e.g., skill-based issues), while the rest of the effort is spent on more strategic coaching (e.g., working with TAP participants to identify appropriate developmental experiences, working with the Steering Committee to make these happen, and working with the participants to ensure that they extract all the nuggets of developmental learning from each experience). By having professional Development Guides assigned to high-potential individuals, Bristol-Myers Squibb is making a major commitment to the development of its people.

Appendix 14-1: Helping Acceleration Pool Members Flourish

A Guide for Managers and Mentors

The acquisition of new, different skills is essential if today's rising stars are to become tomorrow's successful executives. In our current world of brilliant, technically gifted young stars, this equates to telling the smartest kid in the class that he or she needs to study harder. Let's face it—the best and brightest generally know they're good, and a common call to "leadership development" is widely perceived by them as a rite of passage and not a real opportunity to learn important new skills (despite what your pool members might be telling you). Make no mistake—the kinds of egos that flourish among the most senior executives are also generally healthy and growing among budding leaders. These individuals typically have found success already (and in many cases wealth). But what they generally don't realize is that the formula for success is about to change—dramatically.

Ask a professional athlete about the difference between college and the next level, and you'll hear things like, "I never expected it to be this fast," "The competition is so intense—everyone is great," "I have to train harder than ever to be successful," and so on. Ask experienced executives about their first general management-level role, and you'll hear similar remarks. Rarely do the occupants of high posts describe how ready they were to take on their first high-profile role. To the contrary—we routinely hear stories of executives who describe the profound learning (and associated stress) they encountered in their early executive experiences.

Table 14-2 lists some of the transition problems that Acceleration Pool members commonly experience. As appropriate to the job and the individual, these transition problems should be discussed with pool members when they start a new assignment. Also, an effective manager or mentor keeps an eye out for inappropriate reactions to these executive transitions.

Table 14-2: Key Executive Transitions and Likely Reactions

Managers Moving from . . .	to Executive Jobs with . . .	Often Have These Reactions/Outcomes . . .
Single-function management, limited span of influence	Multiple-function management, wide span of influence	• Directive approaches, reluctance to delegate and empower others; difficulty navigating complex internal environments. • Slow to build meaningful internal partnerships.
Controllable environment—more personal influence on group success	Uncontrollable environment—more detachment from day-to-day operations—less able to influence group success through individual action	• Difficulty delegating/empowering teams. • Ego problems—desire to gain personal credit for group accomplishments. • Do-it-yourself solutions in lieu of coaching and developing others.
Limited-scale consequences for leadership failures	Far-reaching consequences associated with leadership failures	• More personal stress. • Driving others to the breaking point. • Withdrawal under pressure.
Basic P&L responsibility	Heavy business judgment responsibility; accountability for shareholder satisfaction with financial performance	• Financial "cramming." • Overemphasis on financial leadership (at the expense of people leadership) due to a personal need to develop financial acumen. • Poor business judgment.

Table 14-2: Key Executive Transitions and Likely Reactions (cont'd)		
Managers Moving from . . .	**to Executive Jobs with . . .**	**Often Have These Reactions/Outcomes . . .**
Tolerant environment that allows derailers to exist without limiting advancement	Highly visible, demanding environment in which derailers are noticed and resented by many and even mimicked by those closest to the leader	• Cultural damage. • Turnover among top talent. • Propagation of derailers throughout the individual's unit. • Executive failure.

Chapter 15

Optimizing Your Talent Review Discussion

*"We do not receive wisdom. We must discover it
from experiences which no one else can have for us
and from which no one else can spare us."*

—Marcel Proust,
French Author & Novelist

The purpose of the Executive Resource Board (which comprises all or a subgroup of senior executives in the organization) is to steer the identification and accelerate the development of the organization's high-potential leaders. How well the board performs these tasks will be a key factor in ensuring the company's leadership bench strength. The Executive Resource Board must maintain an enterprise perspective on the organization's long-term needs and act as a conscience to other stakeholders when short-term pressures get in the way of identifying or developing Acceleration Pool members (e.g., moves are blocked).

The Executive Resource Board has three main functions relative to succession management: 1) to identify people for development; 2) to fill open positions; and 3) to recommend developmental actions (e.g., assignments and training) regarding the future leaders they have identified. Table 15-1 shows these functions for the Acceleration Pool system and for a traditional replacement-planning system.

☞ denotes that information on this topic is available at the *Grow Your Own Leaders* web site (www.ddiworld.com/growyourownleaders).

Table 15-1: Functions of the Executive Resource Board in Two Different Succession Management Systems	
Traditional Replacement-Planning System	**Acceleration Pool System**
• Identify backups for key positions. • Review job performance of backups and take appropriate actions. • Fill current and anticipated open positions.	• Identify individuals for the Acceleration Pool. • Review performance of Acceleration Pool members (on the job and in terms of their development) and take appropriate actions. • Fill current and anticipated open positions.

Breaking Tradition: The Acceleration Pool System

At first glance the board's responsibilities in an Acceleration Pool system seem very similar to those in a traditional replacement-planning system, but in reality there are three large differences:

1. **Traditional replacement-planning systems identified people for specific positions.** The output of the identification process in a replacement-planning system was a room full of organizational charts or a computer program that reflected management's best guesses at backups for key positions. Each department had its own organizational chart with a "ladder" of boxes (some boxes had names in them; others were blank) below each critical leadership position. The boxes represented candidates who were potential replacements for the leaders at the top. Sometimes, the boxes were color-coded to reflect a candidate's readiness to step up to the next level if a critical opening should occur. It was all very impressive. To fill in the boxes, the senior leadership discussed the strengths and weaknesses of candidates recommended by the incumbents. Typically, some executives had a passion for the replacement-planning process as well as great confidence in their ability to spot potential leaders. Some of the backup decisions were hotly debated, but most were accepted as recommended by the incumbents and approved by their manager or vice president.

Quite often the discussion ended with several empty boxes with no "ready-now" names on the replacement charts. The same person was often listed as a backup for several different positions because senior managers believed that too few candidates were strategic enough, had the right experience, or would be able to stand up to the pressure at the next level. Ironically, while the charts implied planning rigor, thoughtfulness, and a strategically focused organization in control of its destiny, in reality they often did little more than provide a false sense of security. No one told the backups that they had been identified on the replacement charts. And no one paid much attention to the data until it was time to generate a new list of backups.

In an Acceleration Pool system the focus is on filling the pool—not filling specific positions. As described in Chapter 5, considerable data are presented and discussed about each candidate, and pool members are carefully selected. The pros and cons of pool membership are explained to the prospective pool members, who then decide if they want to join. There is a psychological and very real commitment to the individual by the organization. The Executive Resource Board firmly believes that the pool members are their highest-potential people. The board signals that belief by inviting them to join the pool and by telling them what to expect as pool members.

2. **In a traditional replacement-planning system, senior leaders met once or twice each year to check on the progress of key backups.** The principle question often was, "Can he or she be moved?" The board spent relatively little time discussing skill development issues. The discussions that did occur were usually not very organized and focused on sending people to outside programs.

As you will see in this chapter, discussions are both very substantial and well organized regarding Acceleration Pool members' job progress and developmental activities. In addition to having the opportunity to be extremely creative in defining challenging assignments because the focus is on job challenges instead of jobs, the Executive Resource Board can approve attendance at special training programs and assign executive coaches.

3. **In a traditional replacement-planning system, decisions to fill current and forecasted job openings often were made without solid data and with little regard to the backups who had been named previously to fill those positions.** In one meeting during which backups for the entire organization were considered, or in several meetings organized by business units, the board made key decisions about who would run the organization. These meetings often were stressful for the business heads presenting their people plans because

they had to do a lot of "selling." They had to sell their people forecasts for the next year, their evaluations of key people, and their recommendations of whom to promote or move—all in a limited time. Most placement decisions were quickly approved, but some were hotly debated. There often was a lack of independent, factual data on which to make solid decisions. Promotions sometimes were made to assuage egos and meet short-term business needs. Too often, discussions were unfocused and driven by competing agendas. Little attention was paid to the replacement charts.

When good ideas were recommended during discussions of development actions that were needed to fill in skill or knowledge gaps, the responsibility for following through on the recommendations often was unclear. For example, the senior leadership might have reluctantly approved a promotion after discussing the person's narrow organizational knowledge and poor partnering behavior. Seldom would these concerns be communicated to the person's new direct manager, and if they were, the manager often didn't know what to do about them.

In today's Acceleration Pool system, the Executive Resource Board's discussions of open positions are quite different. The process is well integrated with the organization's business planning strategy and process. Board members' roles and accountabilities are substantive and well defined, and they see their function as vital to the company's short- and long-run viability. Most important, the rich discussions of individuals are well organized, with considerable documentation available on all candidates and the positions to be filled. Critical short- and long-term development issues are fully discussed in a planned manner that leads to executable actions. Creative development options are considered with specific responsibilities for actions documented.

Members of the Executive Resource Board have two main—and sometimes conflicting—responsibilities in these discussions:

- They want to fill the top positions with the best people so the organization will prosper.

- They want to provide opportunities for people in the Acceleration Pool to expand their skills and knowledge by giving them challenging assignments.

They accomplish these placement responsibilities at meetings held at least twice a year—and sometimes as often as once a month. Most of the time, the board also considers development actions appropriate for pool members. Depending on the organization, this discussion of appropriate placement and development actions might be called a talent review, a succession review, a Human Resource review, an executive resource review, or a replacement-planning review. We will refer to this discussion as the talent review meeting of the Executive Resource Board.

Outcomes of a Successful Talent Review Meeting

Successful talent review meetings:

- Find the best individuals from within or outside the Acceleration Pool to fill currently open positions and positions that will be open in the next year.

- Review the growth of Acceleration Pool members.

- Decide to move Acceleration Pool members to new assignments as appropriate for their development.

- Decide on development actions as appropriate (e.g., individuals are sent to special training activities, provided with executive coaches, etc.).

As a result of their participation in an effective talent review discussion, Executive Resource Board members generally feel that:

- They are involved in an activity critical to the organization's future.

- The best decisions for the long- and short-range good of the organization were made.

- The meeting was well organized and effective (their time was well used).

- Everyone participated fairly and fully.

- All the individuals who were discussed were given equal and fair consideration.

The board should meet at least twice each year. While a semiannual meeting schedule might appear unwieldy, in reality it contributes to efficiency and pragmatic outcomes. It also is becoming a business necessity for organizations operating at "web speed."

The next section of this chapter describes the mechanics of the portions of Executive Resource Board meetings that cover placement and development decisions (the "nuts and bolts" of efficient meetings with rich outcomes). The end of this chapter addresses eight basic principles of a successful Executive Resource Board talent review meeting, including some of the subtleties that sometimes get lost but that make a big difference in the outcome. Recall that in Chapter 5, we discussed the portion of the Executive Resource Board meeting that is devoted to identifying talent.

While different business units can have some latitude around identification strategies, we recommend a common protocol for Executive Resource Board talent review discussions. Offering a discussion template and common decision framework enables board members who also might be on other boards or who are stakeholders in other talent pool discussions to share a common language and understanding of what will be covered. Figure 15-1 illustrates key discussion points to address during Executive Resource Board meetings. These points can be organized in many different ways, and the amount of time spent on each can vary greatly.

The reader might think that we are asking too much of the Executive Resource Board—especially in asking it to consider all the points in step 3 for each pool member they discuss. This review does take time; we've sat in on talent review discussions in large, complex organizations that have lasted three days. Most of the sessions we've seen, however, have lasted only a day. The key is organization, preparation, and leadership of the meeting. We'll now expand on each of the areas listed on the agenda in Figure 15-1.

1. Summarize the inventory of current and projected openings.

In anticipation of the Executive Resource Board meeting, the Human Resource department should construct an inventory of open positions and projected openings brought about by changing organizational requirements, transfers, promotions, retirements, etc. This inventory should include positions within the business unit that are the focus of the meeting as well as positions in other SBUs, divisions, etc. Ideally, documentation of these positions (including simple job descriptions) should be distributed to board members before the meeting.

Human Resource facilitators should also highlight any positions that have previously been identified as key "developmental positions," even if the incumbent appears to be "sitting tight." These positions are a precious organizational resource because they represent prime development opportunities. Thus, development options are limited

Figure 15-1: Sample Executive Resource Board Meeting Agenda and Discussion Themes for a Large Organization

1. Summarize the inventory of current and projected openings.

2. Determine which pool members will be discussed and the order in which they will be discussed.

3. Review the status and possible actions for all designated Acceleration Pool members:

   a. Why are they in the pool, and what are their developmental goals?

   b. Why are they in their current position?

   c. How are they performing relative to job responsibilities?

   d. How are they progressing against developmental priorities?

   e. Are they ready to move?

   f. Are they a potential fit for an opening (see 1 above)? What new openings would be created by such a move?

   g. Will they benefit from working with an executive coach?

   h. What training would be beneficial?

   i. Are they a retention challenge?

   j. Can their current assignments be enriched?

4. Review openings and tentative decisions made during discussion of pool members. Consider diversity issues. Look outside the pool when there is no good fit within it. Make final decisions.

5. Review aggregate trends. Determine group-level development goals, programs, and events.

6. Ask: Should anyone be dropped from the Acceleration Pool?

7. Determine if there are individuals who should be invited into the Acceleration Pool.

8. Debrief the meeting's effectiveness.

9. Reaffirm communication plans.

when adequate (but not stellar) performers fill these roles over a long period. The Executive Resource Board should recommend shifting long-tenured incumbents out of such roles and ideally into positions that provide them with new challenges.

Some organizations build their open position inventory around a simple categorization scheme describing broad challenges associated with open positions (see Figure 15-2). Other tools might include a more extensive taxonomy of job challenges afforded by positions.

Figure 15-2: Sample Open Positions Inventory				
Current Openings				
	"Start-Up"	**"Maintain Business"**	**"Grow Business"**	**"Fix-It"**
Director, Finance		X		
MIS Group Leader				X
Vice President, Sales/Marketing			X	
Plant Manager, Toronto	X			
Brand Director, Benten			X	
Projected Openings (date)				
Vice President, XYZ Ventures (4/02)	X			
District Manager, Seattle (9/02)			X	
Director, Global Accounts (9/02)			X	
Director, North American Distribution (6/02)				X

The meeting should open with a discussion of the inventory or some other grouping of open and projected-to-open positions. Creative thinking about developmental assignments will be stimulated by additional dialog about evolving business needs, structural changes, or market challenges that offer unique job challenges or developmental opportunities relative to specific positions.

2. **Determine which pool members will be discussed and the order in which they will be discussed.**

While each Acceleration Pool member should be discussed, it makes sense to prioritize the discussion of individual members according to the likelihood of their filling open positions. For example, HR might assign top priority to people who are ready for movement now or who are from the business unit being discussed; those who are new in their current job would have a secondary priority. All pool members should be reviewed at least every six months. Any board member should have the prerogative to direct the discussion at any time to pool members he or she feels merit a discussion.

3. **Review the status and possible actions for all designated Acceleration Pool members.**

The board considers each of the following issues for each of the designated pool members.

a. **Why are they in the pool, and what are their developmental goals?**

The following information (organized before the meeting by HR) should be available to the Executive Resource Board:

- Acceleration Pool nomination form.

- Personal Data Form (current personnel information, including career history, education, and training).

- Summary behavioral assessment data (Acceleration Center, 360°).

- Summary of evidence of possible derailers (from the Acceleration Center).

- Development Priority List.

- Completed Development Action Forms.

- Recent performance reviews.

- Special retention issues.

Most of this information is part of the pool member's Career Development Portfolio, which all pool members are responsible for keeping up to date and making available to the Executive Resource Board. Additional information from the pool member's manager or mentor can be brought before the board by asking them for a development status report or by asking the Human Resource department to solicit information.

Because board members review this information before the meeting, a minimum of time is spent on these issues. The information is meant to set up the rest of the discussion. After all, there were good reasons for putting the person into the pool; the board's job is to make good on its commitment to that individual.

b. Why are they in their current position?

What skills and knowledge are the pool members trying to acquire? What are their development objectives? This information should be recorded on each pool member's Development Priority List and on Part 1 of the most current Development Action Forms.

c. How are they performing relative to job responsibilities?

We recommend that board members look closely at trends in positions, responsibilities, and accomplishments. HR might gather and prepare information about performance, but there often are key observations that are unique only to executives who can read between the lines—data that can flesh out subtle details and add important "texture" to round out the formal documentation.

A simple approach to initiating the discussion about an individual starts with the question, "Who is able to share current observations about this person's job performance and progress?" Typically, a number of board members will volunteer to speak, either because they have had the opportunity to observe performance (i.e., because they are an informal/formal coach, manager, or mentor), or because they have been assigned accountability for following that Acceleration Pool member's progress. Here are the topics typically covered in the ensuing discussion:

- Performance—will the pool member meet his or her position/performance goals?

- Successes, problems, issues.

- How well the pool member has demonstrated the organization's values.

- When the person can be moved into the new position or assignment.

d. How are they progressing against developmental priorities?

A review of the up-to-date Development Action Forms for the assignment will answer this question. If some pool members are not progressing as planned or are unable to focus on established development priorities, the board should discuss possible causes for the problem. If the person simply has not been given the time to work on development priorities, or if support resources have not been available, the board should identify aggressive strategies to rectify the situation.

Many organizations gauge an individual's likelihood of dramatic growth against his or her own self-insight and demonstrated commitment to personal development—a view we support. The Executive Resource Board can collect data about these areas from the person's manager and mentor.

A division vice president at a large service organization, with whom we worked, also supports this view. He championed his division's Executive Resource Board and was a fervent believer in the importance of leaders modeling personal development. Acceleration Pool members in his division tended to be individuals who had been identified as "hungry" for learning, rather than the most talented or highest-performing people. In an Executive Resource Board meeting, this vice president spearheaded a move that significantly changed the composition of the division's Acceleration Pool. Two district managers, who were clearly "stretch" candidates, were formally identified as pool members, in part because of the dramatic development they had shown over the previous two years. At the same time, one of the division's most visible high fliers, a young executive, was dropped from the pool because he had failed, on three different occasions, to achieve his personal development objectives. Although at the time he claimed to be too busy, he had missed several opportunities to seek help that would have allowed him to focus on learning needs. As the vice president said, "You can fool me once, maybe twice, but three times sends a very clear message. He doesn't know what he doesn't know—he thinks he has arrived."

Will He *Ever* Be Accountable?

"David" was a 36-year-old marketing vice president for a key product division of a rapidly growing electronics manufacturer. He was known as a fearless, highly entrepreneurial, and ambitious whiz kid. He was also a personal protégé of the CEO. David entered the organization as a high-potential MBA (Stanford) and was promoted through four successively senior roles in seven years. His rapid ascent to the executive ranks was watched with interest by some and with dismay by others.

David had built a reputation for brilliance—as well as defensiveness, unwillingness to take responsibility, and resistance to personal development. Three years ago, he completed a developmental Acceleration Center but cancelled his feedback meeting three times. In fact, he never received the feedback.

David was very effective at "managing up" and had several vocal advocates on the chairman's council. However, with peers his confidence had evolved into arrogance and a sense that he was too busy—or too valuable—to collaborate on agendas other than his own.

David was assigned to a high-pressure, e-commerce initiative that was struggling to succeed. Often he aggressively complained about the highly matrixed resource strategy that had been implemented for this initiative. He had to "borrow" people from all over the organization. Although some of his concerns were legitimate, his inability to mobilize available resources started to become an issue.

Several senior executives were concerned that David's frustration with the difficulty of mustering support might make him vulnerable to offers from competitors. Therefore, the Executive Resource Board discussed moving him to an international role, where his business savvy and strategic sales skills were desperately needed. David even expressed an interest in such an assignment.

The Human Resource group, long frustrated with David's attitude, recommended that he be kept in his role for another nine months to get Year Two results under his leadership, followed by a well-planned transition into his next role. The HR vice president felt that David's cavalier approach to personal development, coupled with his sense of entitlement, provided a poor model for the people he led. While the Executive Resource Board recognized the huge thought-leadership gap in Europe, it agreed with HR's recommendation and kept David in place.

During the next nine months, David's situation became more and more clear as performance results came in. His unit missed key deliveries because equipment and other resources supplied by other parts of the organization were not in place as needed. He finally finished the assignment successfully, but by a narrow margin and with the aid of some high-level intervention.

David eventually moved to Europe, but in a very different position and with considerably more self-understanding. He has reported that his near failure was the best thing that every happened to him because of the self-insights it provided.

e. **Are they ready to move?**

Board members must strike a balance between leaving Acceleration Pool members in an assignment too long and not long enough. Moving an individual into a new role before he or she has a track record of completed job and developmental accomplishments is probably premature. On the other hand, if a pool member has more than three years' tenure in his or her current role without meeting objectives, something else probably is going on. In general, we feel that a pool member needs to prove success with hard results in at least one position every four years. In practical terms this often means a two- or three-year assignment during the four years, but it also leaves time for some shorter assignments in which development outcomes are most important. Of course, it all depends on the available assignments. Sometimes three or even four assignments can be completed in four years.

f. **Are they a potential fit for an opening? What new openings would be created by such a move?**

Each pool member should be weighed as a potential fit against the current and projected openings summarized early in the meeting. Of course, as people are matched against open positions, new positions (i.e., their incumbent positions) become available for other Acceleration Pool members. See Chapter 10 for a discussion of assignment alternatives.

g. **Will they benefit from working with an executive coach?**

It must be noted that executive coaching is not a replacement for training and challenging assignments, nor should it replace coaching by the manager or mentor. With that caveat executive coaches often can offer invaluable support and guidance. Assigning an executive coach to a pool member also sends a message that the organization values the individual because it is willing to invest in his or her future.

Best-practice uses and recommended situations for optimizing executive coaches are discussed in detail in Chapter 13.

Executive Coaching: When It Can Make a Difference

During an Acceleration Pool review, the Executive Resource Board's discussion focused on the readiness of "Renoldo," a relatively young and inexperienced operations manager, to step up to a much broader district manager role. Renoldo's readiness had immediate implications, as "Kara," the incumbent district manager known for her charismatic, visionary leadership style, was on the verge of transferring to a senior corporate marketing role as part of *her* acceleration plan.

As the Executive Resource Board thoroughly reviewed Renoldo's assessment and performance data, a profile of his strengths and development needs emerged. They found that Renoldo was an extremely diligent manager whose strength was his ability to get along with people at all levels of the organization. He had unique credibility with the union. However, he clearly had development needs in strategic orientation and his ability to "sell the vision." Furthermore, his comfort on the floor, combined with his operational focus, sometimes led him to inadvertently disempower his managers, who sometimes perceived his involvement with the line as reflecting a lack of trust in their leadership. Renoldo's development gaps jeopardized his prospects of being accepted by the prospective work group as the new district manager. This very high-performing group was accustomed to a results-oriented, creative, and strategically focused leader—and expected no less from Kara's successor. The Executive Resource Board feared that Renoldo, a relative unknown, might lose the group's respect before he had a chance to understand his new (stretch) role.

The board ultimately promoted Renoldo but also opted to provide an executive coach to help him get off to a fast start in his transition to the new role. This coach, known for "on-boarding" new executives, interviewed direct reports, peers, and superiors from Renoldo's current role as well as from his future leadership assignment. After the interviews the coach presented relevant positive and negative feedback from past associates as well as expectations, opportunities, and land mines that Renoldo would face in his new leadership challenge. Based on this evaluation, the executive coach and Renoldo codesigned a 100-day plan to maximize his early effectiveness and credibility. The plan centered on Renoldo's need to sustain strategic focus, rather than his natural inclination to troubleshoot tactical problems. Renoldo also put an action plan in place to think through and package one key message or vision in every organizational communication.

Renoldo would have eventually learned his new terrain, but it was clear to the Executive Resource Board that the executive coach became his guardian angel through Renold's first months in the role. The coach partnered with Renoldo as he found his own style with the new group. The coach also helped Renoldo overcome development needs through awareness and tactics aimed at ensuring his strategic credibility with a group that needed to know where it was going at all times. The Executive Resource Board unanimously agreed that there had been other "Renoldos" in the past who had faltered during similar leadership transitions largely because they had not been proactively equipped to succeed.

h. What training would be beneficial?

In most organizations the Executive Resource Board is responsible for assigning pool members only to special training programs, such as university executive courses or action learning programs (as described in Chapter 12). However, it is very appropriate for the board to discuss and recommend transition or prescriptive training. These recommendations are passed to the pool member's manager and mentor for consideration.

i. Are they a retention challenge?

What are the retention issues? Is the individual likely to leave soon? If so, what can be done to prevent it? Should the organization exercise any proactive retention strategies? This challenge is addressed in more detail later in this chapter.

j. Can their current assignments be enriched?

If Acceleration Pool members have not been identified for a new role, the Executive Resource Board should consider whether enough *ad hoc* experiences or special opportunities are in place to ensure truly accelerated development. If the aggressiveness of the development path is questionable, the board might recommend to the pool member's manager and mentor that changes in job responsibilities should be considered. They can offer their ideas, but it's up to the manager and mentor to decide on action. For instance, perhaps the Acceleration Pool member can be assigned to short "fix-it" budgeting or planning responsibilities to provide new challenges. Or the individual can be given a short-term learning assignment, such as troubleshooting problems or shoring up resources in a struggling unit. (Accelerated growth through short-term developmental experiences is discussed in Chapter 11.)

The board should also consider teaching experiences, which are best used to leverage strength. Teaching experiences give pool members a platform for exercising unique talents or technical knowledge in a manner that builds their reputation and confidence and, at the same time, offers continuous learning to others. (See the discussion in Chapter 11 of teaching others as a developmental experience.)

4. Review openings and tentative decisions made during discussion of pool members. Consider diversity issues. Look outside the pool when there is no good fit within it. Make final decisions.

By this time names will have been tentatively penciled in for most of the open positions. The board should reexamine the candidate slots to fill the open and projected positions with an eye toward diversity issues and the realization that it might need to stretch some people to fill positions. The board also needs to consider people outside the Acceleration Pool. This is always the most heated portion of the talent review discussion. Often, someone outside the Acceleration Pool is a more natural fit for a position because of the person's direct experience in the area. This person might be a direct report to the open position as well as a solid corporate citizen. The Executive Resource Board must weigh the issues: Does it opt for the person outside the pool who is probably the popular choice, or does it stretch a pool member for the long-term good of the organization? Such choices typically bring out valid points on both sides. There are no right or wrong answers; the quality of the consensus hinges on the quality of the board's discussion.

The Importance of Holistic Discussions

During discussions of individual Acceleration Pool members, the focus should be on understanding the "whole" person, with emphasis on behavioral examples and concrete measures of progress rather than subjective, emotional opinions. While these discussions should go deep, depth need not imply length. With a strong facilitator helping to keep the board on track and with common meeting formats, such discussions can be efficient and relatively brief (i.e., approximately 15 minutes per pool member, discussed in detail).

One of our favorite stories about the power of assessment data involves a well-regarded high flier working for a large computer manufacturer. "John" was being considered for a newly designed, highly strategic executive role in which he would be responsible for the entire life cycle of one of several computer platforms, including R&D, manufacturing, and marketing/distribution. Skill requirements of the platforms varied, depending on the technical complexity and age of the platform design as well as the level of interdependency on multiple internal partners. In all the new roles, it would be essential for the leader to possess strong partnership skills.

John was viewed as the clear choice for the most strategic and technically complex of the platform positions. He was considered one of the highest-potential leaders in the organization, in large part because he had recently turned around a failing key business by emphasizing process excellence and fostering a culture of trust and involvement.

To facilitate placement, Acceleration Center data for each candidate were systematically reviewed with the Executive Resource Board, which included the company's president. Experience and performance history were also key data points. John's assessment data sparked controversy when it was presented to the board. While he performed extremely well in leadership competencies and demonstrated strong interpersonal skills (he was an exceptional listener), his performance in the decision-making, arena was mixed. John was proficient in tactical decision making, but showed a high development need in several strategic decision-making areas. Furthermore, his cognitive testing data suggested slightly below-average critical thinking skills. As these data were presented, the company's president shook his head and commented that the "Acceleration Center missed on this guy—he is one of the best we have." Other board members agreed.

The facilitator hypothesized that John had achieved his noteworthy results through strong leadership and influence skills, but the board did not accept that explanation. Nevertheless, the facilitator stood by consistent data from the Acceleration Center. John's inventory responses predicted fine leadership skills as well as pragmatic, but not conceptual (i.e., strategic), thinking. The president stood firm in his position that John was a top choice for the biggest and most challenging platform—and the review moved onto other candidates.

John's mentor, "Paul," was not at that meeting but did attend the next one, where all candidate data were summarized one more time prior to the board making its final decisions. To the board's surprise, Paul wholeheartedly agreed with the assessment profile. Even more telling, he supported the facilitator's hypothesis for John's success—that John was, in fact, a charismatic leader who accomplished much through high-performing teams. On Paul's advice John was not offered the original platform position, which required a highly strategic and conceptual thinker. Instead, he was promoted to an alternative position, which involved a mature design and a complex process and which would leverage his ability to mobilize resources.

Ironically, John also agreed with the assessment feedback. He was grateful to have been assigned to a role that offered him a new challenge and at the same time drew on his strengths. Ultimately, John was extremely successful in this role and advanced both his career and the organization's objectives. He and Paul agreed that he would have struggled in the other role.

5. Review aggregate trends. Determine group-level development goals, programs, and events.

Immediately following the discussion of pool members as individuals is the appropriate time to consider them as a group. Review aggregate data about pool members to identify themes and trends in organizational strengths and challenges. Evaluate the diversity of Acceleration Pool membership relative to strategic goals. Consider common development needs. For example, a review of Acceleration Pool members at a major consulting organization revealed an alarming lack of web-based knowledge and skills. The lack of readiness among even the highest-potential associates to adapt their consulting advice to more Internet-driven, high-tech solutions appeared to be an enterprisewide phenomenon. As a result, the organization decided to spend several million dollars to create an e-commerce design and implementation curriculum for its consultants—not just those with high potential.

6. Ask: Should anyone be dropped from the Acceleration Pool?

Acceleration Pools are designed to be fluid, with people moving in and out based on evolving needs. There are clearly legitimate circumstances for moving someone out of the Acceleration Pool (e.g., when progress has plateaued). However, be careful to avoid reactive conclusions or adopting a "revolving door" approach to Acceleration Pool membership. While it often is tempting to challenge people's continued membership in the pool because of occasional questionable performance or a recent failure, it is important to recall the original rationale for placing the person in the pool. It is also essential for the board to consider the causes of poor performance: Was the individual put in over his or her head? Was there sufficient support for acceleration expectations? Or is there truly a motivational or skill mismatch between the person's goals and those of the organization?

7. **Determine if there are individuals who should be invited into the Acceleration Pool.**

The discussion of who will fill specific positions will unintentionally bring to the board's attention other, heretofore-unsung individuals who might be appropriate for acceleration. See Chapter 5 for a discussion of identifying high potentials.

8. **Debrief the meeting's effectiveness.**

At the conclusion of each meeting, the Executive Resource Board should review meeting outcomes, quality of content, and suggestions for continuous improvement. And once each year, the board should monitor its own adherence to the principles, for a successful meeting.

9. **Reaffirm communication plans.**

See principle 8 in the next section, Principles for a Successful Meeting, for a discussion on this.

Principles for a Successful Meeting

As the Executive Resource Board moves through the meeting agenda, its members should keep these eight key principles in mind:

1. Ensure that the right players are in your meetings and that they understand their roles, responsibilities, and accountabilities.

2. Don't forget the fundamentals of effective meeting management.

3. Ensure that Executive Resource Board members maintain an enterprise-level perspective.

4. Consider executive judgment as legitimate input, as long as it is supported with behavioral evidence.

5. Beware of biases and old assumptions.

6. Carefully consider whether high potentials are set up for success.

7. Remember that strategic succession management is retention insurance.

8. Don't neglect the communication strategy.

These are discussed in more detail in the remainder of this chapter.

1. **Ensure that the right players are in your meetings and that they understand their roles, responsibilities, and accountabilities.**

The Executive Resource Board meeting provides a unique focus on the organization's people strategy. Because every meeting will require strategic placement decisions that will affect the organization's ability to achieve bottom-line business objectives, it is important that everyone— up to and including the chief executive—actively participates. And all must understand their roles as well as the responsibilities they entail. Here are some of the roles we have seen in various organizations:

- **CEO/Senior Executive**

  - Board Leader.

  - Strategic Process Champion—Maintains relentless focus on succession management goals, values, and process execution.

  - Visionary—Paints a picture of the future and sells it.

  - Devil's Advocate—Challenges conventional thinking and current paradigms.

  - Chief Mentor—Guides board members and Acceleration Pool members.

  - Liaison—Provides an ongoing communication link between Acceleration Pool review activities and members of the senior team not on the Executive Resource Board.

- **Executive Resource Board Member**

  - Stakeholder—Participates in the process as both a (talent) supplier and customer.

  - Observer—Actively observes and evaluates performance, potential, and developmental progress of pool candidates/ members.

  - Tactical Driver—Orchestrates and facilitates process implementation.

  - Best Practice Advisor—Monitors process integrity, ensures continuity/common processes across the organization.

It is important to note that one board member can assume several roles, and not all organizations have all roles filled.

Simple role clarity, process goals, and discussion ground rules often make the difference between open, candid discussions and "old boy" debates that elicit more cynicism than insight. Effective succession management architects ensure that all participants in the talent review process understand the purpose, importance, and expectations around their contributions. Specifically, board members must understand exactly what is expected from them before, during, and after the talent review.

Each board will have its own unique group dynamics. Articulating the ground rules contributes to synergistic, productive group dynamics. Conversely, neglecting to declare ground rules, even when they seem obvious, will lead to unwanted behaviors, such as guarded input and reluctance to challenge, and a disproportional influence of senior members or outspoken, opinionated members. Effective ground rules include:

- **Exercising discussion etiquette**—All members contribute; no one dominates airtime.

- **Maintaining confidentiality**—All discussions stay in the room.

- **Being behavioral**—Advocacy or dissent for individuals must be supported with behavioral evidence. If no examples can be produced, evaluations are regarded as unreliable.

- **Maintaining data integrity**—Unequivocal adherence to data-access policies; no sharing of information for any other purpose or with any other group.

- **Leaving personal feelings/friendships at the door**—Maintain sensitivity toward others, but lose the "blinders" of past friendship (or frustration) when discussing candidates.

A newly established Executive Resource Board might want to charter itself as a team. The chartering process will help the board establish its mission and operating principles (i.e., ground rules) and define formal and informal role expectations. Agreements should be documented and communicated to all stakeholders. Once all the rules and roles have been clarified, the members might want to try an interesting exercise: offering board members the chance to discuss dysfunctional behaviors to be avoided during meetings. These often will come easily because people usually remember situations in which others demonstrated poor

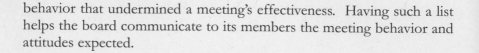

behavior that undermined a meeting's effectiveness. Having such a list helps the board communicate to its members the meeting behavior and attitudes expected.

Dysfunctional Meeting Member Behaviors That Undermine Meeting Effectiveness

Bully—Influential member who aggressively pushes own ideas, preferences, and perceptions; is a poor listener.

Wimp—Easily influenced; holds few strong convictions about anyone.

Good Old Boy—Insists that personal perceptions are correct, despite having no evidence to support them; discounts behavioral evidence as insignificant compared to own experience-based judgments; allows affection for people to dominate judgments of potential.

Expert—Know-it-all who uses technical knowledge and expertise to persuade others.

Bored—Talks to neighbors, frequently makes jokes, steps out often to take calls, or nods off when conversation centers on people whom he or she doesn't know.

The Unknown Member—Offers no opinions; does not speak up even when he or she disagrees.

Box Checker—Desperately wants to end the meeting; hurries the meeting along; agrees too quickly; prefers speed over effectiveness.

---

2. Don't forget the fundamentals of effective meeting management.

Protocol does not equal bureaucracy; a little structure goes a long way. Effectively facilitated Executive Resource Board meetings have the following characteristics:

- Focused, agenda-driven discussions with clearly defined outcomes.

- Defined review protocol, including consistent format for discussing each individual. This format should facilitate balanced representation of relevant performance data, executive observations, and assessment information.

- Diligent documentation of recommendations and accountabilities.

- Summary review of trends, organizationwide opportunities, and training opportunities.

While those characteristics might seem obvious, sustaining this level of structure with an outspoken, opinionated group of executives is easier said than done. It usually requires a well-respected facilitator who is able to channel executive energy in a constructive manner. Although a facilitator should be seen as unbiased, he or she must also be perceived as a credible partner, empowered to be "politically incorrect" in order to challenge executive stakeholders when *their* biases and individual agendas emerge. Usually, a very senior, well-respected Human Resource executive is asked to facilitate meetings; that person also can provide continuity and information about open positions, development assignments, and best practices across organizational boundaries. Sometimes the senior manager at the meeting facilitates. Increasingly, at the start of an Acceleration Pool process, the consultant who helped design the process facilitates the first few Executive Resource Board meetings to provide a model for the person who will have ongoing responsibility.

A key facilitation challenge is balancing process discipline with the need for executive stakeholders to engage in a rich, free-flowing discussion about individual talent and organizational needs. The use of classic data integration principles associated with the assessment center method (Thornton & Byham, 1982) will enhance a facilitator's ability to achieve the appropriate discussion depth.

3. **Ensure that Executive Resource Board members maintain an enterprise-level perspective.**

For most of the year, Executive Resource Board members get results through relentless focus, passion, ownership, and advocacy of opportunities in their area of functional/geographical/product responsibility. During board meetings they must transcend that more limited point of view and adopt a field of vision that represents the overall organization's best interest. This often means supporting the rotation and promotion of their own key players into roles outside their jurisdiction—even into other business units. Remember: The population in the Acceleration Pool often is accurately described as "corporate property," whose members are beyond the unique province of any specific business unit, function, etc.

Conceptually, Executive Resource Board members understand that supporting acceleration might involve tough decisions that could have a detrimental effect on their own areas of responsibility. While they might understand the importance of broader-based, organizationwide concerns, it often is difficult for them to rise above issues that are more parochial. For example, most executive compensation systems breed provincial behavior. Nevertheless, when senior officers visibly support a long-term perspective on the use of people, other board members will be more likely to step up to a long-range, enterprisewide perspective. Over time, it should be a zero-sum game (i.e., board members will give up their best but will also get another board member's best).

Obviously, there are other inherent challenges to maintaining an enterprise-level perspective. The first is rooted in fundamental human nature. Loyalty (as well as dependence on key contributors) makes it difficult for board members to distinguish those who are indispensable to them today from those who are indispensable for the organization's future growth and success.

Second, flawed nomination processes, mixed messages regarding the importance of succession management, or poorly communicated expectations will generate dysfunctional competitive behaviors. For example, we once saw a CEO request 10 identified high potentials from each of three business units. These individuals were to enjoy special focus and resources. However, it was widely acknowledged that Business Unit A had much deeper talent than the other two. Nevertheless, the CEO, in an attempt to maintain "fairness" across business units, insisted on maintaining a quota of candidates from each business unit. This resulted in frustration and open cynicism about the organization's commitment to maintain a legitimate Acceleration Pool process, missed opportunities to focus on key talent, and widespread recognition that some of the organization's best performers were being left out of the Acceleration Pool.

4. Consider executive judgment as legitimate input, as long as it is supported with behavioral evidence.

For all the right reasons, HR facilitators diligently focus executive stakeholders on objective, behavioral performance and assessment data when discussing an individual's potential. However, their efforts to avoid sweeping conclusions based on hearsay, opinion, and conjecture can impede the introduction of informal (but important) executive observations. Executive observations offer a unique and often accurate perspective to a talent review discussion.

To optimize the value of executive insight, it is important to communicate clear expectations about the "packaging" of judgments or opinions. First, executive stakeholders should be encouraged to use common terminology when discussing Acceleration Pool members— the executive descriptors adopted by the organization (see Chapter 6).

Second, and even more important, executive stakeholders should challenge one another to advocate or defend their input with specific behavioral examples. Doing so reflects the philosophy of assessment center data integration, which demands an etiquette of challenge and behavioral defense of evaluative statements. Making executives understand that *behavioral examples* are simply brief descriptions of what someone said or did contributes to constructive discussions that focus on fact instead of conjecture.

Obviously, in the context of a talent review discussion, evaluative comments might launch into or follow a behavioral example. Here is an example: "I believe Eric is very entrepreneurial *(evaluative comment)* because in our business ventures meeting last week, he offered more ideas than everyone else combined. Further, at the end of the meeting, two executives publicly thanked him for his role in the meeting. One specifically commented that the meeting's success could be largely credited to the individual who thought to invite Eric *(behavioral example)*."

5. Beware of biases and old assumptions.

Accurate judgment regarding candidates' potential and progress can be distorted by a variety of biases, including implicit preferences (e.g., individuals under 40; favored backgrounds, such as marketing or sales; and the "looks like me" phenomenon). Furthermore, executives have long memories—even when their assumptions about a candidate's skills or motivations are obsolete, labels and impressions often live on. This applies to reputations that both underestimate or overstate an individual's potential. If old information is introduced into the discussion about an individual, board members should challenge its appropriateness or give it less weight.

The senior author vividly remembers an Acceleration Center for a large retail company in which a certain individual did very well in all areas assessed. A regional personnel vice president happened to be at the center and was asked why the person had not been promoted more rapidly. (The pool member was about 10 years behind his cohorts.)

The vice president explained that he was the person's district manager when the individual joined the company. An early decision made by the person was to order a large number of college sweatshirts in anticipation of the local college doing very well during the football season. As it turned out, the college didn't have a very good season, and the sweatshirts didn't sell. Because of the individual's decision, the company took a large loss. The regional personnel vice president admitted that every time he looked at that individual, he always remembered the sweatshirts.

6. Carefully consider whether high potentials are set up for success.

Do you remember any high fliers who failed to live up to their predicted potential because the organization squandered the opportunity to optimize their development? Perhaps the organization fell into the trap of moving them too quickly to achieve real learning or accountability for actions, or maybe the individuals didn't have sufficient support to rebound from an earlier failure. Or perhaps they were given mixed messages about priorities or faced organizational systems that were inconsistent with stated values.

There are many examples of high-potential people who fell short but who might have succeeded had they been set up with the right support systems. An important ingredient of a successful Acceleration Pool system is a solid understanding of skill gaps and motivations or personality traits that are likely to enhance or derail progress. Insights gained through in-depth discussion of performance trends and the challenges offered by an assignment can help an Executive Resource Board to provide highly individualized support systems.

7. Remember that strategic succession management is retention insurance.

The motivations and career aspirations of potential Acceleration Pool candidates often are an afterthought in talent review meetings. While participation in Acceleration Pools is certainly elective, it also should be attractive in terms of being flexible enough to address people's unique needs and goals. Furthermore, Executive Resource Boards might want to consider explicit, aggressive retention strategies for individual pool members who are frequently courted by competitors or other outside organizations.

Two common motivational challenges presented by high-potential Acceleration Pool candidates are mobility constraints and a sense of professional identity/affiliation with a specific function or role type. To address the first challenge, organizations can consider creative strategies to overcome expressed mobility constraints. While some organizations rigidly view mobility as a minimum requirement for participation in an Acceleration Pool, others want to optimize the likelihood of participation by offering alternatives that will enable high fliers to take developmental assignments without uprooting their school-aged children. Although jobs often require a full-time local presence, many developmental assignments can be accomplished with a combination of remote and on-site presence. Such "commuter" arrangements are becoming more common. Individuals might also have the option of working at home when their presence at the workplace is not essential. In general, most Acceleration Pool members will appreciate the organization's proactive support of family and personal needs and will recognize it as an expression of perceived value.

The issue of professional affiliation can present more of a challenge. At DDI, for example, many of our strongest consultants—and likely future leaders—have an intense affinity for a specialized line of work. These individuals have spent years completing advanced degrees and are published thought leaders in their occupational niches (e.g., succession management, selection, leadership training, and organizational development). For some, their sense of identity is closely tied to their expertise.

On one hand it is reasonable to ask people who take pride in their technical affiliation to step out of their niche in order to build their cross-business exposure and broader general management skills. However, it is foolhardy to ignore the preferences of the very individuals who are most attractive to our competition. As a result, we have learned that benefits associated with rotational assignments outside an individual's technical preference need to be thoughtfully communicated and framed in terms of the clear upside for both the person and the organization.

Timing is crucial—there are definite windows of time in which the organization is most vulnerable to talent raids or other unwanted turnover. Naturally, it is wise to take extra care to involve Acceleration Pool members in strategic career decisions when they have attractive alternatives.

8. Don't neglect the communication strategy.

Packaging the Executive Resource Board's recommendations to Acceleration Pool members should be a specific point of discussion in the talent review meeting. The board must carefully consider who will best convey—and frame—the learning objectives for new assignments, particularly if there is a need to sell the opportunity to the pool member. This interaction also affords a constructive opportunity for feedback as well as positive messages about the individual's perceived value. Most Acceleration Pool members are very hungry to understand how senior leaders see their progress and potential.

Remember, too, the importance of communication to managers, mentors, and other organizational stakeholders who will be expected to facilitate the growth of Acceleration Pool members. Their expectations for supporting growth must be clarified and their buy-in assured.

Summary

When we consult with organizations on their succession management system, we always ask to sit in on a talent review meeting. Our observations of a meeting tell us about every aspect of the process—the amount of backing by top management; whether the company has well-defined, on-the-mark competencies; accuracy of selection into the pool; quality of diagnosis of development needs; quality of development prescriptions; support by all parts of the organization; and overall success. If the CEO is there and actively participating, if hard data are available on pool members and are used correctly and fairly in making decisions, if the meeting follows an agenda in which everyone is involved, and if there are short-term sacrifices being made to further the development of pool members, we can predict the program will be a success. Talent review meetings are an accurate gauge of an organization's succession management process.

Chapter 16

The Role of the CEO and Measures of Acceleration Pool Success

Jack Welch, the CEO of General Electric, believes that his most important job is motivating and assessing GE leaders and future leaders. He feels so strongly about it that he spends about 50 percent of his time on people issues. Welch likens his role in succession management to that of a gardener. "You have to go along with a can of fertilizer in one hand and water in the other and constantly throw both on the flowers." He emphasizes that all of the plants in his garden need to be watered and nurtured (i.e., developed), but that some plants require extra fertilizer and attention to ensure that they will fully blossom. Equally important, Welch notes that some plants need to be weeded out so that the strongest can thrive and achieve their potential (Hymowitz & Murray, 1999, pp. B1, B4).

From our benchmarking for this book, we have overwhelmingly concluded that the most important factor in the success of a succession management program is the attention and backing provided by the CEO or COO (or the top executive of an SBU if the Acceleration Pool is confined to that unit). As a matter of convenience in this chapter, we'll call the top executive "the CEO."

To assure the success of a succession management program, the CEO must work closely with other top company executives to accomplish several important initiatives:

☞⌐ denotes that information on this topic is available at the *Grow Your Own Leaders* web site (www.ddiworld.com/growyourownleaders).

1. **Establish defined succession outcomes.**

   The management team must agree on the outcomes expected from the succession management system. The succession outcomes need to be in line with the organization's strategy. The entire management team must clearly understand why succession management is important to the short- and long-term success of the organization. Otherwise, they won't make the short-term decisions necessary to make the system work (e.g., moving people more rapidly through positions, taking people who aren't completely ready for their new positions), nor will they agree to release the best people for developmental assignments for the good of the organization (even if the move is to another SBU). Measurements might include the length of time that executive positions are open before being filled, percentage of senior management positions filled from outside the organization, retention of pool members, etc. (See Appendix 16-1 for a discussion of measurement options.)

2. **Demand measurement.**

   Someone should be responsible for periodically measuring the succession management system against the goals set by the organization. The CEO should demand that a periodic report be made.

3. **Ensure alignment with key stakeholders.**

   A CEO alone can't make an Acceleration Pool system work. We have seen programs fail when this has been tried. All key executives will be affected by the system, and all are important to its success. They must see the value of the system in relation to organizational goals.

4. **Create a vision for the Acceleration Pool system and how it will operate.**

   Along with the executive team, the CEO makes basic decisions about the number of Acceleration Pools, the size of each one, the investment in special training programs for pool members, and how quickly each pool will be implemented. There's no "standard" Acceleration Pool and, for that matter, no standard succession management system. Systems must be adapted to organizations depending on the organization's size and structure and the speed at which people need to be developed. It should be noted that different parts of the organization might have different requirements relative to speed.

5. **Establish the Executive Resource Board.**

The CEO has the responsibility of establishing the Executive Resource Board. Who will be on the Executive Resource Board? If there is more than one pool, will there be more than one board? Key decisions must be made around who will facilitate the discussion of who gets into the pool and how they will develop. As discussed in Chapter 15, the facilitator needs to be a well-respected, credible, and unbiased individual. This person can be from the Human Resource group, an outside consulting organization, or the Executive Resource Board. If need be, the CEO can do the facilitating.

6. **Assure that the best people get nominated for the pool.**

The CEO needs to sell the importance of getting the best and brightest into Acceleration Pools. Because of parochial short-term thinking, SBU heads or other managers might be reluctant to share their high potentials. The CEO must show the importance of selection by personally being involved in reviewing people nominated for the pool and by asking questions of the nominators to identify people who might have been overlooked. The CEO needs to be a protector of standards—not letting people into the Acceleration Pool for the wrong reasons (e.g., someone who has been around a long time or whom everyone expects to be a successor).

7. **Make a priority of succession management activities, such as Executive Resource Board meetings, and be an active member of the Executive Resource Board.**

The presence of the CEO at these meetings is all-important to give the proceedings prestige and to show the CEO's commitment. Nothing reflects concern and interest more than being an active member of the Executive Resource Board. It puts the CEO at the heart of the action in making decisions relative to the selection of pool members, their placement, and development. The CEO brings a unique grasp of organizational issues and direction. Without the CEO, the board can fragment into warring factions, with each protecting its own turf.

CEOs as Process Champions

Some chief executives really take their role as process champion seriously. We have worked with at least a dozen CEOs or presidents who have insisted on completing the same assessment and feedback experience requested of their leaders. Others so appreciate access to rich assessment data that they act as assessors or are engaged in the assessor discussions.

Consider the following:

- A Japanese president of a multinational pharmaceutical company wanted to try a rigorous assessment before asking his senior team to complete the process. The HR director likened this president to a medieval king who would have refused a personal taste tester.

- The North American and international presidents for a major automobile manufacturer each personally spent more than one week, along with their respective strategy boards, in data integration sessions for candidates responsible for newly defined strategic roles.

- Two board members (including the CEO) of a luxury automobile company chose to learn how to interpret assessment results by first completing the assessment themselves. This assessment was designed to support several selection decisions as well as to identify those with hidden potential. After receiving their own feedback, the board members leveraged their new knowledge in a marathon session, reviewing profiles for more than 20 members of their senior staff.

- Presidents of several manufacturing plants of a North America-based, Japanese-owned organization came together in a data integration and enterprise-level decision-making process for key executive selections. These presidents each described significant enhancements to their own interviewing and selection skills because of their participation in the professionally facilitated review session.

- Two CEOs each used assessment data to support the executive selection decisions associated with their respective reengineered organizations. Independently, each described the pressure and magnitude of responsibility he felt as reminiscent to past military leadership experiences in Vietnam. These individuals viewed the quality and accuracy of these decisions as their key legacy.

- The CEO for a $5 billion health care organization personally piloted each aspect of a holistic selection process, including simulations and personality and cognitive inventories, before asking the same from the top 100 executives in his soon-to-be-restructured organization. His goals included validating the relevance of the process, gaining intimate understanding of the meaning of results (through his own feedback), and developing a starting point (his own profile) for ensuring complementary skills and values on the newly configured executive team. After receiving his own feedback, this CEO personally engaged in reviewing assessment and performance data for every executive who participated in the process. After the reorganization was complete, he also openly shared his feedback with his new senior team.

8. **Personally encourage and coach senior managers to make decisions that will benefit pool members' development.**

Effective CEOs know about the opportunities for developing key talent, and they pass this knowledge along. They recognize that for a pool member to develop, a manager often must accept someone who is less than qualified. Effective CEOs not only apply pressure to managers to make the appropriate decisions, they also coach them in how to effect the change without negative impact to the manager's organization.

9. **Act as a mentor for one pool member.**

While having the CEO as a mentor is extremely positive for the pool member, it is also an opportunity for the CEO to "walk the talk." If the CEO can devote the appropriate time and energy to a pool member, managers below the CEO would have difficulty saying that they're too busy. At management meetings the CEO should make a point to comment on any of his or her activities involving the pool member; this will serve to remind managers of the CEO's ongoing commitment.

10. **Support the Acceleration Pool system in all promotion decisions.**

Force promotion decisions onto the Executive Resource Board. Don't promote people outside the agreed-upon promotional system. When a promotion decision is being made, the CEO should always ask if the person is on the Acceleration Pool list. If not, was an Acceleration Pool member considered? On what basis was the decision made? While it's not necessary that Acceleration Pool members fill all jobs, pool members should at least be considered. The CEO who circumvents the Acceleration Pool is punching a hole in the system; when enough holes are punched, the system will begin to fall apart.

11. Assure that diversity goals are met.

While delegated to the Executive Resource Board, diversity responsibility ultimately rests with the CEO. The CEO should ask for yearly statistics and take actions as needed.

12. Meet one-on-one with pool members as often as possible.

Remember when you were just starting up the organizational ladder and were maybe lucky enough to have a brief conversation with the CEO? It made you feel great, didn't it? The same magic works today although many organizations are much less formal and have fewer communication barriers. Outstanding CEOs (and their key managers) make a point to talk with Acceleration Pool members every chance they get. They schedule breakfasts, lunches, and dinners with individuals and small groups of pool members. Such meetings give CEOs a chance to share ideas with the pool members, but most important, they provide opportunities to find out what is really going on in each pool member's world. Asking a question like, "What are you up to?" is all that it takes to get a meaningful conversation going. Of course, such meetings provide yet another opportunity to observe and evaluate pool members, although caution should be exercised to avoid generalizing from a single, limited observation.

13. Attend and participate in Acceleration Pool training events.

We have long noted that the more the CEO and other top officers are involved in an Acceleration Pool development event (action learning or other executive training programs), the higher attendees rate its value. This is true in every organization we have observed, in all parts of the world. To instill the desired motivation and retain valuable people, organizations want pool members to identify with the company, to be concerned with its worldwide challenges and obstacles, to enjoy its success, and to psychologically feel like an owner of the company. To accomplish this, pool members need to feel that they are getting the inside story. CEOs can meet this need better than anyone else in the company. CEOs are admired—pool members want to understand their thinking and learn from their successes and mistakes. Pool members want to feel that the torch is being passed to them.

For all these reasons and many more, it is critical for CEOs to make appearances at training and other Acceleration Pool events. The best CEO appearances we have witnessed were those built around answering questions submitted in writing from the audience. The CEOs were absolutely honest and forthright. Adequate time was allotted to give extended answers, and the CEOs often stayed around for lunch or cocktails so people could follow up on issues.

Another successful strategy used by many executives and CEOs is the use of stories about personal experiences. They are powerful teaching tools during a program. See "The Pepsi Challenge" anecdote at the end of this chapter.

CEO Traps

While we were benchmarking for this book, we also observed a number of common traps that many CEOs fall into relative to succession management. Here are some of their most common mistakes:

1. **Thinking that having a good succession management system will lead to success.** The existence of a well-designed succession management system is important, but merely having a system does not mean that it is working. Many CEOs breathe a great sigh of relief after they implement a new system, but then they don't follow up. Their measure of success is the number of people in the system rather than the quality of people available to fill positions. It's important to set measurable goals for the system and monitor its effectiveness through periodic reports.

2. **Assuming short-term issues are more important than succession management.** The quarterly pressure of meeting corporate operating numbers, the implementation of an important organizational change, competitive pressures, and many other factors can cause a CEO to put off succession management activities. The thinking is "Why worry about the future? If we don't do well this quarter, there might not be a future." There are tough calls to make, and the pressure to make shortcuts or postpone can be immense. But the best CEOs we interviewed really believe that the future of their organization is in the hands of the people they will develop; therefore, they make time for succession management activities. The best CEOs feel that there's nothing more important for the long-term viability of their organization than developing high-potential people. Many of them

also believe that the stock market is increasingly concerned about the depth of talent in publicly held companies and that this factor is considered when evaluating them. All the CEOs we talked to said that, increasingly, their boards are pressuring them to make sure that an effective succession management strategy is executed.

3. **Thinking that they know who all the high-potential people are.** Some CEOs delude themselves into thinking that they have a good feel for the up-and-coming people in the organization. They tend to select people for the Acceleration Pool based on their personal knowledge or observations; they don't force a true look throughout the entire organization for candidates. This allows an "old boy" system to prevail and can give the lawyers and accountants who interact with the CEO an advantage over line managers.

4. **Considering only individuals who have been personally observed.** This is somewhat related to CEO Trap 3, but it particularly pertains to situations in which the CEO relies very heavily on chance observations of people. The CEO might observe someone making a presentation and reach a conclusion about that person. That presentation would, at best, offer only a glimpse of the individual's talents. The person might have been poorly prepared for the presentation or, conversely, might have been extremely well coached. In either case the CEO's initial impression about the person's skills might be far off the mark. Also, what about others who didn't have the chance to make a presentation and who might be equally or better qualified? CEOs can't feel that they really know what's going on in their organization based solely on their personal observations. There must be other systems in place to help them be sure they get the right people into the Acceleration Pool.

5. **Choosing people who could handle last year's problems.** An effective Acceleration Pool produces people who can handle future challenges, which are often very different than the challenges facing current executives. Effective CEOs periodically check on the criteria for selection into the Acceleration Pool as well as the executive descriptors used to guide development to see if they are visionary.

6. **Creating a pool whose members mirror the CEO.** A CEO with an engineering background might tend to favor individuals with a similar background. The same holds true for CEOs with financial or scientific backgrounds. Early experiences might have been vital in preparing the CEO for his or her current position, but they might not

be appropriate in today's business world, given the rapid, often unforeseen changes in business direction and the speed at which individuals must move through the organization.

7. **Not getting to know people in the Acceleration Pool.** The CEO will be involved in decisions about Acceleration Pool members' promotion and development. It is certainly helpful if the CEO actually knows the people whose future he or she is affecting. Effective CEOs make an effort to know pool members. When visiting regional or overseas offices, they make a point to talk to pool members and to see them in presentations and in other venues. One CEO we know tries to have a one-on-one dinner with a pool member in each town that he visits.

8. **Stopping all recruiting and development of high potentials during a business downturn.** It's very tempting to respond to a bad business cycle by putting the brakes on recruiting or developing people. Both are mistakes in the long term. If you stop recruiting, in the future you will have a shortage of high-potential people who are ready to step into open positions. If you stop development, you frustrate people and increase turnover. Also, you prevent people from being ready to step up when the next upturn comes about. It is certainly appropriate to cut back on recruiting and development efforts, but stopping them altogether is, in most cases, the wrong quick fix.

9. **Not letting people learn from their mistakes.** There's an old story about a middle manager who goes to the CEO's office expecting to be fired because a business decision he made caused a $1 million loss for the company. Instead of getting fired, the individual gets another meaningful job when the CEO explains, "Why should we fire you? We've just invested $1 million in your education!" Many CEOs aren't so forgiving; consequently, they lose good people and foster a work culture of fear that stifles creativity and bold decision making. When a person makes a wrong decision, that poor judgment must be considered as part of the individual's total performance and his or her ability to learn from mistakes.

10. **Being impatient.** CEOs often become frustrated and give up their efforts when the succession management program fails to immediately yield a number of people who are ready to fill executive positions. Remember, just as it takes time to cultivate a garden, people need time to grow and develop. Succession management is a multiple-year strategy.

Another thing that can frustrate a CEO is having a number of people nominated for the Acceleration Pool who are not top-quality candidates. When this happens, the Executive Resource Board must spend excessive time sorting through people and making pool selections. This will cease to be an issue as the nominators learn the criteria used by the Executive Resource Board and as the board works out its own procedures.

The Pepsi Challenge

For two years before Roger Enrico became PepsiCo's CEO, he spent more than 120 days coaching and mentoring high-potential PepsiCo executives and challenging them with action learning assignments. Noel M. Tichy describes how Enrico operated:

> Enrico's methodology was one of intense interaction. He would begin the program with five days at a remote site, where he would spend from 8:00 a.m. until late at night every day talking to the participants individually and as a group about his own personal experiences rising through the ranks in PepsiCo. He talked about his successes and his failures and the lessons he had learned from them. He talked about how he solved problems, met challenges, and viewed the world. "I try to talk . . . the way former PepsiCo CEO Don Kendall talked to me—frankly, openly, matter-of-factly. He didn't pontificate; he told stories" (Tichy & DeRose, 1995), says Enrico.

> He also pressed them for their own ideas and reactions, and to take seriously their responsibilities as leaders of PepsiCo. His opening line at many of these sessions was: "No longer can you look upward and blame the idiots at the top of the company for what is wrong. You're now one of them" (Cohen, St. Clair, & Tichy, 1997). Bill Nictakis, a vice president of marketing at Frito-Lay, says Enrico's remark changed his view of his role, but it "scared the hell out of me. All of a sudden, my job wasn't just to manage volume variance: I had to think about planning strategies for five years from now" (Tichy & DeRose, 1996).

> As the vehicle for learning, Enrico required each participant to bring with him or her a real project that had the potential to dramatically affect PepsiCo's revenue, quality, costs, or customer satisfaction. They each laid out their challenge to the group, including Enrico, and then they all discussed how it might be refined and accomplished. The participants then would go back to their jobs for ninety days and try to implement their projects, using the ideas and lessons they had

learned at the workshop. While the participants from one group were back at their jobs working on their projects, Enrico would start up a new group with a new set of projects. Meanwhile, he remained available for consultation and assistance. At the end of ninety days, each group would reconvene with Enrico for three days to get feedback, report their progress, and review what they had learned (p. 49).

Enrico has continued his commitment to executive development since becoming CEO. His personal involvement provides a "Pepsi Challenge" for other large companies.

Developing a Teachable Point of View

Roger Enrico's leadership seminars did not just happen. They were part of PepsiCo's efforts to get a broad range of senior leaders to share their vision and experiences as part of an executive development process. Paul Russell, PepsiCo's director of executive development, has changed the company's widely benchmarked executive development system from a program based on the models and experiences of university professors and gurus to a program that is "by PepsiCo, for PepsiCo." The new program uses a variety of executives to lead programs and coach individuals. But Dr. Russell doesn't just schedule executives into courses—he spends several days in one-on-one sessions helping them develop a "teachable point of view." A common format is using a statement of the leader's personal philosophy followed by 15 to 20 major ideas that support the philosophy. Personal anecdotes illustrate each of the ideas.

Summary

We are not suggesting that a CEO give succession management first priority—just that it receives appropriate priority. The CEO and other executives must determine the priority relative to the organization's short- and long-term goals. Then the CEO's job is to see that the succession management program gets the attention appropriate for the priority.

Too often, the CEO fools himself or herself into thinking that things are going well relative to succession management when, in reality, they are not. This often happens when the CEO delegates too much succession management responsibility to others. It is perfectly appropriate for the CEO to get help from consultants or others in setting up the system and to delegate its operation to HR or other parts of the organization. But the CEO can delegate neither the attention required to create a "grow your own" organizational culture nor the backing to be sure that the Acceleration Pool system works.

Appendix 16-1: How to Measure the Success of an Acceleration Pool System

Operating an Acceleration Pool system is expensive in terms of time required of people in the pool and those who support their development. It is important, then, for an organization to measure the system's effectiveness. We also advise breaking out subgroups from the pool to get more specific data on each group. For example, you might break out data on pool members from lower or higher levels of the organization, or from different SBUs. Or you might separate the data on people having "average" high potential from those with exceptionally high potential. The data on each group might reveal very different results. Only by constantly measuring a wide range of factors can the Acceleration Pool system be improved and the enthusiasm for it sustained.

Listed below are some possible areas of measurement. Some produce "hard numbers," such as turnover of pool members, and some produce opinions. All will be helpful in monitoring the progress of your Acceleration Pool system. Organizations should tailor their measurement to their particular needs and succession system.

• Retention of pool members (voluntary and involuntary turnover).

• Long-term performance of those selected from the pool (relative to others).

• Percentage of nominated people selected for the pool.

• Number of people in the pool (against goal).

• Growth rate of the pool.

• Advancement of pool members (number moved upward each year).

• Percentage of times (against the goal) that senior positions are filled by non-pool members from within the organization.

• Percentage of times (against the goal) that senior positions are filled from outside the organization.

• Average time in position.

• The length of time executive positions are open before being filled.

• Cross-unit movement.

- Quality of people in the pool (e.g., job performance problems, performance ratings, problems in selling people to managers for assignments).

- Percentage of positions identified as "best development opportunities" that are filled by pool members.

- Changes in average 360° feedback results of participants over time.

- Diversity of pool members (race, gender, geography, function, SBU, educational background, etc.).

- The reactions of people in the pool (survey results):

  - Satisfaction with their development.

  - Do they have development priorities?

  - Percentage of development objectives completed.

  - Do they feel like they are learning and being developed?
    How many learning priorities were met in the past year?

  - Motivational level relative to their job and the organization.

  - Motivation for development.

  - Degree to which participating in the pool met their expectations.

  - Potential barriers to development, especially in the work environment.

  - Quality of development help received from manager.

  - Quality of mentoring.

  - Number of meetings with mentor.

  - Number of meetings with manager about development.

  - Follow-through on development assistance.

  - Difficulties/Problems.

  - Perception of improvements in their skills.

- The reactions of supervisors/managers (survey):

  - Satisfaction with the Acceleration Pool system.

  - Quality of pool members.

  - Pool members' ability to learn.

  - Pool members' motivation to develop.

- Number of meetings with pool members each month regarding development.
- Hours spent each month aiding pool members' development.
- Hours spent each month getting to know individuals better.
- The reactions of managers two levels up (survey):
  - Satisfaction with Acceleration Pool system.
  - Quality of pool members.
  - Pool members' ability to learn.
  - Pool members' motivation to develop.
  - Number of meetings with pool members each month regarding development.
  - Hours spent each month aiding pool members' development.
  - Hours spent each month getting to know the individuals better.
  - Perceived ROI or impact on the bottom line.
  - Perceived impact on ROI 5–10 years from now.
- The reactions of mentors (survey):
  - Satisfaction with Acceleration Pool system.
  - Quality of pool members.
  - Pool members' ability to learn.
  - Pool members' motivation to develop.
  - Number of meetings with pool members each month regarding development.
  - Hours spent each month aiding pool members' development.
  - Hours spent each month getting to know individuals better.
  - Benefits gained by participating in the mentoring process.
  - Nature of the mentoring relationship (type of activities, most helpful activities).
  - Barriers to effective mentoring.

- The reactions of the Executive Resource Board (survey):

  - Satisfaction with Acceleration Pool system.

  - Quality of candidates for the pool.

  - Availability of qualified people from the pool to fill executive slots.

  - Quality of diagnosis of pool members' development needs.

  - Adequacy of information about pool members' development.

  - Sufficient information about pool members to make assignments.

  - How meetings are run.

  - Attendance at meetings.

  - Board members' commitment to their tasks.

  - Follow-through on development needs.

  - Quality of developmental suggestions.

  - Degree to which the pool supports the organization's vision, values, and critical success factors.

  - Perceptions of leadership bench strength (changes and current level).

  - Managers' success in developing pool members.

We are not suggesting that an organization look at all these factors, but we do advise that more is better. It's good to get multiple views of the system because part of the succession management system might be working well, while another part might be in trouble.

Chapter 17

Getting Started

"The journey of a thousand miles starts with a single step."

—Chinese Proverb

For two years before writing this book, we presented the Acceleration Pool concept to organizations around the world and fielded countless questions about Acceleration Pool systems, especially implementation issues. In this last chapter we present answers to the most common ones on the assumption that you might have the same questions. We have grouped the questions in some general areas to make it easier to find questions of concern. At the end of the chapter, we again state the philosophy behind the Acceleration Pool concept and provide advice on its implementation.

Other Frequently Asked Questions About Acceleration Pools*

Who Should Go into the Pool—Issues about Having a Pool

1. **We have a vice president who is doing an adequate job at the general management level. We don't see him moving up. Is he a viable candidate for the Acceleration Pool?**

   Ask yourself this question, "Do you need to accelerate this person's development?" In this case, the answer is probably no. Therefore, the individual should not be in your Acceleration Pool.

* See Chapter 4 for more questions regarding Acceleration Pools.

☞ denotes that information on this topic is available at the *Grow Your Own Leaders* web site (www.ddiworld.com/growyourownleaders).

2. **There's a manager who is not performing in the current job as effectively as he or she might. Is this person a candidate for an Acceleration Pool?**

   No. One criterion for getting into the pool is good performance in the current job. The person should be developed to the fullest extent possible for current job requirements.

3. **What about the expense of having foreign nationals in an Acceleration Pool?**

   Organizations must accept that having certain people in the Acceleration Pool will be more expensive. For example, if pool members are in the home office, there's probably less movement of families—and, therefore, much less expense—than if they're in a regional or overseas office. Although it will be more expensive, it's in every company's best interest to cast as wide a net as possible to find and develop the best people.

   A common mistake that organizations make is to treat pool members in foreign locations differently than pool members near corporate headquarters. With today's modern communications, however, there's no reason that they should be. They now can be electronically brought in on meetings and can be mentored by phone or videoconferencing. The expense of bringing foreign nationals to training programs is small relative to the overall benefit of having people with diverse backgrounds available for promotion. In general, we have found that while it is common that pool members are treated differently when they go overseas, there's generally no good excuse for it. Rather, the fact that they're out of sight is often used as an excuse for not following through on organizational commitments.

4. **Must you be in a leadership job to be in an Acceleration Pool?**

   People who show high-level leadership potential in their jobs—although they don't have the title of *supervisor* or *manager*—are often appropriate candidates for an Acceleration Pool. In general, we feel the scope of job challenges is more important than the title.

5. **What if you feel someone has leadership skills, but they turn down an offer to be in the Acceleration Pool, professing a lack of interest in leadership?**

   It is a mistake to try to force someone into an Acceleration Pool who doesn't want to be there. However, there's nothing wrong with giving people a sample of leadership responsibilities without putting them into a pool. Often times, once people taste the fruits of leadership (e.g., responsibility for a project and the satisfaction that comes from helping people grow), joining the Acceleration Pool becomes more appealing to them.

6. How do you get around the issue of managers promoting their friends and not giving everyone a fair chance?

The first step is to look at the selection system. The more selection decisions are based on the requirement of providing behavioral backup for ratings, the fairer the selection system will be. When they have to discuss their nominations, managers who are basing them on friendship or loyalty will recognize that they don't have the "facts" to document the high ratings necessary for someone to be considered for the Acceleration Pool. The more the selection discussion is focused on behavior built around key development areas, the more accurate it becomes.

The second step is to get the CEO or COO to continually reinforce high selection standards through word and deed. Probably the most important thing senior managers can do in filling positions is to skip over "nice guys" in favor of more highly qualified, upwardly mobile individuals who are below them. The CEO can also seek people with potential from other parts of the organization or other companies who can make a great contribution to the organization.

Number and Size of Pools

7. Can an organization have more than one Acceleration Pool?

Yes. It depends on the size and structure of the organization. For example, in a large company each strategic business unit (SBU) could have its own pool, with another organizationwide pool preparing candidates for the very top of the organization. See Chapter 2 for more information.

8. How many people should be in an Acceleration Pool?

The answer depends on the size of the organization and its need for senior managers. Increasingly, leadership obsolescence (not just numbers of leaders) is emerging as a factor. However, the primary determinant is the availability of people to work with the pool members. Organizations are limited by the number of mentors they can provide, their tolerance for moving people throughout the company, the number of appropriate international assignments, and other related issues. Companies have anywhere from 1 to 2 percent of their employees in their Acceleration Pool, depending on their need. Most Fortune 500 companies have about 1 percent of their employees in their succession management system.

9. **Approximately 50 percent of the senior executives in my company will leave in the next three years. In total, that comes to 100 senior managers. Our president has said that he wants a 3:1 ratio of candidates to open positions. Does that mean we need 300 people in the Acceleration Pool?**

It would be nice to have three different people ready for each open job, but that would be a very difficult—and expensive—goal to attain. Fortunately, you don't need 300 people, because people can be considered for several different jobs. That's why Acceleration Pools target *job levels,* not specific positions. In this case, we would recommend a pool of about 150 people. You might be interested to know that, of its thousands of managers, GE targets only 500 people for special development.

Operation of the Executive Resource Board

10. **Should the semiannual Executive Resource Board meetings focus only on Acceleration Pool members?**

The answer to this question varies according to the organization, but most companies would not concentrate only on Acceleration Pool members. The Executive Resource Board makes decisions on all management promotions anticipated for a given time period. While Acceleration Pool members are always considered for open positions and their development is discussed during these meetings, the board might well choose candidates from outside the pool to fill some open spots if it thinks doing so is in the best interest of the organization. See Chapters 2 and 14 for more information.

11. **Do members of the Executive Resource Board know the members of the Acceleration Pool?**

In almost all organizations, the Executive Resource Board (which comprises the very senior management of the company) makes special efforts to get to know Acceleration Pool members. One way to do this is through events held exclusively for Acceleration Pool members.

However, this is more likely to happen when each executive makes a concerted effort to observe the pool members on the job or in special assignments.

12. What happens if a vacancy arises when someone is currently on an assignment that's not yet completed?

This is a more common situation than you might expect. Both management and the individual will be torn between wanting to give the promotion immediately and waiting for the person to get the most from the development experience provided by the current assignment. Most organizations opt to give the promotion, thinking that "a bird in the hand is worth two in the bush." If this route is pursued, methods should be put in place for the individual to follow up on the impact of any decisions made on the previous job.

13. What about the use of multiple-perspective (360°) data in talent review meetings?

We recommend against using 360° data in the talent review process because the data often are not comparable among individuals (depending on the rigor of the administration). However, we think that all pool members (and perhaps many outside the pool) should have the opportunity to gather 360° developmental insights from their colleagues. Using the results, the pool members can work with their manager, mentor, or assigned HR professional to establish development priorities. These development priorities can then be shared with the Executive Resource Board.

14. If there are multiple Acceleration Pools, are there multiple boards similar to the Executive Resource Board?

Yes. The CEO and Executive Resource Board compose the governing body for the high-level Acceleration Pool. The ranking leader of an SBU or other organizational unit would assume the same responsibilities as the CEO with regard to his or her unit's Acceleration Pool. There is usually overlap in the membership of Executive Resource Boards.

Administration of Acceleration Pools

15. Are Acceleration Pool members paid a premium compared to others in the same positions?

Acceleration Pool members should be paid at the going rate for an assignment. The fact that they are on a fast track, moving through organizational levels more quickly, should in itself accelerate their compensation. When Acceleration Pool members take a lateral assignment, they don't necessarily get a pay raise; however, someone must explain the longer-term advantages of the assignment.

16. How often will talent reviews be conducted?

In some organizations the president or CEO conducts an Acceleration Pool review twice a year. In other organizations a portion of each month's regular executive operating meeting is devoted to reviewing Acceleration Pool candidates. See Chapter 15 for more information.

17. Where are Acceleration Pools budgeted?

About half of the organizations we surveyed carry the unique expenses of their Acceleration Pool on the corporate budget and don't charge these costs back to the SBUs. These expenses include operating the Acceleration Center, operating action learning or other special programs conducted for pool members, sending people to university programs, etc. The rationale for central budgeting is that, when individuals come into the Acceleration Pool, they become "corporate property" and can be moved to any position within the organization. Thus, the corporation should pay for their unique expenses. These organizations feel that it's hard enough to get SBUs to make appropriate personnel changes in support of the Acceleration Pool, so they don't want to make it any harder by saddling the SBU with an unbudgeted expense. Further, these organizations fear that allocating Acceleration Pool expenses back to the SBUs or other organizational subdivisions might cause SBU leaders to make short-term decisions to save money by not nominating or developing high-potential people.

The other half of the organizations we surveyed charge unique experiences back to the SBU budgets on a *pro rata* basis.

18. **How does an organization measure the success of an Acceleration Pool?**

   Success is measured by the quality of people ready for promotion to senior management positions, not by counting the number of people in a program. There are many other measures that can help improve the effectiveness of a system. See Chapter 16 for a discussion of measures that can be used to monitor the success of individual Acceleration Pool members.

Manager and Mentor

19. **What kind of training and development are required for the manager and mentor?**

   As discussed in Chapter 14, we feel that at the very least, the manager and mentor should participate in an orientation session lasting two or three hours. During this session their roles are clearly explained and common issues discussed (e.g., What if the Acceleration Pool member doesn't come to you very often? or What do you do if an Acceleration Pool member is falling behind in his or her work?).

   We also recommend that the immediate manager be trained in a behavior modeling-based program that develops skills in coaching, supporting, and developing direct reports. ☞

20. **What do you do if the manager of an Acceleration Pool member would not be effective in developing the individual?**

   Sometimes it is necessary (or perhaps preferable) to bypass the immediate manager altogether and have the second-level manager work directly with a pool member. The second-level manager then performs all the planning and coaching that was discussed in Chapter 14 (in the section titled Immediate Managers Provide Guidance, Resources, and Encouragement). This is typically the case when the immediate manager does not have good leadership or coaching skills, when management knows the immediate manager will be moved soon, or when the immediate manager is too busy to develop people. It might also be appropriate to rely on the second-level manager when the pool member is working independently of the immediate manager but still reporting to that person. Finally, regardless of whether the second-level manager is the primary development contact, he or she can draw on a wealth of experience to serve as a rich source of tactical and "political" advice to pool members. ☞

Diagnosis of Development Needs

21. Our organization has used multiple-perspective (360°) instruments for more than 10 years. Some managers have had four or five feedback sessions. How should this old 360° data be used?

Obviously, the most recent data are the most important because they address competencies that are more similar to those required at higher organizational levels. Also, the more recent data reflect what the manager learned from the earlier 360° feedback. Above all, the most recent data represent the best prediction of future behavior. For example, a person who has shown improved leadership skills in every job should be expected to continually grow in leadership skills.

Most professionals who give Acceleration Center feedback would like to see all 360° data that an individual wants to share, but the sharing is totally up to the individual. The wider the range of data available about an individual, the richer the developmental insights.

Talent Development

22. Must everyone in the pool have a development assignment in another unit or SBU?

It is often advisable to move people around in an organization. However, this is often impossible. A task force assignment, a coordinating job, or a series of well-planned experiences can often suffice if pool members know what they are expected to learn. This is why we recommend that Development Action Forms be completed before these events.

23. Should a person who is being stretched in a high-risk assignment be told about the risk of failure?

Management must be very clear about what the pool member is being challenged to do—specifically, what the performance requirements and development goals are. It's easy to confuse development targets with performance targets in discussing positions. Both are important, and both need to be discussed. Pool members should be told that they wouldn't have been offered a stretch assignment if management didn't think they could succeed. They also should be told which of their strengths they will have to rely on to succeed.

24. Can people really change their behavior in a meaningful way?

Given an accurate diagnosis, the motivation to change (i.e., complete understanding of how important it is to change), the right resources, and ongoing encouragement, people at all levels of an organization can change significantly in most competencies and derailers (see Chapter 9). We've seen some wonderful examples of such change and commensurate organizational success. We will always remember a high-potential scientist who had everything going for her except her interpersonal skills. Her employees supported this by saying that she treated them like inanimate objects from the laboratory. Normally, she wouldn't have been asked to join an Acceleration Pool, but she was brought in as an exception because of her outstanding technical skills and strong commitment to development. The results of the Acceleration Center were certainly no surprise to the scientist, and she set out a comprehensive plan to change her behavior, starting with enrolling in a weeklong behavior modeling-based program designed to develop supervisory skills. After the training the scientist contracted with her manager to immediately apply the leadership skills on the job. She conducted her own 360° studies to monitor reactions to her behavior, and within a few months things had changed in her unit to the point that her direct reports actually sent her flowers. When she told us about the event, she burst into tears, saying that it was the most important thing that had ever happened in her life—more important than getting her Ph.D. or any of her other technical achievements. Because she was able to get over this interpersonal skills hurdle, she started to move up in the organization and is now in a high-level position.

Older managers can also change their behavior in addition to learning new technologies. A large manufacturing organization decided to set up an e-commerce subsidiary to manage its purchasing of raw materials. Vendors would bid over the Web. "George," who had a long series of success in the purchasing organization, was the logical candidate, but there was tremendous concern over whether his thoughtful, systematic way of making decisions and dealing with issues would fit into a high-pressure, web-based, hyper-speed environment. Management felt that his style wasn't right and hired a younger, more energetic person to manage the subsidiary. However, the younger man quit within three months because he didn't fit in the organization, and George was named interim manager. Before officially giving the assignment to him, management discussed with George his perceived weaknesses. He assured them that there would be no problem. And, indeed, the "weaknesses" were not a problem! His direct reports later revealed that George pushed them to make faster decisions and take action more quickly. One might think he was able to change because a latent personality attribute was allowed to surface. But we know the change resulted from a very thoughtful decision on George's part to identify the kind of behavior that would be required and then to develop it. He had no mentor in the organization, but he had a friend who worked in a hyper-speed organization who gave him advice almost daily about handling situations. Not only was George named permanently to the position, he also became a hero within the organization.

One thing that should be noted from these anecdotes is that the success of these individuals came from a combination of competencies. They might have lacked competencies in some areas, but they had a great deal of motivation, good planning skills, self-insight, and other qualifications that helped them succeed.

Legal Issues

25. What are the equal employment opportunity implications of an Acceleration Pool?

It certainly can be argued that getting into an Acceleration Pool gives a person an advantage toward promotion; thus, if a pool includes disproportionately few members of protected classes (e.g., women and minorities), an organization might find itself in legal trouble. This situation can occur even when the organization has the best intentions, so it always must be able to defend its system for selecting people into the pool. In Chapter 6 we recommend involving a selection expert in setting up the system for nominating and inviting people into the Acceleration Pool. With an EEOC challenge, the company would have to defend its criteria for selection as being job related and its methodology for making decisions as being fair—providing equal opportunity to every individual. To minimize the threat posed by these kinds of legal challenges, it's extremely important to rigorously document the process of setting up the Acceleration Pool system and to make sure the elements of the system are followed. Also, we advise performing a yearly audit of the organization's compliance with the planned selection system and annually monitoring Acceleration Pool diversity. These findings should then be reported to the Executive Resource Board.

On the other hand, most organizations use Acceleration Pools as a cornerstone of their diversity efforts. Having a diverse pool is a tangible sign that the organization is putting its money where it is needed relative to diversity.

26. How does the European Union Data Protection Act of 1998 affect Acceleration Pools?

Organizations with pool members working in a European Union (EU) country fall under this act. They must set up procedures to get required clearances and often to qualify for "safe harbor" status in terms of storing and using employee information. For more information on this act, refer to the information in the following box.

European Union Data Protection Act of 1998 and the Implications for Succession Management

All organizations with employees in the European Union need to be aware that there are restrictions on using employee data inside and outside the EU. The act, which became effective January 2001, determined protection principles relative to personal data that is held and shared within all large organizations. The act states that personal data should be:

- Obtained and processed fairly and lawfully.
- Held only for lawful purposes, which are described in the register entry.
- Used or disclosed only for those compatible purposes.
- Adequate, relevant, and not excessive in relation to the purpose for which they are held.
- Accurate and, where necessary, kept up to date.
- Held no longer than is necessary for the purpose for which they are used.
- Available to individuals so they can access information held about them and, where appropriate, correct or erase it.
- Surrounded by proper security.

The personal data covered in this law include data obtained through interviews, assessment centers, aptitude tests, multiple-perspective (360°) surveys, performance appraisal reports, succession management forms, or anything that can identify an individual. Personal data relate to a living individual who can be identified from the data. It can include any expression of opinion about the individual and any indication of the intention of the data controller in respect of the individual. Personal data do not have to be particularly sensitive information and can be as little as a name and address.

To be able to share this data, organizations having operations within the EU should start to initiate the proper accumulation of permissions from employees.

Organizations that manage their succession management system from locations outside the EU need to be particularly concerned about the act's provisions relative to data transfer. Take, for example, a U.S.-based company that wants to bring back assessment center reports or appraisal data on individuals working in the EU for its overall manpower or succession management planning. The company must get written permission from those individuals and certify in writing that it subscribes to strict data controls.

As with any legislation, many are trying to clarify the law's exact meaning and methods of compliance. We suggest that you ask your international law department to keep an eye on developments. The Resource Center at Development Dimensions International is compiling public information about the act and compliance to it. If you would like access to this collection, please e-mail us at ddiresctr@ddiworld.com.

Making the Transition to an Acceleration Pool

27. What help does an organization need in starting an Acceleration Pool?

Organizations have a great deal riding on the success of their Acceleration Pool—the future of the enterprise. Thus, it's very understandable when an organization is concerned about whether it can successfully pull off a major change such as installing one. We sincerely hope that we've provided in this book much of the information an organization would need, but we recognize that there are hundreds of issues that we couldn't deal with because of space considerations.

Whether an organization needs outside help in starting an Acceleration Pool depends on the experience and knowledge of the organization's internal professionals and their ability to devote the time necessary to quickly install a system. As in most situations, using outside consultants has the greatest payoff during the planning of the Acceleration Pool system because they will ensure that all elements are considered during development and that the process is tailored to the organization's specific needs. The worst thing an organization can do is to completely adopt the system used by another company. We've never seen two companies whose needs were exactly the same.

28. Should the Acceleration Pool system be piloted before being rolled out to the company at large?

There are three advantages to piloting:

• To see if the idea works.

• To focus on the greatest need (e.g., a senior manager for overseas assignments). It is better to address the greatest organizational need than to impose a solution on parts of the organization that don't really need it.

• To provide an opportunity to improve supporting systems, such as selection and performance management, before implementing the Acceleration Pool system throughout the company.

A major disadvantage to conducting a pilot might be the seemingly (to other business units) unfair concentration of effort in one part of the organization while leadership needs exist everywhere else as well. Another disadvantage is that by focusing on only one unit, an organization might miss people with leadership potential who might be appropriate for that unit because they are outside the pilot's narrow net.

Support Systems

29. To have an effective Acceleration Pool, what personnel systems should be in place and working well?

You need four HR systems to support an Acceleration Pool:

• **Performance management (performance appraisal)**—The organization's performance management system gives Acceleration Pool members performance targets and feedback relative to job assignments. It also provides guidance and reinforcement for the managers and mentors of the pool members. In today's fast-paced, high-volume work environment, little development takes place without accountability.

- **Selection**—The selection system helps the organization determine who would be appropriate for an Acceleration Pool. There must be a common organizational process and standards for ongoing talent identification used throughout the organization.

- **Development**—Effective transition and prescriptive development programs must be in place and operating frequently enough to meet Acceleration Pool members' needs. The DDI web site includes advice on evaluating your transition and prescriptive training. ☞

- **Compensation**—The organization's compensation system must be agile enough to allow for the accelerated development of pool members. Pool members need to be paid relative to their responsibilities—no matter how quickly they move through salary levels. ☞

The Human Resource Department's Role

30. What are the roles and responsibilities of the Human Resource department?

The primary role of HR is to make sure that the Acceleration Pool system works. HR representatives are essential, often behind-the-scenes drivers of the process. They are the catalysts that make things happen. Their responsibilities vary greatly among organizations, but can typically include:

- Setting up the Acceleration Pool:

  - Managing the Acceleration Pool nomination process.

  - Making sure all candidate data are available for review by the Executive Resource Board.

  - Making the Executive Resource Board aware of individuals whose background and performance indicate that they should be considered for the Acceleration Pool, but who have not been nominated.

- Helping pool members diagnose development needs:

  - Scheduling attendance at Acceleration Centers.

  - Interviewing for needs around challenges and organizational knowledge.

  - Helping them create Development Priority Lists.

- Ensuring that the Executive Resource Board runs smoothly:
  - Scheduling the board's meetings and preparing the agendas.
  - Making sure that all data on Acceleration Pool members are up to date and available.
  - Taking notes or recording decisions made by the board.
  - Conveying the board's decisions to the individuals (e.g., discussing entrance into the Acceleration Pool; explaining reasons for an assignment).
- Acting as a development resource:
  - Counseling/Coaching managers and mentors involved in the system.
  - Suggesting developmental actions or resources that can meet pool members' priority needs.
  - Monitoring the relationship of pool members, their managers, and mentors. If a relationship gets off track, it is HR's responsibility—either through direct intervention or by having higher management intercede—to see that the relationship gets back on track.
  - Operating as an advocate for Acceleration Pool members who need it (e.g., helping them access alternatives when their mentor relationship is not working).
  - Keeping top management informed if anything goes wrong with the system.
- Monitoring and evaluating the system:
  - Delivering an annual report on how the system is working and the extent to which quantifiable objectives are being met.

Often, one person takes on all these responsibilities and more as needed. That person might have any of a variety of titles, such as director/manager of succession management, secretary of the Executive Resource Board, etc.

Our Grow-Your-Own Philosophy

We feel that the philosophy behind the Acceleration Pool system is the important thing—not the implementation details. We summarize that philosophy as follows:

- The Acceleration Pool system must link to the organization's business strategy and flow naturally from the business planning process.

- An Acceleration Pool system has no chance to succeed unless top management owns it and is committed to growing talent from within. Executives must be involved in all aspects of the system, from selecting Acceleration Pool members to their progress reviews to placement and promotion decisions. Senior managers should personally know pool members and have continual contact with them. Many managers and mentors will fulfill their responsibilities only if top management's attention and reinforcement motivate them to do so.

- Acceleration Pool members are responsible for their own development. This includes involvement in prioritizing development needs and setting up development opportunities. They need guidance in how to fulfill these responsibilities, and they need to understand their role relative to their manager and mentor. Pool members also must be involved in any decisions that would affect their family or personal situations (e.g., entering the pool, assignments).

- Pool members' immediate managers play a key role in their development. These managers must be sure that their pool members understand the purpose and importance of each developmental event, get the help and resources they need to learn, and then apply that learning. Training for the immediate managers is a requisite if they are to help their charges succeed.

- Turnover and personal needs of an individual should be checked when he or she enters an Acceleration Pool and at least once a year thereafter to be sure that assignments and training recommendations are in sync with the person's personal needs.

- An effective system for identifying and selecting people into an Acceleration Pool is essential to the pool's success. In fact, time spent on selection has a greater payback to *overall* organizational success than money spent on development.

- An effective system to diagnose pool members' competencies pays off in terms of more effective and efficient development. Although a variety of strategies can be used, we recommend using an Acceleration Center, which combines the most effective assessment methodologies.

- Development planning should take place when a pool member understands his or her job responsibilities and understands the amount of help available from managers and mentors.

- Acceleration Pools must operate with minimal bureaucracy. Any forms that need to be completed should be simple and available on the organization's intranet, along with directions for their use and completed models. Pool members should be able to use the intranet to maintain their Career Development Portfolio.

- All aspects of an Acceleration Pool program need to be extremely efficient. Meetings of pool members, their manager, and their mentor must be well planned and efficient in order to optimize participants' input and decision making. Model agendas should be on an organization's intranet as an aid.

- Use existing HR systems, improving them as necessary. It's not a good idea to overlay existing HR systems with special systems developed for the Acceleration Pool. If an organization does not have a good performance management system, one should be developed for the entire organization. It can be tested on Acceleration Pool members.

- The role of the Human Resource department is not to own the Acceleration Pool system, but to *make it work* by ensuring that all forms are completed, data are obtained, people are trained, and commitments are met. The CEO owns the system.

Summary

The philosophy spelled out above and the beliefs outlined in the introduction have been our guide in developing the Acceleration Pool system described in this book. We are proud of how we've been able to overcome many of the traditional problems of succession planning and executive development with the Acceleration Pool system. But we admit that there's still room for improvement and refinement—and we're working on it. The important thing is that organizations take effective action—**now!** Taking no action will lead to problems with growth and profit in the near future, caused by the inability of organizations to take advantage of opportunities. In the longer run, taking no action will sap the ability of organizations to staff current operations and possibly lead to organizational decline. Resurrecting tired, old methods is not the answer, such as replacement planning and development planning forms, which are completed with little understanding of the individual's needs or opportunities for development and with no follow-up after they are completed. New thinking is required that puts equal emphasis on selection and development and takes into consideration contemporary issues, such as the difficulty and expense of moving people and the strong desire of high-potential individuals for continuing their learning and development. We believe that the Acceleration Pool idea is the contemporary answer to the needs of many organizations. We don't expect your organization to follow every suggestion in this book, but we hope that we have made some contribution to your thinking on this subject.

We sincerely believe that the competitive wars of the 21st century will be won by organizations that are ready with the skilled and motivated management talent they need to take advantage of the opportunities that are over the horizon. We hope we have furnished some ideas to help your organization be part of the elite group of companies that will thrive by having the executive resources you need through improved, more accurate systems of hiring people from the outside and, most of all, *Growing Your Own Leaders.*

References

American Management Association. (1996). *Corporate downsizing, job elimination, and job creation* (survey). New York: Author.

American Management Association. (1997, October). Special report on recruitment and retention: Strategies for managing retention. *HRfocus, 74*(10), S3–S5.

Axel, H. (1998). Strategies for retaining critical talent. *HR Executive Review, 6*(2).

Bassi, L., Cheney, S., & Lewis, E. (1998, November). Trends in workplace learning: Supply and demand in interesting times. *Training & Development, 52*(11), 51–75.

Bernthal, P.R., Rioux, S.M., & Wellins, R. (1999). *The leadership forecast: A benchmarking study* (MICABERSR5). Pittsburgh, PA: DDI Press.

Black, J.S., & Gregersen, H.B. (1999, March–April). The right way to manage expats. *Harvard Business Review, 77*(2), 52–63.

Borman, W.C., & Brush, D.H. (1993). More progress toward a taxonomy of managerial performance requirements. *Human Performance, 6*(1), 1–21.

Brake, T., Walker, D.M., & Walker, T. (1995). *Doing business internationally: The guide to cross-cultural success.* Burr Ridge, IL: Irwin.

Bray, D.W., Campbell, R.J., & Grant, D.L. (1974). *Formative years in business: A long-term AT&T study of managerial lives.* New York: Wiley.

Byham, W.C. (1996). *Developing dimension-/competency-based human resource systems* (Monograph No. XXIV/BPMN24 0496). Pittsburgh, PA: DDI Press.

Byham, W.C., & Moyer, R.P. (1996/1998). *Using competencies to build a successful organization* (Monograph No. XXV/BPMN25R). Pittsburgh, PA: DDI Press.

Byham, W.C., & Pescuric, A. (1996, December). Behavior modeling at the teachable moment. *Training, 33*(12), 50–56.

Byham, W.C. (with Cox, J.). (1988/1991). *Zapp!® The lightning of empowerment.* New York: Harmony Books.

Campion, M.A., Campion, J.E., & Hudson, J.P., Jr. (1994). Structured interviewing: A note on incremental validity and alternative question types. *Journal of Applied Psychology, 79*(6), 998–1,002.

Campion, M.A., Palmer, D.K., & Campion, J.E. (1998). Structuring employment interviews to improve reliability, validity and users' reactions. *Current Directions in Psychological Science, 7*(3), 77–82.

Challenger, Gray & Christmas. (1997). *Challenger Index.* Chicago: Author.

Chambers, E.G., Foulon, M., Handfield-Jones, H., Hankin, S.M., & Michaels, E.G., III. (1998). The war for talent. *The McKinsey Quarterly, 3,* 44–57.

Cohen, E.D., St. Clair, L., & Tichy, N.M. (1997). Leadership development as a strategic initiative. *Handbook for business strategy 1996* (p. 151). New York: Faulkner & Gray.

Corporate Leadership Council. (2000, April). *Challenges in managing high-potential employees: Results of the council's membership survey.* Managing High-Potential Employees Series, Vol. I (Rep. No. E00-006). Washington, DC: Author.

Corporate Leadership Council. (2000, November). *Toward effective management of high potential employees: Identifying and developing early- and mid-career talent.* Managing High-Potential Employees Series, Vol. II (Rep. No. E00-026). Washington, DC: Author.

Csoka, L.S. (1998). *Bridging the leadership gap* (Rep. No. 1190-98-RR). New York: The Conference Board.

Development Dimensions International. (1997, June). *Selection.* Baptist Health System, Inc. (MKTTSRR02-06972MA). Pittsburgh, PA: DDI Press.

Development Dimensions International. (1997, September). *Start-Up and Selection.* Equate Petrochemical Corporation (MKTSURR01-09972MA). Pittsburgh, PA: DDI Press.

Development Dimensions International. (1998, August). *Targeted Selection*® (Return on Investment [MKTTSRR03-08980MA]). Pittsburgh, PA: DDI Press.

Development Dimensions International. (1999, April). *Targeted Selection*®. Oracle (MKTTSRR05-0499.0MA). Pittsburgh, PA: DDI Press.

Development Dimensions International. (1999, August). *Selection.* MediaOne Group (MKTSERR01-0899.0MA). Pittsburgh, PA: DDI Press.

Development Dimensions International. (1999, November). *Targeted Selection*® Evaluation Summary (MKTTSRR01-1199.0MC). Pittsburgh, PA: DDI Press.

Development Dimensions International. (2000, December). *Selection.* Kraft Foods North America (MKTGACA01-1200MA). Pittsburgh, PA: DDI Press.

Development Dimensions International. (2001). *Appliance manufacturer's executive mentoring program.* Unpublished study.

Ellinger, A.D., Watkins, K.E., & Bostrom, R.P. (1999, Summer). Managers as facilitators of learning in learning organizations. *Human Resource Development Quarterly, 10*(2), 105–122.

Gatewood, R.D., & Feild, H.S. (1987/1990). *Human resource selection.* Chicago: The Dryden Press.

Gaugler, B.B., Rosenthal, D.B., Thornton, G.C., III, & Bentson, C. (1987). Meta-analysis of assessment center validity. *Journal of Applied Psychology Monograph, 72*(3), 493–511.

Goleman, D. (1995). Emotional intelligence: *Why it can matter more than IQ.* New York: Bantam Doubleday Dell.

Gottfredson, L.S. (Ed.). (1986). The *g* factor in employment. *The Journal of Vocational Behavior, 29*(3), 293–450.

Graddick, M. (1998). *Leveraging assessment for greater impact.* (Presentation material from The 26th International Congress on Assessment Center Methods: Assessment Center Technology for the New Millennium.) AT&T.

Guion, R.M. (1998). *Assessment, measurement, and prediction for personnel decisions.* Mahwah, NJ: Lawrence Erlbaum Associates.

Hauenstein, P., & Byham, W.C. (1989). *Understanding job analysis* (Monograph No. XI/CPMN15-019010MA). Pittsburgh, PA: DDI Press.

Hogan, R. (2000). *Hogan leadership forecast: Leadership advisor report.* Tulsa, OK: Hogan Assessment Systems.

Hogan, R., Curphy, G.J., & Hogan, J. (1994, June). What we know about leadership: Effectiveness and personality. *American Psychologist, 49*(6), 493–504.

Hogan, R., & Hogan, J. (1997). *Hogan development survey manual.* Tulsa, OK: Hogan Assessment Systems.

Howard, A., & Bray, D.W. (1988). *Managerial lives in transition: Advancing age and changing times.* New York: The Guilford Press.

Hunter, J.E., & Hunter, R.F. (1984). Validity and utility of alternative predictors of job performance. *Psychological Bulletin, 96*(1), 72–98.

Hymowitz, C., & Murray, M. (1999, June 21). Raises and praise or out the door: How GE's chief rates and spurs his employees. *The Wall Street Journal,* pp. B1, B4.

Janz, T. (1982). Initial comparisons of patterned behavior description interviews versus unstructured interviews. *Journal of Applied Psychology, 67*(5), 577–580.

King, S. (2000). *On writing: A memoir of the craft.* New York: Scribner.

Kogan Page Limited. (1999/2000). *International Executive Development Programmes* [Online]. Available: www.venda.com/vendanet/iedp/

Landy, F.J., Shankster, L.J., & Kohler, S.S. (1994). Personnel selection and placement. *Annual Review of Psychology, 45,* 261–296.

Leonhardt, D. (2000, May 24). Testing for common sense. *The New York Times,* p. C1.

McCall, M.W., Jr. (1997). *High flyers: Developing the next generation of leaders.* Boston: Harvard Business School Press.

McCall, M.W., Jr., & Lombardo, M.M. (1983). Off the track: *Why and how successful executives get derailed* (Tech. Rep. No. 21). Greensboro, NC: Center for Creative Leadership.

McCall, M.W., Jr., Lombardo, M.M., & Morrison, A.M. (1988). *The lessons of experience: How successful executives develop on the job.* New York: Lexington Books, The Free Press.

McManis, G.L., & Leibman, M.S. (1988, April). Succession planners. *Personnel Administrator,* 24–30.

Mitrani, A., Dalziel, M.M., & Fitt, D. (Eds.). (1992/1996). *Competency-based human resource management: Value-driven strategies for recruitment, development and reward* (p. 60). London: Kogan Page Limited.

Muoio, A. (Ed.). (1999, July/August). Unit of one: The art of smart. *Fast Company, 26,* 85, 96.

Ohlott, P.J. (1998). Job assignments. In C.D. McCauley, R.S. Moxley, & E. Van Velsor (Eds.), *The center for creative leadership handbook of leadership development* (pp. 127–159). San Francisco: Jossey-Bass.

Orpen, C. (1985). Patterned behavior description interviews versus unstructured interviews: A comparative validity study. *Journal of Applied Psychology, 70*(4), 774–776.

Peterson's. (1999). *Bricker's International Directory* [Online]. Available: www.petersons.com/brickers/bsector.html

Rich, J.T., & Saunier, A. (1999). *The point is better talent.* (Presentation material from The 1999 Seminar on Succession Planning and Top Talent Development: New Rules/New Tools.) The Conference Board; Sibson & Company and McKinsey & Company.

Rioux, S.M., & Bernthal, P.R. (1999). *Succession management practices survey report, 2*(1). (MICABERSR4). Pittsburgh, PA: DDI Press.

Schmidt, F.L., Ones, D.S., & Hunter, J.E. (1992). Personnel selection. *Annual Review of Psychology, 43,* 627–670.

Stewart, T.A. (1999, October 11). The leading edge: Leaders of the future—Have you got what it takes? *FORTUNE, 140*(7), 318, 320.

Taylor, P.J. (1994). *The transferability of behaviour modelling training across organisations and cultures.* Unpublished paper presented at the 4th Conference on International Human Resource Management, Queensland, Australia.

Thornton, G.C., III, & Byham, W.C. (1982). *Assessment centers and managerial performance.* San Diego, CA: Academic Press.

Tichy, N.M., & Cohen, E. (1998, July). Leadership 2000: The teaching organization. *Training & Development, 52*(7), 27–33.

Tichy, N.M., & DeRose, C. (1995, November 27). Roger Enrico's master class. *FORTUNE, 131*(11), 105.

Tichy, N.M., & DeRose, C. (1996, May). The Pepsi challenge: Building a leader-driven organization. *Training & Development, 50*(5), 58.

Tichy, N.M. (with Cohen, E.). (1997). *The leadership engine: How winning companies build leaders at every level.* New York: HarperCollins.

Wright, P.M., Lichtenfels, P.A., & Pursell, E.D. (1989). The structured interview: Additional studies and a meta-analysis. *Journal of Occupational Psychology, 62,* 191–199.

Glossary

Acceleration Center[SM]: Modern-day assessment center that uses professional assessors, highly realistic job simulations, and a wide variety of other assessment methodologies to accurately diagnose a person's appropriateness for a position as well as his or her development needs. Acceleration Centers compel prospective pool members to deal with issues and situations typical of general manager and executive positions.

Acceleration Pool[SM]: A systematic method for identifying and developing high-potential people to fill targeted levels of management (e.g., senior management, general management). Development of pool members is accelerated through stretch job and task force assignments that offer the best learning and highest-visibility opportunities.

Acceleration Pool member: The high-potential individual within an Acceleration Pool whose development is placed on a fast track for a targeted level (usually general management or above).

Action learning: Usually a team project in which participants tackle actual business problems or challenges outside their area of expertise. Team members deal with strategic issues important to the organization and develop decision-making tools and methods. Participants also can learn the importance of networking and understand the different styles and methods represented by others on the team.

Behavior-based interviews: Interviews that gather specific examples of past behavior to predict future behavior at higher levels of management. The methodology is based on the tenet that interviewers who are trained to collect and evaluate job-relevant behavior in a standardized fashion are more accurate in their evaluations. The data gathered in behavior-based interviews can be used to evaluate executive descriptors (i.e., competencies, derailers, job challenges, and organizational knowledge).

Career Development Portfolio: Documentation maintained by each Acceleration Pool member to track his or her development needs and accomplishments. Often stored online, the Career Development Portfolio is accessible only to each respective Acceleration Pool member and members of the Executive Resource Board.

Clinical psychologists: Licensed professionals who conduct assessments to aid in the development or selection of specific individuals. Assessments are typically done through personality inventories and clinical interviews.

Cognitive ability test: An assessment tool that provides basic measures of intelligence.

Competencies (also known as *dimensions*): Clusters of behavior, knowledge, technical skills, and motivations that research has found to be related to job success or failure and under which data on behavior, knowledge, technical skills, or motivation can be reliably classified. Competencies is one of the four executive descriptors.

Development Action Form: A form that encourages pool members to think about how they will achieve the targeted development (job challenges, organizational knowledge, competencies, and derailers) as well as how they can apply the newly learned development targets in the workplace and measure the effectiveness of the application. This form helps to ensure that development focuses on behavior change and is bottom-line oriented. It also helps the individual generalize the learning to fit other situations. A separate form should be completed for each area to be developed.

Development planning meeting: Generally held when the pool member first enters the pool and at least once a year thereafter (but always at the start of a new assignment). The meeting is held to review roles and expectations, review performance objectives for assignments, determine how development goals that were set by the Executive Resource Board and agreed to by the pool member will be met, decide on additional development objectives, plan action, and set dates for follow-up meetings.

Development Priority List: A list created by each pool member (with the aid of an HR professional or a professional who interprets Acceleration Center and 360° feedback) that prioritizes development needs in each of the four executive descriptor areas—job challenges, organizational knowledge, competencies, and executive derailers. The list is reviewed by the Executive Resource Board to ensure that the chosen priorities fit with the organization's strategic direction. The list is altered over time to incorporate new insights into a person's development needs.

Development sign-off meeting: Occurs between the pool member, manager, and mentor at the end of an assignment or development project. This meeting covers such topics as achievement of (or failure to achieve) the targeted development goals, what factors facilitated learning, insights into the development process, future applications of the learning, and possible improvements in the development process. The development sign-off meeting is usually held in conjunction with a discussion of the next development need.

Diagnosis of development needs meeting: Meeting between the pool member and a professional from the Acceleration Center and/or designated HR representative, or between the pool member and his or her mentor, to discuss development needs and determine development priorities (completing a Development Priority List).

European Union Data Protection Act: Legislation that determined protection principles for employees relative to personal data that are held and shared within all large organizations within the purview of the European Union (EU). This act became effective January 2001. It states that personal data should be:

- Obtained and processed fairly and lawfully.

- Held only for lawful purposes.

- Used or disclosed only for those compatible purposes.

- Adequate, relevant, and not excessive in relation to the purpose for which they are held.

- Accurate.

- Kept up to date.

- Held for no longer than necessary.

- Available to individuals so they can access information held about them and, where appropriate, correct or erase it.

- Surrounded by proper security.

Executive coach: A professional who is brought in to work one-on-one with a pool member. Coaches help Acceleration Pool members to expand self-awareness and understand their development needs. They also help pool members overcome obstacles to progress and help them to measure and monitor growth against desired goals. Coaches act as catalysts or facilitators of individual development and performance. They are seen as strategic business partners whose business experience, diagnostic insight, and proactive guidance offer tangible value to leaders. Perceived "value-added" and "good chemistry" qualities are keys to successful coaching relationships.

Executive derailers: One of the four executive descriptors. Derailers are certain qualities and learned behaviors that can cause executives to fail. They can include personality traits and dispositions that get in the way of effective performance.

Executive descriptors: Characteristics that define an effective executive. They generally fall into one of four categories: job challenges, organizational knowledge, behaviorally defined competencies, and executive derailers.

Executive Resource Board: A senior management committee, generally comprising the CEO and/or COO and unit or SBU heads, that is responsible for an organization's Acceleration Pool system. The Executive Resource Board reviews the nominations to an Acceleration Pool against defined criteria and makes the final decisions about who is to be admitted. The board also makes job and task force assignments, sends people to special training programs, and assigns executive coaches to develop pool members based on assessed needs. When more than one pool exists within a company, the organization usually has a different board for each pool (and a different name, although there is some overlap in membership).

Group self-mentoring: Involves 15 to 20 high potentials who self-mentor as a team, with a senior manager acting as a facilitator and coach. Participants meet to bring up issues and share suggested answers, while the senior manager facilitates the meeting process and helps the group to discover the answers on their own.

High potentials: Individuals who are perceived as being likely future executives in an organization. Each major part of the organization nominates high potentials to fill an Acceleration Pool, basing their choice on job performance and agreed-upon criteria of potential. In the pool the high potentials develop new skills and knowledge and take on new responsibilities, giving them the experience they will need to lead in the future as well as encouragement to stay with the organization.

HR representative: The Human Resource representative who is assigned to the Acceleration Pool and who acts as catalyst, quality control expert, and "expert source of information" on all aspects of the system. The HR representative is responsible for the day-to-day administration of the Acceleration Pool system.

Job challenges: One of the four executive descriptors, job challenges are the kinds of on-the-job situations that someone entering top management should have experienced or at least have had some exposure to (e.g., negotiating agreements, implementing a plan to cut costs, being involved in a merger or acquisition).

Long-term mentor: Assigned to a pool member for 2 to 10 years. Helps to plan development activities and monitor the Acceleration Pool member's progress against those activities. While long-term mentors perform all the same tasks as short-term mentors, they also are more likely to provide career advice, help pool members to network, create growth opportunities outside of normal job responsibilities, report the pool member's achievements to top management, and offer advice regarding the organization's politics. Long-term mentors also can help pool members cope with the personal challenges they encounter by providing long-term support and positive reinforcement.

Manager: The individual to whom the Acceleration Pool member reports. The manager's role is to establish an environment for development and to provide guidance, coaching, feedback, and encouragement.

Mentor: A manager at a level equal to or higher than the pool member's manager and often from a different organizational unit, who guides the development of Acceleration Pool members. The mentor's role is to provide guidance, support, and organizational and business insights.

Multiple-perspective (360°) interviews: A systematic means of gathering interview-based competency and derailer information from a number of people who work with the person being assessed. The approach used in these interviews is similar to that used in multiple-perspective surveys, except that the information is gathered via interviews rather than questionnaires.

Multiple-perspective (360°) surveys: A questionnaire assessment tool that elicits a comparison of self-perceptions with the perceptions of others who are familiar with the target person's behavior relative to targeted competencies and derailers.

Nomination meeting: A meeting between the potential pool member and a member of the Executive Resource Board or designated HR representative. Its purpose is to offer Acceleration Pool membership. The pros and cons of membership are discussed, and the pool member decides whether to join the pool.

One-on-one training: Personalized training involving an instructor and an executive. For any given course or program, the instructor covers essentially the same material that is covered in the classroom, but in a greatly abbreviated version that meets the executive's specific business and personal needs. One-on-one training works particularly well when behavior skills are being developed, such as interviewing, completing performance management forms, negotiating, and coaching.

Organizational knowledge: One of the four executive descriptors, organizational knowledge refers to the degree of understanding that senior managers must have about how the organization operates. Includes areas such as functions, processes, systems, and products and services.

Personal attributes: Personality traits and dispositions (i.e., tendencies) that either facilitate executive success (i.e., enablers) or impede executive performance (i.e., derailers).

Personality inventory: An assessment tool that provides insights into underlying personality characteristics (e.g., sociability, adjustments, etc.) relative to derailers.

Prescribing solutions for development needs meeting: This meeting is generally held with a member of the Executive Resource Board, a designated HR representative or the pool member's mentor, and the pool member. It explains the purpose and importance of an assignment or special training event, obtains the pool member's commitment, and defines specific development goals for the pool member.

Prescriptive training: Training built around an Acceleration Pool member's specific needs, as delineated by his or her Development Priority List. For middle managers and below, the training can be delivered to groups of pool members with common needs, or they can participate in internal or external open-enrollment or electronically delivered programs (e.g., web-based training). More senior managers can be developed through attendance at short programs run by universities or consulting companies and through one-on-one training—often combined with coaching.

Progress check meeting: A meeting between the pool member, manager, and mentor to monitor the pool member's progress toward job performance objectives and development objectives and to determine any needed support.

Short-term mentor: Assigned to a pool member for one to three years. A short-term mentor helps to plan development activities and monitor an Acceleration Pool member's progress against those activities. Often, the short-term mentor is a role model for a competency that a pool member needs to develop. The short-term mentor also monitors the relationship between the pool member and his or her immediate manager.

Simulation: An assessment tool used in Acceleration Centers. Simulations enable a participant to "try on" a role and exhibit behavior required in the target job or job level. Individuals must perform a series of tasks, such as handling a disgruntled employee, making strategic decisions, preparing and delivering a presentation to top management, etc.

Special training: Training designed specifically for Acceleration Pool members, such as Acceleration Pool orientation, action learning team projects, and action learning individual projects. These events are generally held away from work, push participants hard, provide short training nuggets, and help people develop their interpersonal competencies and decision-making skills. A variety of training methods are used.

Talent review meeting: Meeting held by the Executive Resource Board to find the best people from within or outside the Acceleration Pool to fill current open positions and positions that will be open within the next year. This meeting also determines the specific development goals and assignments for Acceleration Pool members as appropriate for their growth and development needs (e.g., special training, executive coaches, etc.).

Targeted Selection®: A behavior-based interviewing system developed by Development Dimensions International. The key elements—competency and other executive descriptor targets, a systematic and consistent interviewing system that pins down behavior, and the integration of data— are combined in a program that assures accurate, carefully considered, and high-quality hiring decisions.

Transition training: Training that helps rising leaders develop the skills and knowledge they need as they move up the organization (e.g., into middle or senior management). Transition training programs provide information on roles, competencies, and systems associated with the new organizational level.

Acknowledgements

For two years *Grow Your Own Leaders* has been an iterative work. During that time we called upon a number of people to lend their considerable talents to this book. Some worked on the project since its inception, while others stepped up as they were called upon. We want to recognize these people and their specific contributions here:

Helen Wylie—Majordomo, Linchpin—Helen has 12 boxes of drafts as a testament to the volume of work she put into this project. For two years she fielded, typed, edited, spliced, and coordinated the input of the three authors and incorporated their myriad (and often major and barely legible) revisions. She was dogged in her determination that we delivered what we promised when we promised it. She made sure we were aware of impending deadlines. Then, when the DDI editorial and graphic groups got involved, Helen faced—and met—an expanded challenge to coordinate activities. Over the course of this project, Helen cheerfully and tirelessly devoted a vast amount of time—including long days and frequent weekends—to getting the book completed. Without Helen, *Grow Your Own Leaders* couldn't have been written.

Bill Proudfoot—Chief Editor—Bill was an integral part of the core team that held the entire project together. Bill put in countless hours editing, proofing, and polishing multiple iterations of the manuscript before managing it through formatting and proofing and then into printing while under some very tight deadlines. *Thanks* can't begin to express our appreciation for the work that Bill did. Suffice to say that we couldn't have produced this book without him either.

Janet Wiard—Graphic Designer—Another major player in the production of this book. Janet's patience and dedication are unsurpassed. She spent many hours designing and then reworking layout and cover designs to give the book its finished look. She also typeset the manuscript chapter by chapter, proving herself to be quite adept with the formatting software. Without Janet's technical skills and eye for design, *GYOL* would still be a manuscript.

Claire Werling—Research Associate—Claire enthusiastically tackled the often nebulous—and frustrating—task of researching, identifying, and verifying the references in this book. She painstakingly matched each reference to its corresponding passage in the text. We applaud Claire's dedication and commitment to making sure that all the references were correct and accurate. We appreciate her help more than she'll ever know.

We offer special thanks to **Shawn Garry, Peter Haapaniemi, Amy Plitt,** and **Chris Neuf** for their editing and proofreading efforts and to **Ginny Morgan** and **Tammy Watkins** for inputting revisions and transcribing the authors' dictation.

We also want to thank **Dave Biber** for his cover ideas; **Paul Bernthal, Carla Fogle, Sue Huber, Jennifer Lukondi,** and **Angela Magliacane** for their research assistance; **Lisa Malley** for her expertise with 360° surveys, **John Buffington, Jr., Brian Hilker, Paul West,** and the **CSI Printing Team** for the book production; and **Suellen Fitzsimmons** for her photography.

Many DDI associates volunteered to review iterations of the manuscript. Their feedback was instrumental to improving the content of *Grow Your Own Leaders.* They include **Rick Anderson, Loren Appelbaum, David Black, Doug Bray, Tacy Byham Lehman, Bruce Court, Jac Cuney, Ron Dalesio, Dave Fisher, Andrew Gill, Susan Haid, Eric Hanson, Mike Hoban, Ann Howard, Bill Jackson, Margot Katz, Michael Lehman, Dana McDonald-Mann, Sheryl Riddle, Bob Rogers, Mary Jo Sonntag, Adrian Starkey,** and **Rick Swegan.**

We would also like to thank our former DDI colleague, **Rodney Warrenfeltz,** and **Suzan McDaniel,** both of Hogan Assessment Systems, for their thought leadership, partnership, and willingness to share their latest ideas in executive assessment and development.

The following reviewers provided us with valuable input and feedback: **Michael Coates,** Cummins Business Services; **Harvette Dixon,** PPG; **Eric Elder,** Bristol-Myers Squibb; **Mark Evans,** Great American Knitting

Mills; **Alan Foss,** PPG; **Kenneth Hall,** University of Pittsburgh; **Tom Jeswold,** PNC Bank; **John Lankford,** Comcast; **Roderick Lincoln,** Cytec; **Manuel London,** SUNY-Stony Brook; **David MacDonald,** Steelcase; **Antigoni Mallen,** AT&T Wireless; **Amber McDougall,** Australia Post; **Steve McMillen,** Hillenbrand Industries; **Robert Parks,** Eli Lily (retired); **Tim Poshek,** Milwaukee Journal Sentinel; **E. Barry Richmond,** Great American Knitting Mills; **Edward Roth** (retired) and **Steve Leavey**, U.S. Postal Service; **Paul Russell,** of PepsiCo; and **Tim** (and **Danielle**) **Walker,** Bristol-Myers Squibb.

We also thank the following individuals and their organizations for providing us with case studies and examples from their organizations: **Harvette Dixon,** PPG; **Eric Elder,** Bristol-Myers Squibb; **Jamie Forst** and **Sharon Clay,** Rolls-Royce, plc.; **Diana Kamyk,** Bayer USA; **Steve Leavey** and **Sherry Barber,** U.S. Postal Service; and **Paul Russell** and **Lucien Alziari,** PepsiCo.

We also want to thank our families for their support and patience as we worked on this project.

And last, but certainly not least, we thank **Jack Horner Communications, Nancy Fox,** and **Rich Wellins** for their PR, consulting, promotional, and marketing efforts of *Grow Your Own Leaders*.

About Development Dimensions International

For more than 30 years, Development Dimensions International (DDI) has helped many of the world's leading organizations hire, develop, and retain their best people by specializing in:

- Competency-based recruitment and selection systems that identify people with the right skills and motivations—people who can grow, learn, and succeed with the organization over the long term.

- Leadership development through succession management, assessment, and training.

DDI has worked with more than 19,000 organizations around the world and with clients from every industry. To meet our clients' global needs, DDI operates 70 offices and affiliates in 22 countries, offering programs in 10 languages.

DDI operates Acceleration Centers in several U.S. cities as well as in Europe, Asia, and Australia. These assessment center facilities enable companies to evaluate leadership potential at all organizational levels. DDI's Acceleration Centers are used by many of the world's largest private and government organizations as a key element of their succession management program.

At least 8,000 organizations have used DDI programs to help their leaders move into supervisory, management, and executive positions and to overcome diagnosed skill gaps. In addition to our well-known behavior modeling-based programs for frontline leaders (Interaction Management®: Tactics and Strategies for Effective Leadership), DDI offers the Strategic

Leadership Experience^SM, a unique program designed to help middle and upper managers make the transition to senior strategic leadership. The program features a computer-based management simulation. DDI also develops tailored action learning programs for executives.

DDI leads our industry in creating web-based leadership training and hiring tools, offering systems that stand alone on the Web and systems that combine various delivery methodologies.

For more information about programs and services available from DDI, visit our web site at www.ddiworld.com or call us between 7:30 a.m. and 5:30 p.m. (Eastern Standard Time) at 1-800-933-4463 in the United States or 1-800-668-7971 in Canada.

As always, we welcome your comments on *Grow Your Own Leaders*. Please feel free to write us at:

Development Dimensions International
1225 Washington Pike
Bridgeville, PA 15017

or e-mail us at:
bbyham@ddiworld.com

About the Authors

William C. Byham, Ph.D.

William C. Byham is chairman, CEO, and cofounder of Development Dimensions International (DDI), a global human resource consulting firm specializing in leadership development and selection system design and implementation. Before founding DDI in 1970, Dr. Byham was manager of selection, appraisal, and general management development for J.C. Penney Company.

At both J.C. Penney and DDI, Dr. Byham pioneered a number of important human resource technologies that have had a significant impact on how people are managed. These technologies include the assessment center method, behavior-based interviewing, behavior modeling, behavioral job analysis methodology, and Acceleration Pools. These technologies have been described in 20 books and 170 monographs and articles written by Dr. Byham.

Dr. Byham is particularly well known for his work with the assessment center method. For more than 30 years, he has been the principal researcher and developer of the technology. He has written and edited two books discussing research and application, *Assessment Centers and Managerial Performance* (coauthored with George Thornton) and *Applying the Assessment Center Method* (coedited with Joseph Moses).

Dr. Byham is also well known for his work on improving organizational effectiveness. He has coauthored three books on teams and five books on empowerment, including **Zapp!**® **The Lightning of Empowerment,** a worldwide best-seller.

Dr. Byham and his DDI colleagues have developed executive development programs to diagnose leadership deficiencies as well as programs to fill leadership gaps in thousands of organizations around the world. He has published 17 articles on the upcoming shortage of skilled and experienced executives and steps that organizations can take to prevent the problem.

An internationally renowned educator, consultant, and speaker, Dr. Byham has received numerous honors. A few of these include the Distinguished Contribution to Human Resource Development award from the American Society for Training & Development, the Distinguished Professional Contributor award from the Society for Industrial and Organizational Psychology, and the Distinguished Contributions to the Practice of Psychology award from the Society of Psychologists in Management.

Audrey B. Smith, Ph.D.

Audrey B. Smith is consulting vice president of the Staffing and Assessment Consulting group and Executive Succession Management group at DDI. Dr. Smith directs the activities of consulting teams that deliver executive development and succession management consulting services and leadership assessment center technology. Her work has focused on the design, implementation, and validation of Acceleration Pool systems; selection systems, including executive team reengineering applications; developmental assessment; and executive coaching.

Dr. Smith has worked with many clients throughout the world, including General Motors, Northern Telecom, BMW, PPG Industries, the U.S. Postal Service, Steelcase, Whirlpool, the United Nations, United Airlines, Toyota, and Unisys Corporation.

Dr. Smith earned her doctorate and master's degrees in industrial/ organizational psychology from Colorado State University, where she taught courses in psychometrics and industrial and organizational psychology. Her bachelor's degree is from Pennsylvania State University. Before joining DDI in 1989, Dr. Smith worked for Rockwell International as a training and management development specialist.

Matthew J. Paese, Ph.D.

Matthew J. Paese is practice leader of Executive Succession Management at DDI. He is responsible for the development, research, sales, and delivery of DDI's executive succession management methodologies. Dr. Paese directs consultants, executive coaches, and senior assessors in implementing assessment, selection, and development initiatives that are aimed at senior-level populations in major corporations throughout the world. Dr. Paese has designed and implemented many large-scale succession management initiatives, ranging from Acceleration Pool implementations to executive assessments and coaching. He has also led strategic consulting services to support succession management design efforts. Dr. Paese also maintains a number of executive coaching relationships with senior executives in a variety of industries.

Dr. Paese has consulted extensively with General Motors, Steelcase, Cisco Systems, Toyota, Eastman Chemical, Quest Diagnostics, United Airlines, and many other global clients.

Dr. Paese earned his doctorate and master's degrees in industrial/ organizational psychology from the University of Missouri-St. Louis, where he also taught courses in industrial and organizational psychology and organizational behavior. He earned his bachelor's degree at St. Norbert College in De Pere, WI. Before joining DDI in 1994, Dr. Paese was with Anheuser-Busch, where he managed executive assessment and development programs and implemented organizational development initiatives throughout the corporation.

Other Books from DDI

Also available are the following books on empowerment, teams, selection, and performance management by William C. Byham, Ph.D., and other associates:

Empowered Teams: Creating Self-Directed Work Groups That Improve Quality, Productivity, and Participation by Richard S. Wellins, William C. Byham, and Jeanne M. Wilson

HeroZ™—Empower Yourself, Your Coworkers, Your Company by William C. Byham with Jeff Cox (available in English, French, German, Spanish, Korean, Chinese, Arabic, and Portuguese)

Inside Teams: How 20 World-Class Organizations Are Winning Through Teamwork by Richard S. Wellins, William C. Byham, and George R. Dixon

Landing the Job You Want: How to Have the Best Job Interview of Your Life by William C. Byham with Debra Pickett

Organizational Change That Works: How to Merge Culture and Business Strategies for Maximum Results by Robert W. Rogers, John W. Hayden, and B. Jean Ferketish, with Robert Matzen

The Selection Solution: Solving the Mystery of Matching People to Jobs by William C. Byham with Steven M. Krauzer

The Service Leaders Club by William C. Byham with Ray Crew and James H.S. Davis

Shogun Management™: How North Americans Can Thrive in Japanese Companies by William C. Byham with George Dixon

Succeeding With Teams: 101 Tips That Really Work by Richard S. Wellins, Dick Schaaf, and Kathy Harper Shomo

Team Leader's Survival Guide by Jeanne M. Wilson and Jill A. George

Team Member's Survival Guide by Jill A. George and Jeanne M. Wilson

Zapp!® Empowerment in Health Care by William C. Byham with Jeff Cox and Greg Nelson

Zapp!® in Education by William C. Byham with Jeff Cox and Kathy Harper Shomo

Zapp!® The Lightning of Empowerment—revised edition by William C. Byham with Jeff Cox (original edition available in English, French, German, Japanese, Dutch, Chinese, Korean, Portuguese, and Spanish)

Zapp!® The Lightning of Empowerment—the video

These publications can be ordered from DDI's Client Services group either by calling 1-800-334-1514 from 8 a.m.–5 p.m. (Eastern Standard Time) Monday through Friday, by faxing to 724-746-3903, or by sending an e-mail to csiclientservice@ddiworld.com.